BLACK

THOUGHT

MATTERS

Also Available from Bloomsbury:

Multi/Race/Less/Ness, Jon Ivan Gill
Black Bodies, White Gazes, George Yancy
Alienation and Freedom, Franz Fanon

BLACK THOUGHT MATTERS

Africana Philosophy and Freedom

LAROSE T. PARRIS

BLOOMSBURY ACADEMIC
LONDON · NEW YORK · OXFORD · NEW DELHI · SYDNEY

BLOOMSBURY ACADEMIC
Bloomsbury Publishing Plc, 50 Bedford Square, London, WC1B 3DP, UK
Bloomsbury Publishing Inc, 1359 Broadway, New York, NY 10018, USA
Bloomsbury Publishing Ireland, 29 Earlsfort Terrace, Dublin 2, D02 AY28, Ireland

BLOOMSBURY, BLOOMSBURY ACADEMIC and the Diana logo are trademarks
of Bloomsbury Publishing Plc

First published in Great Britain 2026

A catalogue record for this book is available from the British Library.

A catalog record for this book is available from the Library of Congress.

ISBN: HB: 978-1-3505-3653-1
PB: 978-1-3505-3654-8
ePDF: 978-1-3505-3655-5
eBook: 978-1-3505-3656-2

Typeset by Newgen KnowledgeWorks Pvt. Ltd., Chennai, India
Printed and bound in Great Britain

For product safety related questions contact productsafety@bloomsbury.com.

To find out more about our authors and books visit www.bloomsbury.com and
sign up for our newsletters.

For my parents, Dulcie and Canute Parris, who lovingly ushered me into the life of the mind through lessons about our Ancestors' struggles and triumphs. For our Mighty Ancestors whose expansive vision of humanity and tireless commitment to forge a better world inspire me to fight and write every day.

Contents

Preface ix

Acknowledgments xix

PART ONE AFRICANA PHILOSOPHY, ENLIGHTENMENT, AND FREEDOM

1 **Unveiling the History of Black Thought: Lewis Gordon's** *an Introduction to Africana Philosophy* 3

2 **Leonard Harris's Philosophy of Struggle** 49

3 **Creolize the Academy** 73

4 **The Specter of Africana Thought in Juliet Hooker's** *Theorizing Race in the Americas* 89

5 **"Young, Gifted" and Woman, Reading Rosa Luxemburg through Lorraine Hansberry and the Black Radical Tradition** 101

PART TWO THE BEAUTIFUL STRUGGLE: DIALOGUES IN BLACK THOUGHT

6 **Interview with Jina Fast** 125

7   Interview with A. Shahid Stover 147

8   Interview with Lewis R. Gordon 167

References 179
Index 189

Preface

Media images from the summer of 2020 are unforgettable. In the wake of George Floyd's murder by Minneapolis police, millions of anti-racist activists in over ninety countries[1] defied COVID-19 lockdown strictures to proclaim that Black Lives Matter. Defiantly assembled in close proximity, they marched and shouted, "I can't breathe," to decry Western hegemony's white supremacist anti-human agenda: Black dehumanization, criminalization, and extermination through systemic anti-black violence. With this same life-affirming spirit of resistance, I avow that Black thought matters. Why does the philosophical thought of Africans and African descendants throughout the diaspora matter? Because Black thought has established the ideological foundation for the ethical and political mission of Black liberation movements by emphasizing the intrinsic value of Black life and advancing a radical egalitarianism wherein all lives can truly matter. Proclaiming Black thought's significance is an act of dissent in today's increasingly authoritarian world order as all areas of Black/Africana Studies are under siege. Collectively, these sociopolitical and cultural developments reflect the paradox at the heart of Black thought's persistent marginalization, for Africana philosophers have exerted a tremendous influence on the history of ideas and the movement of human progress from ancient times to the present. Absent the epistemological innovations of Black thinkers, the high culture of classical antiquity would not have developed. Black thought has not only mattered since the dawn of human achievement in ancient Kemet,[2] but it has served as a catalyst for ensuing intellectual endeavors:

Before any other people, the Egyptians introduced the concept of eternal life and immanent moral justice, opening the way for humanist universalism … In this light, one can clearly see the degree of progress represented by the invention of the 'immortal soul' and the idea of individual rewards and punishments, founded on a universal morality that scrutinizes the motives and intentions of human actions … [This] universalist moral breakthrough of the Egyptians is the keystone of all subsequent human thought. (Amin 1989: 107)

Indeed, over three thousand years ago the ancient Kemites made unprecedented strides in the attainment and production of human knowledge. They laid the epistemological foundations for mathematics, literary expression, philosophy, and the sciences; and erected enduring monuments of architectural genius. Of these prescient Kemites, the fifth-century BCE Greek historian Herodotus plainly stated that "it is certain that the natives of this country are black with the heat" ([c. 450 BCE] 1997: 130). Despite Herodotus's eyewitness account, Eurocentric historians from the nineteenth century to the present day have consistently dismissed the ancient testimonies of Plato,[3] Herodotus, and later Diodorus,[4] which collectively underscore how the Greeks not only benefited from their Kemetic teachers' wisdom, but also incorporated their erudition into the material, cultural, and symbolic life of classical antiquity.

I begin with the whitening of Kemet to demonstrate how the construction of historical knowledge has been subject to epistemic colonization — a project that necessitated the Europeanization of Kemetic thinkers to further the hegemonic project of white/European epistemological, sociohistorical and cultural dominance. The British historian Martin Bernal (1937–2013) emphasizes that modern Eurocentric historians praised the Greeks as philosophers, artists, and mathematicians while disparaging their reliability as historians, simply because these Hellenic thinkers paid tribute to their black Kemetic mentors.[5] This repudiation of ancient Greek historiography has engendered a false Eurocentric narrative that effectively disavows Herodotus's claims of Kemites who:

were the first to discover the solar year, and to portion out its course into twelve parts. They obtained this knowledge from the stars. (To my mind they contrive their year more cleverly than the Greeks … dividing the year into twelve months of thirty days each, add every year a space of five days besides, whereby the circuit of the seasons is made to return with uniformity). The Egyptians … first brought into use the names of the twelve gods, which the Greeks adopted from them; and first erected altars, images, and temples to the gods; and also first engraved upon stone the figures of animals … Concerning Egypt itself I shall extend my remarks to a great length, because there is no such country that possesses so many wonders, nor any that has such a number of works which defy description … ([*c.* 450 BCE] 1997: 119–20, 138)

Herodotus continues praising the Kemites for a society "swarming with medical practitioners" specializing in ophthalmology, dentistry, neurology, and internal medicine; boasting mechanical acumen in their use of battlements and machines to build the pyramids; originating a pantheon of twelve gods with religious and cultural rituals adopted by the Greeks; training in anatomy and physiology in their embalming practices; and differentiating between sacred and secular writings (ibid.: 164–5, 190, 138, 153, 140). Given the breadth of the Kemites' scientific, medical, religious, and literary sagacity, it seems obvious that modern Eurocentric historians theorized Kemet as an atypical Caucasian/Eurasian civilization in Africa in order to claim ancient black achievement as their own. This three-centuries-long historiographical project of deracinating the Kemites from their African origins has effectively severed these ancient people's ethno-racial, cultural, and geographical ties to the African continent in the collective Western consciousness, to the extent that the "destruction of the African past" (Robinson 1983: 81) has had devastating consequences on the generalized perception of Africa, Africans, and African descendants throughout the globe. We are erroneously perceived as an ahistorical people whose entry onto the world stage began with the degradation of chattel slavery, and the subjugation of Western imperialism and colonialism. How can we account for this blatantly reactionary transmutation of the Kemites racial identity from the nineteenth century onward? And what ideological, cultural, and material forces led to the whitening of these ancient African people? Briefly reviewing twentieth-century African-centered and Afrocentric scholars'[6] challenges to this revisionist historiography reveals how the erasure of ancient Black history and, by extension, Black thought legitimized the brutality of the chattel slavery and Western imperial-colonial systems, thereby solidifying the myth of African racial inferiority.

W. E. B. Du Bois's (1868–1963) theoretical critique is instructive on this point. He elucidates the ideological, socioeconomic, and cultural forces during the chattel slavery and second wave imperialist eras that led nineteenth-century Egyptologists[7] to reject ancient Greek testimonies of the Kemites as black African people:

> The Greeks looked upon Egypt as part of Africa not only geographically but culturally, and every facet of history and anthropology proves that the Egyptians were an African people varying no more from other African peoples than groups like the Scandinavians vary from other Europeans…There can be but one adequate explanation of this vagary of nineteenth-century science: it was due to the slave trade and Negro slavery. It was due to the fact that the rise and support of capitalism called for rationalization based on degrading and discrediting the Negroid peoples. It is especially significant that the science of Egyptology arose and flourished at the very time that the cotton kingdom reached its greatest power on the foundation of American Negro slavery. We may then without further ado ignore this verdict of history, widespread as it is, and treat Egyptian history as an integral part of African history. (1946: 99)

Du Bois reveals how nineteenth-century science, or scientific racism (which will be addressed in Chapters 1, 2, and 4) rationalized the dehumanization of Africans under chattel slavery while supporting Egyptology's anti-African theoretical orientation. These related developments led to Kemet's elision as the progressive African civilization that propelled classical antiquity toward sociocultural maturity. Du Bois's analogy, that likens the Eurocentrist separation of Kemet from black Africa to a fabricated divide between Scandinavians and other Europeans, provides an apt conceptual bridge to the portrayal of the ancient Kemites in twentieth- and twenty-first-century films where Caucasian/Eurasian casting persists. One need only recall that the majority white casting of *The Ten Commandments* (1956) has been consistently replicated in more recent Hollywood productions. *Exodus: Gods and Kings* (2014), *Gods of Egypt* (2016), and *The Mummy* (2017)—all portray dynastic Kemites as a Caucasian/Eurasian master class with black African servants (this will be discussed in Chapter 2). This trend in popular culture indicates that the debate over Kemet's African identification is far from over, since Eurocentrism's hegemony has perpetuated the conceptual, cultural, and epistemological excision of Kemet from its autochthonous roots on the African continent. Du Bois's 1946 critique of the intertwined ideological and material forces that led to the whitening of Kemet, while noteworthy, is not unprecedented. As the consummate historian and Africana philosopher that he was, he assumed the theoretical mantle of the eighteenth- and nineteenth-century Black vindicationists who preceded him in upholding the cause of African historical recuperation.[8]

Late twentieth-century Afrocentric thinkers forwarded Du Bois's and the Black vindicationists' discursive legacy by persistently agitating for Kemetic historiographical restoration. In forwarding this ideological mission, Yosef Ben-Jochannan (1918–2015), Leonard Jeffries (1937–), and Molefi Asante (1942–), among others, challenged the racial chauvinism of white academics who defamed their research as lacking theoretical rigor and accuracy. Consequently, Afrocentricity's counter-hegemonic epistemology came under attack during the culture wars of the late 1980s and 1990s. These scholar-activists were not deterred; they inspired generations of college students to view the academy as a potential site for committed ideological, sociopolitical and cultural agitation. Although Ben-Jochannan and Asante had published carefully researched historical studies on Kemet in the 1970s and 1980s,[9] it was not until the publication of *Black Athena* (1987) by Bernal that US academics debated rather than derided the historical arguments at the heart of Afrocentric scholarship. More specifically, the widely cited fray between Martin Bernal and Mary Lefkowitz—two white academics—shone a spotlight on Afrocentricity's theoretical subversion of the Eurocentric historical paradigm that, ironically, would never have taken root if modern historians had believed ancient Greek reflections on Kemet. The Afrocentrics' and Bernal's shared arguments attest to the fact that the anti-black, Eurocentric strain of modern Western historiography has entrenched a colonialist image of Kemet as an anomalous European/Eurasian civilization on the African continent. That *Black Athena* received serious critical appraisal while the scholarship of Bernal's Black contemporaries was marginalized and vilified, did not escape Bernal. He concedes that "if a Black were to say what I am now putting in my books, their reception would be very different. They would be assumed to be one-sided and partisan, pushing a Black nationalist line and therefore dismissed" (1989: 20). Such was the fate of the aforementioned Black vindicationists, including the trailblazing champion of Negro History Week, Carter G. Woodson (1875–1950).

Woodson grasped the insidious psychological effects of Eurocentric education's intrinsically white supremacist methods of inculcation when he prophetically opined, "If you can control a man's thinking, you do not have to worry about his actions … If you make a man feel that he is inferior, you do not have to compel him to accept inferior status, for he will seek it himself" ([1933] 2012: 55). With this statement, Woodson articulated the mission of late nineteenth-century white American elites who attended the 1890 Mohonk Conference on the Negro Question. There, these white leaders outlined specifications for educational curricula that exploited connections between pedagogical indoctrination and identity formation among African Americans who were just three decades removed from chattel enslavement. According to the former New York State Regent Adelaide Sanford, the conference's all-white body of clergy, educators, philanthropists, and politicians specifically proscribed the teaching of Black history in order to disconnect Black communities from their African heritage, foster ignorance of their history before slavery and, most importantly, prevent Black communities from gaining control of their schools.[10] Clearly, these nineteenth-century white leaders understood that African-centered curricula could empower and embolden Black students, so they insisted on an industrial, Christian-based education to cultivate "subservience, passivity, and docility" amongst those who potentially threatened the system of white supremacy (Kazembe 2021: 131). The Mohonk Conference's white supremacist agenda reveals that educational bans against the teaching of Black history were combined with vocational and religious training to intensify the institutionalized oppression of African Americans in the late nineteenth century and into the twentieth century. As a settler-colonial and former slave-holding nation, the US system of education is no different from that of any other colonialist society. From the nineteenth century on, most American students have been steadily exposed to the tenets of white racial chauvinism through pedagogy that highlights the contributions of white Americans and Europeans while maintaining a conspicuous silence on any aspect of Black achievement. This structural epistemic violence is what generations of

Black students in the United States have been forcibly subjected to. The most recent iteration of this anti-black educational agenda is reflected in the controversy over the high school Advanced Placement (AP) course in African American Studies. While states like Florida have banned the course outright, those states that offer it could only do so by following the college board's mandate to delete content on Black Lives Matter, intersectionality and feminist thought. Through these examples, we can see how the epistemic anti-black violence endemic in the US education system is but one iteration of unceasing attacks on Black life that have become increasingly prevalent.

Black thought matters because it established the contours of human knowledge production during antiquity and, in the modern era, Black thought continues to be a driving force in the realization of humankind's most lauded humanist principles: egalitarianism and freedom. If we are to promote true egalitarianism, both domestically and globally, Black thought must be seen as indispensable to this charge. In this regard Part I of this work covers Black thought's contributions to discourses on enlightenment, egalitarianism and freedom. Chapter 1 delves into this subject through my engagement with Lewis Gordon's seminal study, *An Introduction to Africana Philosophy* (2008), which offers meta-epistemological and meta-philosophical ruminations on Black thought's foundational impact on philosophy writ large, intellectual history, the social sciences, literature and political theory. I extrapolate on Gordon's work to show that Africana philosophers have forwarded the aforementioned progressive ideals more vigorously than most of their white/European counterparts. Chapter 2 focuses on the intellectual activism and philosophical work of Leonard Harris, one of the academy's founding fathers of Africana philosophy, through a brief overview of his professional agitation for Africana philosophy's formal recognition and through close readings of his most recent work, *A Philosophy of Struggle* (2020). I present Harris's struggle philosophy as the much-needed antithesis to classical philosophy's preoccupation with theoretical abstraction because he wields philosophical discourse in the fight for human liberation.

Chapters 3, 4, and 5 apply Africana philosophy's inherently transdisciplinary methodology to discussions of curricular expansion, theoretical occlusion and radical social history respectively. The third chapter presents a close reading of Jane Anna Gordon's *Creolizing Political Theory: Reading Rousseau through Fanon* (2014) and advocates for broader implementations of transdisciplinarity, or theoretical creolization, to challenge delimiting disciplinary practices that relegate the works of Black thinkers to Ethnic Studies when their works should be taught in a variety of academic fields. Chapter 4 presents a critique of Julier Hooker's *Theorizing Race in the Americas* (2017), due to the author's cursory juxtapositional readings of works by the Africana philosophers Frederick Douglass and W. E. B. Du Bois. The fifth chapter presents a reflection on the lives, activism and writings of Rosa Luxemburg and Lorraine Hansberry through the lens of the Black radical and Black feminist thought traditions.

Part Two is composed of interviews with three different philosophers whose work centers the importance of Black thought. These radical thinkers "do philosophy" by contributing to contemporary discourse and by living their political and ethical principles as a form of praxis. Chapter 6 features an interview with Jina Fast, author of *Decolonizing Existentialism and Phenomenology: The Liberation of Philosophies of Existence and Identity* (2023). Fast offers compelling insights on the practice and teaching of philosophy, just as she does on academia, feminism, Africana philosophy and American society as a whole. In Chapter 7, the existential philosopher A. Shahid Stover, author of *Being and Insurrection* (2019) and *Epistemic Ruptures, Insurgent Philosophy* (2022), discusses his journey as an autodidact and independent scholar through varied stages of literary engagement; from his early days as a journalist and a hip-hop intellectual to the current horizon of his emancipatory commitment as an avant-garde Black radical theorist. In Chapter 8 we are graced with the revelatory insights of Lewis Gordon whose trailblazing work in Africana philosopohy and Black existentialism, tireless international activism, and committed institution-building have had a tremendous impact on public philosophy, as well as on Fast's, Stover's, and my own intellectual journeys.

Regarding terminology, I use "Black" and "Africana" interchangeably to denote people of African descent and our intellectual productions. Uppercase "B" is used to connote the agential and self-conscious embrace of Black identity, while lowercase "b" in "black" is used to maintain an author's original usage, or as in the case of the Kemites, to denote black skin color. "Negro" also appears in keeping with the terminological accuracy of its respective time. The term "African" describes those thinkers hailing from the continent of Africa; "African

American" for those of African ancestry in the United States; and "Afro-Caribbean" for those of African ancestry residing in the Caribbean or having Caribbean roots. Enlightenment appears with a lowercase "e" to de-center the eighteenth-century European enlightenment as singular in its philosophical exegesis on reason's triumph over religiosity. Instead, just as the preceding pages emphasize how Kemetic enlightenment inspired the ancient Greeks, Chapter 1 details the early modern period of intellectual advancement occasioned through the Moors' Islamic enlightenment of Medieval Europe. Throughout this work I use "thought" and "philosophy," as well as "thinker" and "philosopher" interchangeably since most abstract reflection engages philosophical questions, concepts, and concerns.

My rationale for choosing such a broad array of Black philosophers from Africa and the African diaspora is to underscore the untold impact Black thought has had on humankind's cultural, intellectual, and sociopolitical advancement. It is my hope that this study will inspire ongoing critical dialogues about the historical and epistemological significance of Black thought, thereby remedying its persistent marginalization, negation and erasure in the academy and beyond. For as El Hajj Malik El Shabazz, Malcolm X, so wisely counseled, "it is so important for you and me to spend time today learning something about [history] so that we can better understand the present, analyze it, and then do something about it" (1967: 5).

Notes

1 See Pressman and Devin, "Profile: The diffusion of global protests after George Floyd's murder," 558.

2 Kemet, meaning black lands or dark lands, is the indigenous geographical moniker for ancient "Egypt," which is the Greek name for the region along with "Egyptian" for its people. Lewis Gordon, *An Introduction to Africana Philosophy,* 2; and Molefi Asante *Kemet, Afrocentricity and Knowledge.*

3 Refer to Plato's *Timaeus,* 52–3, where the Greek statesman Critias recounts Solon's conversation with a Kemetic priest who referred to the Greeks as "children," since they had no ancient knowledge of their own. The Kemetic priest further reminds Solon that it was not until the Greeks were given access to the Kemites' religious texts—housed in their temples—that the Greeks were exposed to such spiritual edification.

4   See Diodorus Siculus's descriptions (in Book I) of the Greeks benefiting from Kemetic knowledge in astronomy, historiography, pantheism and ecology—adopting the term "earth mother" from the Kemites to honor the earth's generative life force.

5   Bernal, *For the people: Black Athena Live*, October 25, 1987 [Video] YouTube: https://www.youtube.com/watch?v=dt1NyAqUL6Y

6   The late nineteenth- and early twentieth-century scholars George Washington Williams (1849–1891), Leila Amos Pendleton (1860–1938), Carter G. Woodson (1875–1950), George M. James (1893–1956), John Henrik Clarke (1915–1998), John Hope Franklin (1915–2009), and Cheikh Anta Diop (1923–1986) may also be considered African-centered in that they historicized the Kemites as a black African people. Afrocentricity refers more specifically to an epistemological and sociocultural movement of the 1980s and 1990s in which the scholarship of Yosef Ben-Jochannan, Molefi Asante, and Leonard Jeffries became central. Afrocentrists, whether in the academy or without, resurrected aspects of the 1970s Black is Beautiful movement: donning African clothing, sporting natural hairstyles, and wearing African inspired jewelry and medallions.

7   Egyptology, as an academic discipline separate and apart from African history writ large, arose in tandem with the eighteenth-century Napoleonic expeditions and promoted anti-black myths about Kemet's being an extension of European and/or Near Eastern civilization for two reasons:

   a. Napoleon's disbelief that black Africans could have created the advanced civilization of Kemet, symbolized by the pyramids at Giza and the Sphinx; and

   b. To "whiten" the Kemites and create a colonialist historiographical narrative that supported the exploitation and dehumanization of Africans during the chattel slavery era.

8   The Black vindicationist canon includes Phillis Wheatley's, *Poems on Various Subjects, Religious and Moral* (1777); David Walker's *Appeal* (1832); and Edward Blyden's, *The People of Africa* (1871) among other literary, historical, and political works. See also the introduction of this author's *Being Apart* (2015).

9   Refer to the following works by Dr. Ben: *African Origins of the Major Western Religions* (1970); *Africa, Mother of Western Civilization* (1971); and *Black Man of the Nile and His Family* (1972). Molefi Asante's earlier works include *Afrocentricity: The Theory of Social Change* (1980); *The Afrocentric Idea* (1987); and *Kemet, Afrocentricity and Knowledge* (1990).

10 Molefi Kete Asante. (February 27, 2015). *MKA Institute Presents Adelaide Sanford* [Video]. YouTube. https://www.youtube.com/watch?v=2Lrp 2TSuJf8.

Acknowledgments

A shorter version of chapter one was originally published under the title of "Revisiting Humanity's Roots: Establishing Africana Philosophy's Metaepistemological and Metaphilosophical Foundations," by LaRose T. Parris, in *Entre Letras,* vol. 9, no. 1, January/June 2018: doi. org/10.20873/uft.2179-3948.2018v9n1p.92,

"Creolize the Academy: Embracing Transdisciplinarity to Revive the Humanities and Promote Social Justice" was originally published as "Creolizing the Academy: Embracing Transdisciplinarity to Revive the Humanities and Promote Critical Pedagogy" in the *Review of Education, Pedagogy, and Cultural Studies,* by LaRose T. Parris, vol. 40, no. 1, January 30, 2018, *Taylor & Francis Online,* doi.org/10.1080/107144 13.2018.1409518, reprinted by permission of the publisher (Taylor & Francis Ltd, http://www.tandfonline.com).

An abridged version of chapter four was originally published under the title of "The Present Absence of Africana Thought in Juliet Hooker's *Theorizing Race in the Americas,* by LaRose T. Parris, in the APA blog *Black Issues in Philosophy* on February 5, 2019.

Chapter 5 was originally titled *"To Be Young, Gifted and Woman,"* by LaRose T. Parris, and first appeared in *Creolizing Rosa Luxemburg* (2021), published by Rowman & Littlefield, all rights reserved.

PART ONE

AFRICANA PHILOSOPHY, ENLIGHTENMENT, AND FREEDOM

1

UNVEILING THE HISTORY OF BLACK THOUGHT: LEWIS GORDON'S *AN INTRODUCTION TO AFRICANA PHILOSOPHY*

[The seeker of wisdom is the one/the philosopher is the one] whose heart is informed about these things which would be otherwise ignored, the one who is clear-sighted when he is deep into a problem, the one who is moderate in his actions, who penetrates ancient writings, whose advice is [sought] to unravel complications, who is really wise, who instructed his own heart, who stays awake at night as he looks for the right paths, who surpasses what he accomplished yesterday, who is wiser than a sage, who brought himself to wisdom, who asks for advice and sees to it that he is asked advice.[1]

During Lewis Gordon's keynote address for Columbia University's 2017 "Burning Issues in African Philosophy" speaker series, he quoted the *Inscription of Antef* to expound on how far philosophy has strayed from its originary aims of theoretical expansion and societal amelioration. The Kemetic sage's words resounded as a counterpoint to what Gordon identified as academic philosophy's current state of decline. He asserted that Antef's focus on conceptual innovation and intellectual enlightenment—"[the philosopher's] heart is informed about these things which would otherwise be ignored … is clear-sighted when he is deep into a problem … who surpasses what he accomplished yesterday … to bring himself to wisdom"—is no longer heralded as apotheotic in the academy. To extrapolate further the philosopher's mission of outlining the contours of human existence and freedom, delineating the constitution and breadth of knowledge, and exploring the intricate facets of human reality, is now subordinate to higher education's neo-liberal imperative: the demonstration of skill as a tangible and verifiable market commodity. Gordon avers that the professionalization of philosophy has caused the important reflective and conceptual work of philosophers to be subsumed by the very decadent disciplinary practices that their open inquiry once precluded (Gordon 2006: 26–8, 42).

Viewing philosophy in this totalizing manner—as the sole method of advancing the neo-liberal imperative of profit through professionalization—renders a potentially vast terrain of theoretical inquiry into a particularized domain of ideology. This tendency of deploying philosophy to meet specific ideological aims is not new: eighteenth-century European thinkers merged philosophical concepts with pseudoscientific[2] claims to sanitize and justify the racist dehumanization inherent to the Western imperialist/colonialist projects and the chattel slavery system. This discourse of scientific racism, which has antecedents in sixteenth- and seventeenth-century theories of ethnobiological determinism,[3] has had a lasting epistemic impact and continues to shape global knowledge production, sociocultural formations, and geopolitical relations. As Emmanuel Eze (1963–2007) notes:

> Enlightenment philosophy was instrumental in codifying and institutionalizing both the scientific and popular perceptions of the human race. The numerous writings on race by Hume, Kant, and Hegel played a strong role in articulating Europe's sense not only of its cultural but *racial* superiority … "reason" and "civilization" became almost synonymous with "white" people and northern Europe, while unreason and savagery were conveniently located among the non-whites, the "black," the "red," the "yellow," outside Europe. (1997: 5)

Hume's, Kant's, and Hegel's potent blend of philosophical and scientific bigotry has provided an epistemological foundation for racist ideas to thrive and adapt from the eighteenth-century onward. The widespread influence of Hume's, Kant's, and Hegel's collective thought has legitimized and justified African, Asian, and Indigenous dehumanization, which are foundational to African racial slavery, Western imperialist expansion, and contemporary forms of institutionalized oppression. Since eighteenth-, nineteenth-, twentieth-, and twenty-first-century works of racist thought have become forms of hegemonic discourse, their studied denigration of African people's humanity has lent a false credence to spurious tenets of white/European exceptionalism. There is therefore a direct epistemic correlation among David Hume's "Of National Characters" (1741), Immanuel Kant's *Physical Anthropology* (1802), Hegel's *Lectures on the Philosophy of World History* (1857), Gobineau's *Essay on the Inequality of the Human Races* (1853), Herrnstein and Murray's *The Bell Curve* (1992), and Wade's *A Troublesome Inheritance* (2014), as they perpetuate the fallacy of European racial superiority through ahistorical inquiry that obviates the intellectual, social and cultural advancements of African people and their descendants across the globe. In the case of the eighteenth- and nineteenth-century thinkers, Hume, Kant, Hegel, and Gobineau, their works exemplify how racist and colonialist thought comprise a mutually-informed modern episteme at the level of knowledge production that has intertwined theoretical and sociopolitical implications. This coloniality[4] of knowledge production has engendered four related axiomatic sociocultural practices that are not only derived from the aforementioned European thinkers' racist views, but they also hold currency in philosophy departments, academia and society more broadly:

1. The categorization of African, Global South and Black, Indigenous, and people of color (BIPOC)as subhuman and, therefore, incapable of rational and intellectual thought;

2. The dismissal and/or repudiation of philosophical discourse written by African, Global South, and BIPOC thinkers;

3. The exaltation of European and white American thinkers as cultural heirs of Greco-Roman philosophical exceptionalism and therefore predestined to direct the history of ideas; and

4. The aggrandizement of white American and European philosophical texts as the epitome of human philosophical expression.

To refute these fallacies and highlight the theoretical import and global discursive impact of Black thought, Gordon cited Antef's quote in his "Burning Issues in African Philosophy" talk to provide textual and historiographical evidence that substantiates ancient Africa as the cradle of human civilization and the font of philosophical knowledge—an argument presented in his groundbreaking work, *An Introduction to Africana Philosophy* (2008).

Gordon's title, *An Introduction to Africana Philosophy,* is a provocative misnomer since the study transcends disciplinary boundaries to present Africana thought's age-old existence by revealing its centrality to the development of Western epistemology. Quite tellingly Antef's assertion that the philosopher is "clear-sighted when he is deep into a problem" and their "advice is [sought] to unravel complications" is consistent with what Gordon and others[5] identify as Africana philosophy's transdisciplinary or creolized methodology, which prioritizes ecumenical inquiry over circumscribed, discipline-specific research. This creolized methodology, combined with Gordon's exposition on the professional developments that dictated *An Introduction's* discursive engagement, allows for a multivalent critique of Africana philosophy's erasure and/or negation in hegemonic discourses. Thus, *An Introduction* simultaneously presents Black thinkers' intellectual productions from ancient times to the present while addressing related questions of motivation, method, and inquiry, as well as Africana philosophy's contingent positionality within the Eurocentric discipline of professional philosophy. Through this creolized meta-philosophical approach, Gordon refashions the metaphor of the Du Boisian Veil to disclose Africana philosophy's ideological impact from antiquity to modernity and, in doing so, he reminds readers of the Veil's illusory paradox: it merely cloaks that which is already evident to the naked eye. To support his proposition of revealing the "old"—Africana philosophy—in the form of something entirely "new"—*An Introduction's* taxonomic survey—Gordon unveils Black thought's centrality to world history, the history of ideas, intellectual history, the social sciences, and, of course, philosophy writ large.

He cites the work of the British political scientist and archeo-linguist Martin Bernal, the Argentinian historian and philosopher Enrique Dussel, and the Congolese philosopher and archaeologist Theophile Obenga to confirm the ancient origins of Black thought while affirming these thinkers' radical etymological interrogation of the word "philosophy" itself. Gordon, Bernal, Dussel, and Obenga interpellate "philosophy" and the reader through an archeo-linguistic method that probes the word "philosophy"—not in its immediate Greco-Latin formation (philia/ brotherly love and sophia/wisdom), or earlier Phoenician and Hittite roots—but in its more ancient Old Kingdom Kemetic origins (2008: 1–2). Gordon reminds readers that the Kemites undertook the work of abstract reflection to comprehend, contemplate, then articulate the significance of tumultuous societal occurrences, like the "cross-fertilization of cultures [and the] collapse in concrete manifestations of authority" (ibid.: 7). The *Inscription of Antef* (1991–1782 BCE) substantiates Gordon's, Bernal's, Dussel's, and Obenga's shared claim that the Kemites originated the contours of philosophical discourse, which provided the epistemological foundation for later Greco-Roman systems of knowledge and applied methods of inquiry. Gordon and company's etymological foray substantiates *An Introduction's* meta-historiographical and meta-philosophical critique of Eurocentric histories that elide or, in the case of Hegel and the American school ethnologists, deny the ancient Kemites African racial identity[6] in order to Asianize or Europeanize their contributions to the development of Western civilization. The collective scholarship of Gordon, Bernal, Dussel, and Obenga also dispels the centuries-old myth that the Greeks invented philosophy, Greek civilization arose "*ex nihilo,* out of nothing or nowhere," and that older African, Asian, and Levantine cultures were inconsequential to classical civilization's evolution (Gordon 2008: 1–2). Thus, *An Introduction's* initial archeo-linguistic inquiry sets the stage for an equally catholic survey that accomplishes two related aims:

1.　Ancient Africa is contextualized as the birthplace and inspiration for classical civilization and philosophical thought.

2.　Eurocentric histories that elide ancient Africa's role in catalyzing the cultural and philosophical progress of Greco-Roman antiquity are refuted and delegitimized.

Before delving in to Gordon's survey of Africana philosophers from ancient to modern times, we must first address the historical developments that engendered the Euromodern world's disavowal of Black thought.

Islamic Enlightenment, La Reconquista, and the Rise of Euromodernity

To fully appreciate the meta-theoretical significance of *An Introduction to Africana Philosophy*, I will elaborate on four epochal historical developments that Gordon identifies as actuating the project of African epistemological erasure:

1. The Moors' conquest and colonization[7] of southern Europe in general and the Iberian Peninsula in particular from 711 to 1492 CE;

2. The assertion of "European" ethnic identity throughout Medieval Latin Christendom in response to Islamic imperial might;

3. La Reconquista's inception of Euromodernity through the age of exploration and the first-wave imperial project of 1492; and

4. Renaissance historians' erasure of the Moors' scientific, philosophical, and technological bequests to Europe during the Medieval age.

First, armed with "lightning speed,"[8] in the century after the Prophet Muhammad's death, African and Arab Muslims had extended the Asian, African, and Levantine borders of the Umayyad Caliphate into southern Europe by conquering the Iberian Peninsula in 711 CE and creating the Mediterranean colony of al-Andalus, which included Spain and Portugal, southern France (for a brief period), Sicily, and Sardinia.[9] These Muslims came to be known by the European-derived moniker of Moors, which stems from the Greek terms *Maurus* and *Mauri*, meaning " 'black' or very dark in color."[10] *Maurus* was adopted by the Romans who "called the entire region of northwestern Africa

Mauretania,"[11] and both Greek and Byzantine writers used *Mauri* as a referent for "the indigenous Berber populations … who were a 'black-skinned, war-like, nomadic … population stretching from the borders of Egypt to Morocco."[12] During the Medieval age of the Moors' European invasions, they also came to be known as Blackamoors, Musulmanes, Mohammedans/Muhammadans, and Saracens.[13] From 711 to 1492 CE they maintained colonial rule of al-Andalus through a three-pronged strategy of governance: modernizing material life through advancements in engineering, agriculture, and architecture; providing cultural enrichment through knowledge dissemination and trade in rare and refined goods; and societal assimilation through religious tolerance (particularly during the Umayyad dynasty) and intermarriage with local nobility.[14] We need to only refer to the findings of Western historians themselves to verify the Moors' instrumental role in guiding Europeans toward the intellectual advancements of the Medieval and Renaissance eras. Watt insists that

> without the Arabs European science and philosophy would not have developed when they did … about 1100 CE [when] Europeans became seriously interested in the science and philosophy of their Saracen enemies, these disciplines were at their zenith; and the Europeans had to learn all they could from the Arabs before they themselves could make further advances. (43)

Watt's assessment is borne out in scholarly consensus that denotes the undeniable influence of Córdoban thinkers, like Ibn Rushd, the Moor, (1126–1198 CE also known as Averroes, to whom we will return shortly). Rushd's legal and philosophical arguments for open scriptural interpretation—in addition to his influential commentaries on Aristotle—shaped the thought of the Latin Averroists, inspired the Christian secularism of St. Thomas Aquinas, and the Protestant reformism of Martin Luther. Muslim thinkers, like Ibn Rushd, introduced Europeans to foundational mathematic, scientific and philosophical knowledge that Europeans emulated, assimilated and disseminated. For this reason Lewis reverses the hegemonic binary of the cultured European and the savage Other, remarking that "the European is not the explorer discovering barbaric peoples in strange and remote places, but is himself an exotic barbarian discovered and observed by enquirers from the lands of Islam" (1982: 11). He later proclaims that "the influence of the West in this period was virtually nil—perhaps for the very good reason that the West had so little to offer" (ibid.: 221). Although Watt and Lewis credit Muslim teachers for instructing Europeans in a range of disciplines, their intentional and exclusive use of the term "Arab" rather than "Moor," which describes the African Berber colonizing clans, reflects the tendency among many modern scholars to deny the Moors' African racial identity by privileging the more ethnically palatable Arabian identification due to its proximity to whiteness. Thus to properly contextualize the Moors' Promethean epistemological impact on European knowledge production during the Medieval and, later, Renaissance periods, we must first address the manner in which the historicization of these "Moorish conquerors" (Trevor-Roper 1996: 119) has been marred by anti-black racism.

Several scholars emphasize this racial bias in the Moors' historicization by providing an analysis of modern sources that "attempt to place an artificial wedge between these early Berbers and Black [Africans]" (Brunson and Rashidi 1992: 55), alongside the following primary Christian and Islamic sources that plainly describe the Moors as black Africans

1. *De Bello Vandalico,* written by the sixth century Byzantine historian Procopius, states that African Berbers were comprised of "a number of 'black skinned tribes' who had gained domination over all of North Africa after the period of the Vandals ascendancy in Africa" (qtd. in Reynolds 1992: 95).

2. The Medieval epic poem, *Song of Roland,* narrates the Moors' ninth century CE invasion of France, and depicts them as "black as melted pitch" and the Moorish armies as "hordes blacker than the blackest ink—no shred of white on them except their teeth" (Goldin 1978: 99, 107).

3. Ibn Hayyan's *Dikr Bilad al-Andalus* (1068), describes the 711 CE invading army of Tarik ibn Ziyad of the Nafza Berbers as "'a force of at least seven hundred Sudanese', an Arabic word for Black people" (qtd. in Brunson and Rashidi 1992: 55).

4. Alfonso X's *Cantigas de Santa Maria* (1270–84) includes drawings of black-skinned Moors engaged in both battle and

> leisure activities, like playing chess and dining. The *Cantigas* also recount the 1086 Almoravid invasion of Yusuf ibn Tachfin, the "warrior-king" who is described as "brown-skinned, small-framed and hook nosed, with heavy eyebrows and woolly hair."[15]
>
> 5. *Primera Chronica General,* also penned by Alfonso X, states that the Moors' "faces were as black as pitch, the handsomest among them was as black as a cooking pot" (qtd. in Smith 1988: 19).

These primary sources attest to the fact that historiography is a propagandistic pursuit in which scholars become "architects of ideolog[ies]" expressing political orientations that, in turn, determine the trajectory of their intellectual productions (Keita 2000: 7). Through such a critique we can apprehend that the Moors' historicization, like that of the ancient Kemites, is indicative of the very epistemic colonization that Gordon's *An Introduction to Africana Philosophy* problematizes.

The Moors' prescient scholarship was matched by expertise in trade and engineering that transformed the economically underdeveloped areas of al-Andalus into a bustling hub of inter-regional commerce, or as the fin de siècle Belgian historian Henri Pirenne called the Mediterranean, "a Musulman lake". ([1939] 2017: 162). Their reconfiguration of Iberian life gave Andalusian citizens access to trade in exotic products like silk, gold, copper, papyrus—all of which allowed for an urbane lifestyle of "gracious living"[16] that was common to the peoples of northern and western Africa, the Levant, and Asia. Moorish updates to the Andalusian infrastructure through engineering advancements included the benefits of Kemetic drainage and irrigation systems of "floodgates, wheels and pumps" (Scobie 1992: 354); and in Córdoba the Spanish names for the irrigations system's component parts—like *noria* (irrigating wheel) and *aljibe* (cistern) were derived from Arabic (Watt 1972: 22). Fresh running water and renewed agricultural production regenerated the formerly arid cities of al-Andalus into a verdant urban "paradise" that yielded exotic crops including sugar cane, rice, oranges, lemons, apricots, artichokes.[17] By the tenth century CE Córdoba held the distinction of al-Andalus' center of scholarship and the city was heralded as "the most splendid metropolitan center" (Roberts 1985: 93) due to its numerous libraries that held more books than existed in all of Europe, fifty hospitals, three hundred mosques, nine-hundred public baths and twenty-seven schools for all social classes.[18] By the eleventh century, al-Andalus became a mecca of intellectualism that attracted scholars and students from all corners of the world, which made the Moors' southern European colony "the most powerful state in Europe" (Roberts 1985: 93). For these reasons, the period from the tenth century to the fifteenth century CE came to be known as the Islamic Golden Age, marking six centuries of Islamic enlightenment that brought significant technological, intellectual, and cultural flowering to Europe during the Medieval Age and the later Renaissance era. It is a great irony that it was African and Arab Muslim conquerors who bequeathed Europeans the material, technological, and epistemological benefits of modern civilized society that have been falsely historicized as autochthonous features of European life: a universalized hospital system, refined architecture and engineering, libraries, universities,[19] and advanced scholarship.

The second development, stemming from al-Andalus's pre-eminence and the Moors' cultural and sociopolitical dominance in Medieval Europe, was the coinage of the term "European" as a generalized ethnic identity that supplanted more region-specific monikers like Iberian, Basque, and Gaul. The word "European" first appears after Charles Martel's victory at the Battle of Tours in 732, and it came to symbolize Latin Christendom's oppositional relationship to Islam. The notion of "Europe" as a distinct ethno-religious and cultural region then arose during the reign of Martel's grandson, Charlemagne (768–814 CE), who is memorialized as the "father of Europe." The term "European" gained even greater currency during the Crusades (1095–1291) and peaked during first and second wave of imperialism (1492–1914) through its binary pairing with the fallacy of African primitivism.[20] Therefore we must note that several centuries of European ethnocentrism arose in response to the Moorish colonization of southern Europe. This was an initially reactionary ethnocentrism that became a chauvinistic and predatory form of Eurocentricity through the related hegemonic pursuits of empire-building, conquest, colonization and African enslavement (Amin 1989: 152–4).

La Reconquista of 1492 was the third historical development that led to African epistemological erasure. To explicate how African people's role in the development of early modern European civilization was subsumed by a historiography of European imperial ascendance, Gordon explains the Reconquest as a pivotal yet cataclysmic turning point that established the "hegemonic symbolic order of Western civilization" (2000: 9). Referencing the work of Walter Mignolo, Enrique Dussel, and Cedric Robinson, Gordon contends that early modern European scholars forged an account of the Reconquest to reconfigure Europe as a discrete continent and global center. This narrative of European dominance necessitated framing the reclamation of Spanish sovereignty as a triumphant era of European exploration, burgeoning capitalist growth, and colonial expansion. These geopolitical and economic progressions effectively altered Europe's topographical reality as a "peninsular projection from [the Asian] continent" that, prior to the Moors' arrival, had been a "colonial backwater" in the midst of ancient and advanced Asian, African, and Levantine civilizations that influenced it (Robinson 2001: 29). With the aggrandizement of Europe as a continental and global imperial power, the mutually dependent myths of European exceptionalism and African primitivism came to represent this watershed moment in global history, despite a historical record of highly advanced and intellectually progressive ancient, medieval, and early modern African civilizations.[21] Gordon clarifies that this epochal shift in global reality has led to the widely held misconception that the term "Africana philosophy" is oxymoronic since "the thought of African thinkers became increasingly a form that lacked matter as millions of Africans were involuntarily shipped and distributed across the globe" (Gordon 2008: 26).

The fourth historical occurrence that rendered ancient African knowledge subordinate to Western thought is the discursive outcome of the preceding three: Renaissance historians' erasure of the Moors' influence on Medieval European life, culture, and scholarship. In addition to Gordon, Mignolo, Dussel, and Robinson, several scholars[22] aver that Renaissance historiography of the Medieval period elides the Moors' advancement of European civilization for two reasons: to deny cultural borrowing from a highly advanced foreign enemy culture and to promote the reclamation of "classical" European roots in Greco-Roman culture, effectively erasing the truth of Medieval Europe's backwardness before Moorish interposition. Watt underscores Europeans' dependence and resentment towards their Muslim teachers as causing the reactionary ethno-racial chauvinism that led to their denial of the Moors' intellectual bequests:

Not merely did Islam share with western Europe many material products and technological discoveries; not merely did it stimulate Europe intellectually in the fields of science and philosophy; but it provoked Europe into forming a new image of itself. Because Europe was reacting against Islam it belittled the influence of the Saracens and exaggerated its dependence on its Greek and Roman heritage. (84)

The Moors' colonization of southern Europe transformed and accelerated Europe's development for centuries to come and therein lies the paradox: absent the Moors' colonial domination, European agriculture, sciences, technology, philosophy, and theology would not have flowered in the centuries leading up to its renowned Renaissance. Given that the pioneering scholarship of African and Arab Moors provided the theoretical foundation for Medieval and later Renaissance-era advancements in multiple disciplines, it seems predictable that European historians would falsely credit the scholarship of their Greco-Roman forebears as the source of early modern Europe's rebirth. As I have outlined, Gordon's initial chapters provide an opening for viewing the Moors' historical erasure through the lens of hegemonic discourses on conquest, enslavement, and colonialism—and how these related forms of domination irrevocably altered knowledge production, its content and dissemination, as well as its integrity and veracity from the late fifteenth century onward.

Within the context of the aforementioned geopolitical and discursive developments, Gordon urges readers to consider the emergence and development of Africana thought and, while it is the principal subject under discussion, he undertakes a "teleological suspension" of philosophy (2006: 34) to accomplish two related tasks. First, in suspending the originary purpose of philosophy, which lies in the abstraction of analytical thought, Gordon analyzes transdisciplinary Africana intellectual productions—philosophical, historical, literary, political, and autobiographical—to unveil a meta-philosophical approach that discloses philosophical reflection in a range of disciplinary sources. Second, by using this creolized method of inquiry to probe varied articulations of Africana thought, Gordon unveils mutual areas of topical convergence among the disciplines of history, philosophy, literature, and the social sciences. The result of this transdisciplinary foray is an edifying investigation of Africana philosophers of all affiliations: pragmatists and prophetic pragmatists, Black feminists and womanists, Afrocentrics, African American and Afro-British (European) continental philosophers, Black radical philosophers and Decolonial Marxists, African American analytical philosophers, Africana existential phenomenologists, Afro-Caribbean philosophers (poeticists and historicists), African humanists, African theorists of invention and critics of invention among others. His scholarly intervention allows Africana philosophers to stand out as crucial intellectual interlocutors who have contributed to the history of ideas through their shared exploration of three related topics:

1. a philosophical anthropology that defines what it means to be a human being;

2. analyses of individual/collective liberation and social transformation; and

3. reflective critiques of reason that, in particular, address reason's correlation to the preceding two themes.

With limited space to write on this encyclopedic study, I will present my analysis in two related ways. First, in addressing the connections among theodicy, modernity and reason, three concepts that have indelibly shaped philosophy and knowledge production, I will offer thoughts on the works of ancient and modern Africana and European thinkers whose writings have contributed to furthering the insights and impact of Africana philosophical thought. Second, through detailed discussions of Africana philosophy's aforementioned three themes, I will examine the works of renowned and lesser-known Africana thinkers whose seminal discursive interventions in the eighteenth, nineteenth, and twentieth centuries have been expanded upon in the decades and centuries since their inception. Like Gordon, I will include each philosopher's date of birth and death to show the millennial span of Black thought, which has left an oft-overlooked mark on the fields of intellectual history and the history of ideas. What follows will illuminate how Africana philosophers have historically advocated for the universal realization of fundamental principles that are primarily credited to their European counterparts: enlightenment, egalitarianism, and freedom.

Theodicy, Reason, and Modernity: St. Augustine, Ibn Rushd, and Zara Yacob

Reviewing Gordon's critique of St. Augustine's (354–430 CE) historicization as a Roman colonial-subject philosopher and discussing St. Augustine's position on theodicy will allow us to fully grasp the fundamental paradox inherent to Africana philosophy's circumscribed academic institutionalization. Despite Africana philosophy's ancient origins, reflected in the thought of Antef and other Kemetic thinkers, and its prescient exploration of themes associated with modern European philosophy, Africana philosophy is widely considered subordinate to and/or derivative of European thought for reasons related to the entrenchment of structural and epistemic racism that have been previously discussed. This blindspot towards the seminal nature of Black thought also holds true for ancient and early modern articulations of theodicy and reason, which were explored in the writings of St. Augustine of Hippo in the fifth century CE; the Medieval treatises of Ibn Rush the Moor (1126–98) from Córdoba in al-Andalus; and the seventeenth-century writings of Zara Yacob (1599–1692) from Ethiopia.

St. Augustine is widely accepted as one of the most influential classical philosophers, yet his European genealogical identification is the direct result of ancient Africa's erasure from the narrative of Western civilizational development. Even though St. Augustine's mother was a North African Berber—the same ethno-racial group as the Moors who would later colonize Spain—most modern biographies depict St. Augustine as "ethnically" Roman. Gordon avers that St. Augustine's Roman identification is symbolic of the ways that contemporary thought on racial, geographic, and cultural difference has been imposed upon ancient peoples for whom such discrete categories of ethnic, morphological, and cartographic particularity did not exist. He reminds us that these anachronistic impositions have caused the whitening, or erasure, of African philosophers, like St. Augustine, since: "the thought of African thinkers became increasingly a form that lacked matter as millions of Africans were involuntarily shipped and distributed across the globe. Suddenly, Africans who spoke and wrote of reason began to disappear as Africans," and that, "St. Augustine is exclusively Roman Christian only through a logic that denies mixture, where he supposedly cannot be Roman and Berber, a product of two sides of the Mediterranean" (Gordon 2008: 26, 89). Since St. Augustine was of mixed African and Mediterranean parentage, his African identity was subordinated to his colonial Roman one. This is clearly evinced in the following biographical excerpt, "scholars generally claim that Augustine and his family were Berbers, an ethnic group Indigenous to North Africa, but were heavily Romanized, only speaking Latin at home as a matter of pride and dignity" (https://en.wikipedia.org/wiki/Aug ustine_of_Hippo#Background). For the authors of this entry, pride and dignity among Africans may only exist through their assumption of a subservient positionality with respect to the Roman colonizing class. The hegemonic historicization of St. Augustine as a Roman philosopher has caused the erasure of this influential thinker's mixed-race, Africana identity. In this regard St. Augustine personifies the historical paradox of Africana philosophy's veiled existence within the discipline of Western philosophy: Africana thought precedes European philosophy by several millennia and became foundational to the latter's subsequent emergence in classical antiquity. Rather appropriately, however, St. Augustine's writings on theodicy have become integral to both Africana and Euromodern thought.

Theodicy is a compound word that means God's justice: "*theo* (god) and *dike* (justice)" (Gordon 2008: 43). Theodicy is invoked when humans question the existence and preponderance of evil in a universe ruled by an omniscient and omnipotent God. St. Augustine addresses theodicy by raising two dichotomous, yet related points: (1) humans cannot be privy to God's will; and (2) that humans were bestowed with the ultimate gift from God—free will. As beings whose freedom is intrinsic to their existence, St. Augustine holds that evil acts are the manifestation and result of human freedom (ibid.: 189). In *City of God* (426 CE), widely regarded as St. Augustine's magnum opus, the philosopher elaborates on his theodicean position. He describes God's omniscience towards our freedom and our free will as both the driving force in human destiny and the central factor in humankind's ineluctable power struggles:

God, whose foreknowledge is infallible, has foreknown the strength of our wills and their achievements, and it is for that reason that their future strength is completely determined and their future achievements utterly assured. That is why, if I had decided to apply the term 'destiny' at all, I should be more ready to say that the destiny of the weak is the will of the stronger, who has the weak in his power. (194)

Here, St. Augustine clarifies that free will dictates human endeavors, including how our interactions and relations are determined by the dominance and/or subordination of one person's will to another's. Additionally, he also underscores how free will is both contingent upon and indicative of our intrinsic freedom. He holds that

the same applies when we say that it is 'necessary' that when we will, we will by free choice. That statement is indisputable; and it does not mean that we are subjecting our free will to a necessity which abolishes freedom. Our wills are ours and it is our wills that affect all we do by willing, and which would not have happened if we had not willed. (195)

St. Augustine's spiritually based theodicean position is quite modern in its connected formulations of human agency, freedom, and responsibility, for he aserts that human beings have the ultimate power to actualize through exercising our freedom. This modern take on human freedom is echoed in the writings of two subsequent Africana philosophers whose exegeses on rationality's relation to faith predate those in European discourse by six centuries and two centuries respectively: Ibn Rush the Moor, (1126–1198), also known by his Latin name, Averroes, from Córdoba; and Zara Yacob (1599–1692) from Ethiopia. Through *An Introduction's* metacritique we find that Africana articulations on the compatibility of reason and faith anticipated those in eighteenth-century European enlightenment discourse. Rushd's legally-inspired disputations urging plurality in Qur'anic scriptural interpretations, along with his famed commentaries on Aristotle's metaphysics, led to four watershed developments in European thought and in intellectual history more generally: (1) the rise of the twelfth- and thirteenth-century Latin

Averroists who revived Christian scholarship on the Iberian peninsula and throughout Europe; (2) St. Thomas Aquinas's thirteenth-century re-framing of Islamic-based arguments in Rushd's *Summa,* which became the ethico-philosophical basis for the Aquinian position on Christian secularism; (3) Martin Luther's sixteenth-century Protestant Reformation and its Rushd-inspired call for "Free inquiry into Scripture"; and (4) European enlightenment thinkers' elevation of rationality over religious fundamentalism.[23] Thus, the prescient ideological insights of Ibn Rushd, an Africana philosopher, birthed seminal philosophical and sociopolitical developments that have defined Western culture for the past nine centuries: scholarly exegeses and popular debates on the divide between sacred and secular life. Gordon alerts readers to the fact that Rushd's philosophical thought presents further historical evidence that the Euromodernity of the late fifteenth-century should not be considered the incipient model of global modernism that it is commonly thought to be, for his influential work, *On the Harmony of Religion and Philosophy* (1198), was published when Rushd's fellow Moors had already transformed southern European life for five centuries through the technological and intellectual advancements of Afro-Arabic modernity.

Three centuries after Rushd's work was published, the Ethiopian philosopher Zara Yacob (1599–1692) expressed similar views, averring that faith should and must be the subject of "critical self-examination" (Gordon 2008: 24). Yacob upholds reason as the reflective pathway to scriptural interpretation through his use of inquiry, or *hatata* in Amharic, and searching, or *hasasa*—a dualistic theoretical method dependent upon the guidance of God.[24] Stemming from his mutually informed practice of scholarly and scriptural research, and conscientious probing, Yacob not only held that faith should be examined, but that the search for truth should become a natural extension of human agency and free will:

Man aspires to know truth and the hidden thing of nature, but his endeavor is difficult and can only be attained with great labor and patience … Hence people hastily accept what they have heard from their fathers and shy away from critical examination. But God created man to be a master of his own actions, so that he will be what he wills to be, good or bad. (qtd. in Kiros 2005: 57)

As Rushd's and Yacob's respective writings show, Africana articulations on the compatibility of reason and faith pre-date (in the case of Rushd) and are concomitant (in the case of Yacob) with Réne Descartes's seventeenth-century writings that inspired later eighteenth-century enlightenment thinkers like Locke and Rousseau. Indeed, Sumner reminds us that "Modern Philosophy in the sense of a personal rationalistic critical investigation, began in Ethiopia with Zara Yacob at the same time as in England and in France" (1994: 20).

Turning to the eighteenth and nineteenth centuries, we find Gordon interrogating Western philosophy's impact on the history of ideas through debates on chattel slavery that dominated public intellectual life and knowledge production in Europe and the United States. He presents close readings of John Locke's *Second Treatise on Government* (1689) and *The Fundamental Constitution of Carolina* (1670), alongside Jean-Jacques Rousseau's *The Social Contract* (1762) to evince how philosophical thought was used to either justify or decry the institution of chattel slavery. Locke argues for the enslavement of prisoners in "just wars of self-defense," while Rousseau holds that surrendered prisoners of war can no longer represent their former states and, due to this change in status, should not be held as slaves. In the case of Locke, Gordon pinpoints the spurious nature of his argument, since enslaved Africans were neither at war with the nations of Europe and the United States, nor had Africans "violated laws of nature" (2008: 33–5). Instead, Gordon stresses that European and American slaveholders loathed relinquishing the enormous capital gains they gleaned from slavery; therefore they alternately rationalized slavery's inhumanity in their political treatises or, in the case of the American founding fathers, used it as a metaphorical embellishment to denounce British colonial rule, a core feature of eighteenth-century American rhetoric. Analyzing the contrasting views of these prominent European thinkers allows Gordon to reveal chattel slavery's centrality to the history of Western ideas. And as one of the preeminent Anglo-analytical philosophers, Locke's influential ideas, along with those of John Rawls and Thomas Hobbes, have been problematized and broadened in the works of the African American analytical philosophers Bernard Boxill, Tommy Lott, Charles Mills, Adrian Piper, and Rodney Roberts who "[apply] Anglo-analytical philosophy to the study of black problems, most significantly those that are a function of the impact of race and racism on the lives of black people" (ibid.: 11).

However, less frequently cited in mainstream studies than Locke's and Rousseau's contrasting views on slavery is the considerable impact of philosophical and scientific racism as an organizing episteme that provided ideological justifications for chattel slavery and European colonialism in the Global South. Scientific racism's specious claims about African peoples' sub-humanity are presented in a hierarchy of races that positions the Nordic European at its pinnacle and Africans at its nadir. Within this theoretical and classificatory framework, European and European American philosophers, like David Hume, Immanuel Kant, Thomas Jefferson, and Georg Hegel, contributed to a significant oeuvre that rationalized the brutality of chattel slavery, colonialism, and systemic oppression. These thinkers' works promulgated monogenetic and polygenetic theories on the causes of racial and morphological differences reflected in racial and "species" differentiation that, together, created the figure of the sub-human Negro (Parris 2015: 25–7). As an invention of Euromodern philosophy and anthropology, this sub-human figure may also be understood as a discursive product of secularized theodicy since Gordon frames manifestations of God's justice in the material world of knowledge production thusly:

> In the modern age theodicy has been secularized. Whereas God once functioned as the object, the rationalization, and the legitimating of an argument, other systems have come into play, such as systems of knowledge and political systems, and they have taken up the void left by God. (2008: 76)

Using this treatment of theodicy's secularization enables us to define more precisely the tacit acceptance of Western epistemologies that have become a false universal standard by which the Global South and its people are invariably measured. This establishment of the Euro-modern world's theodicean status has worked in tandem with Western socioeconomic and political dominance to collectively solidify white/ European American peoples's hegemonic domination of the Global South. Consequently, secularized Western theodicy and hegemony have together spurred a significant discursive response from Africana thinkers in the realm of philosophical anthropology. Through their critical reflections on the meaning of their existence in a racist world, Africana philosophers have disproved the tenets of racist thought and made significant theoretical and disciplinary innovations.

"Am I not a man and a brother?": Philosophical Anthropology

Taken from the seal of the London-based Society for Effecting the Abolition of the Slave Trade, the above-cited query plaintively voices the radical dehumanization of Africans under the chattel slavery system. Many of the enslaved ancestors, like Anton Wilhelm Amo (1703–c. 1759), used their intellectual productions to refute chattel slavery's ideological underpinings in racist discourse. Originally from Ghana, Amo was enslaved in Amsterdam and afforded the benefits of an education. Nevertheless his scholarly achievements surpass those of the average eighteenth-century man of any race. In addition to attending the German Universities of Helmstedt (1721–7) and Halle, where he studied Hebrew, Latin, Greek, and romance languages, Amo graduated with a law degree and penned "Inaugural Dissertation on the Laws of the Moors in Europe" in 1729. He then completed his doctoral degree at the University of Wittenberg in 1734, where he finished his dissertation, "Of the Apartheid of the Human Mind, namely, the Absence of Sensation and the Faculty of Sense in the Human Mind and their Presence in our Organic and Living Body." He then taught at the University of Halle from 1736 to 1738 when his major work, *Treatise on the Art of Philosophizing Soberly,* was published in 1738. Amo began his professorship at the University of Jena, also in Germany, but was forced out due to the increasingly hostile racial climate, a consequence of scientific racism's prevalence and blight on interracial social relations (Gordon 2008: 36–7).

His dissertation's critique of Cartesian duality, on its face alone, disproves European enlightenment theories on African intellectual inferiority, while simultaneously refuting the major organizing principle of Descartes's mind-body binary through the fundamental nature of mind-body relationality—namely physiological interdependence. This aspect of Amo's critique may have resulted from his Akan linguistic and cosmological frame of reference for as Gordon notes "Amo's critique of Descartes suggests that he may have been drawing upon an Akanian understanding of the subject from his early years in what is today Ghana. Since he spoke Akan, the metaphysics of language, so to speak, worked its way into his investigations of philosophy written in Latin" (ibid.: 38). Thus Amo's critique of Cartesian thought is both metaphysical and philosophical.

Following Amo, Quobna Ottobah Cugoano (*c.* 1757–*c.* 1803), also from Ghana, became a leading abolitionist in London and a major contributor to the growing canon of anti-slavery, Black vindicationist letters during the eighteenth and nineteenth centuries. In 1787 Cugoano's *Thoughts and Sentiments on the Evil and Wicked Traffic of Slavery and Commerce of the Human Species* was published and the author, like many other Africana writers, used the autobiographical narrative format to deliver political, philosophical, and moral arguments on the inhumanity of the slave trade. Yet Gordon also reminds us that "Cugoano took the time to develop full-fledged theories to support the arguments he made against slavery, and in so doing he offered some original contributions to philosophy" (2008: 4). Cugoano's interpellation of theodicy is one such philosophical contribution. He raises the theodicean question to verify the fallacy of Eurocentric anthropological schema that labeled him and all Africans sub-human beasts. Like St. Augustine before him, Cugoano attributes the existence of evil to the ineluctability of human freedom. Therefore, the "evil and wicked" slave trade is attributable to white Europeans and Americans whose choice to exalt avarice above morality became proof of willful malice and depravity. Cugoano's belief in their moral frailty serves as the basis for his philosophical anthropology, in which he locates humanity's purpose in the forging of a just world where every human being and all nations must be mutually accountable:

> the several nations of Europe that have joined the iniquitous traffic of buying and selling men, must in course have left their own laws of civilization to adopt those of barbarians and robbers…But whereas every man, as a rational creature, is responsible for his actions, and he becomes not only guilty in doing evil himself, but in letting others rob and oppress their fellow-creatures with impunity, or in not delivering the oppressed when he has it in his power to help them. And likewise that nation which may be supposed to maintain a very considerable degree of civilization [,] justice and equity within its own

jurisdiction, is not in that case innocent, while it beholds another nation or people carrying on persecution, oppression and slavery … ([1791] 1999: 87)

Here Cugoano uses the language and logic of European enlightenment rationality against its purported originators, urging them to reconsider their involvement in the forced kidnapping, bondage, and trade of Africans. He impels his largely European audience to consider their tacit involvement in so brutal a socioeconomic and cultural institution. Cugoano also directly refutes the empirical philosopher David Hume's claim that Africans were not opposed to enslavement as a condition of warfare. Using his first-hand knowledge of Fanti political institutions, Cugoano reveals the illogic of Hume's argument: Since military service was "voluntary, a function of duty and respect" in West African communities it could not be considered equal to mercenary militarism which required monetary remuneration (Gordon 2008: 42). While Cugoano used his autobiography to disprove Hume's conclusions and connect theodicean arguments to a philosophical anthropology premised upon human cooperation in the pursuit of a more humane world, Anténor Firmin grounded his challenges to racist thought in creolized analyses that critiqued and expanded the disciplines of philosophy and the social sciences.

Firmin (1850–1911) was born in Haiti four decades after the enslaved revolutionaries overthrew both French colonial rule and the chattel slavery system, making the former San Domingo the first free Black republic in the western hemisphere which, as Gordon reminds us, stood as "a beacon of hope for enslaved people worldwide" (2008: 57). Just as the nation's name (Ayiti) simultaneously honors the Indigenous Tainos whose genocide was the consequence of Spanish enslavement and disease, it also reflects, "A powerful 'reappearance' of black reality in the New World" (ibid.: 160). After completing his secondary and higher education in Haiti, where he began a professional career as a lawyer, Firmin served as a diplomat in France in 1883 and one year later received an invitation to join the Paris Anthropology Society. Like Amo and Cugoano before him, Firmin's intellectual productions and inclusion in European scholarly circles delegitimized claims of inherent African mental incapacity. Nonetheless, Firmin's white French colleagues in the anthropology society continued to espouse polygenetic theories of human evolution that supported the Aryan race's putative preeminence. Firmin recounts the absurdity of joining a professional organization whose ideological rationale was premised upon his, and all African people's, radical dehumanization: "Does it make sense to have seating as equals within the same society with men whom the science which one is supposed to represent seems to declare unequal?" ([1885] 2002, liv). His formal retort was to write *The Equality of the Human Races* (1885), in direct response to Arthur Comte de Gobineau's widely read *Essay on the Inequality of the Human Races* (1853). Firmin stands as a Haitian philosopher whose 1885 work, illuminates the centurial span of scientific racism's legacy.

With his groundbreaking text, Firmin undertook a theoretical intervention that problematizes methodological approaches in the disciplines of philosophy and the social sciences. First, he addresses the difficulty in studying the human being, "a contradictory subject" who may "lower himself to the lowest depths of ignorance ... [and] ... also rise to the resplendent heights of truth, goodness, and beauty" (qtd. in Gordon 2008: 60). Gordon also presents Firmin's critique of Kantian thought to demonstrate how scientists and philosophers alike tried to reconcile human nature's essential contradiction through formulating "idealistic theories of the human or subjective reductive naturalistic ones" (ibid.: 60). Although both Firmin and Gordon differentiate between Kant's transcendental idealism or moral philosophy, which is rational, and Kantian moral anthropology, which is purely empirical, both philosophers identify a direct link between Kantian moral philosophy and Kantian anthropology. This thematic connection between Kantian philosophy and anthropology explains his "geographical theory of intelligence ... and geographic idealism" (ibid.: 60) that denigrates African people, and is outlined in his *Observations on the Beautiful and the Sublime* (1764):

> The Negroes of Africa have by nature no feeling that rises above the ridiculous. Mr. Hume challenges anyone to adduce a single example where a Negro has demonstrated talents, and asserts that among the hundreds of thousands of blacks who have been transported elsewhere from their countries, although many of them have been set free, nevertheless not a single one has ever been found who has accomplished something great in art or science ... ([1764] 2011: 58)

The preceding discussions of Antef's, St. Augustine's, Rushd's, Yacob's, Amo's and Cugoano's philosophical contributions illuminate the anti-black bias that undergirds Kant's fallacious deduction. What is more the intertexuality between Hume's and Kant's erroneous writings on African racial deficiency, resulting from geographical (tropical) privation, is duplicated in the nineteenth-century writings of Hegel, most notably in his *Lectures on the Philosophy of World History* (1837). To believe that Hume's, Kant's, and Hegel's geographical idealism is s a thing of the past is tantamount to saying that such blatantly racist philosophical anthropology has ceased to exist. One need only recall disparaging Republican comments about immigrants from "sh**hole countries" to verify that the legacy of epistemic racism in Kantian and Hegelian thought remains evident in contemporary discourse.

Second, Firmin's text also addresses the issue of human categorization as it relates to epistemic structures of meaning. Gordon details Firmin's awareness of nineteenth-century anthropological limitations since, as the above-cited excerpt of Kant's writing shows, eighteenth- and nineteenth-century knowledge production was complicit in the formation of the very human subject that it professed to "objectively" study. Gordon also alerts readers to the fact that Firmin's late nineteenth-century metatheoretical critique of the social and human sciences prefigures Michel Foucault's archaeology of knowledge and its relation to inquiry. However Firmin's analysis surpasses that of Foucault's because Firmin directly implicates the pseudo-scientific laws of race, physical geography, and natural history in the creation of implacable "racial impositions" that, in themselves, engender the "genealogical organization of thought on human subjects" (Gordon 2008: 61–2). In other words, Firmin's study delineates the interrelated ways that knowledge production is defined by and through overarching structures of meaning that, in themselves, perpetuate racist logic. Firmin, therefore, explicates how certain forms of anthropological and philosophical knowledge are inherently marred by a racist telos.

Third, the ideas and arguments outlined in Firmin's nineteenth-century text contributed significantly to the development of Africana thought and letters since "Nearly every contemporary debate in race theory and Africana philosophy is touched upon in an insightful way in [Firmin's] tome of more than a century past" (ibid.: 58). Central to such discussions of race theory inspired by Firmin's pioneering research is the scholarship of twentieth-century Afrocentric philosophers, like the Senegalese historian and anthropologist Cheikh Anta Diop (1923–1986) and the African American historian and philosopher Molefi Asante (1941–), both of whom have relocated the history of African and African peoples from "the underside of modernity" (Dussel 1998) to the forefront of modernity through historiographies that center ancient Africa as the birthplace of Western civilization. And while not necessarily considered Afrocentric thinkers in the traditional sense, African philosophers who focus on the theme of invention, like Kwame Gyekye, John Mbiti, and V. Y. Mudimbe, contextualize the Western image of a primitive, ahistorical Africa as the signature fabrication of European thinkers, like Kant and Hegel, who placed Africa and "blackness" in a false binary relationship with Europe and "whiteness" (Gordon 2008: 196–203). The philosophical influence of Firmin's Kantian critique is also evident in the works of two twentieth-century philosophers who specialize in Africana thought: Emmanuel Eze, a Nigerian-American philosopher who wrote extensively on the Kantian foundations of racist thought; and Robert Bernasconi, a continental philosopher who has also written on Kantian philosophical racism and "Sartrean readings of black invisibility and humanism" (ibid.: 120). Firmin's nineteenth-century quest to problematize the racial blind-spots of European continental philosophy has also been reinvigorated in the twentieth- and twenty-first-century works of the following philosophers who contrast the thought of European continental thinkers to that of Africana philosophers, in order to create more progressive and emancipatory critical theory: Drucilla Cornell, David Theo Goldberg, Kathryn Gines, Lewis Gordon, Paget Henry, Renee McKenzie, and Cynthia Willett (ibid.: 121).

Amo, Cugoano, and Firmin should be remembered among other prominent eighteenth- and nineteenth-century Africana thinkers like Phyllis Wheatley, David Walker, Maria Stewart, Frederick Douglass, Sojourner Truth, Alexander Crummel, and Anna Julia Cooper, as they used their oratory and textual platforms to reaffirm the inherent equality of African people throughout the world. In Crummel's case, his founding of the American Negro Academy in 1897 marked a turning point in the creation of an educational institution for African American males that rejected the dominant classist and colorist models of Black achievement (ibid.: 51–5). This is just one example of several social transformation and liberatory efforts that characterized the mid to late nineteenth-century agitation of Africana men and women.

"Aren't I a Woman?": Liberation and Social Transformation

In her historic 1851 proto-intersectionalist speech, Sojouner Truth mined her lived experience as an enslaved woman to forward the egalitarian mission of the nineteenth-century abolitionist and women's rights movements. Truth's "Aren't I a Woman"[25] address crystallizes the manner in which the mid to late nineteenth-century and the first half of the twentieth century represent a pivotal era in the development of Africana philosophy, largely because this centurial span gave rise to three seminal geopolitical and social movements for equality in the United States, Europe, and the Global South: the anti-slavery struggle, women's suffrage, and what was then termed Third World decolonization. During the first half of this historic period Frederick Douglass, like Truth, emerged as a committed anti-slavery and women's rights advocate in the United States. In his characteristically principled and forthright manner, Douglass summed up his unequivocal commitment to social equality in the following aphorism, "Right is of no sex—Truth is of no color" (qtd. in McDowell 1999: xxv). His letters, speeches, and three autobiographies encapsulate the former bondsman's, and later stateman's, articulations of freedom that would lead the African American philosopher Broadus Butler to dub Douglass, "The Black Philosopher in the United States" (1982: 1–2), whose

> inquiry, analysis … and political work [was] directed primarily toward change in the human condition and toward social and legal change in pursuit of a clarification and perfection of the democratic ideal of justice.
>
> That pursuit has combined ontological analysis with moral prescription … Black American thinkers [like Douglass] have contributed profound insights into what America ought to be and, by extension, what the universal condition and quality of existence of humankind ought to be. (Ibid.: 1–2)

Douglass's mission to foster the realization of a genuine American democracy inspired profound meditations on the meaning of human freedom. This philosophical introspection led to his unwavering belief that every individual, irrespective of race or gender, not only has the right to be free, but embodies this freedom as an intrinsic and definitive feature of human existence. Indeed, it is nearly impossible to imagine the nineteenth-century anti-slavery and women's suffrage movements without the "epistemological ruptures" (Parris 2015: 47) of Douglass's numerous public addresses, articles, and editorials in *The North Star*. For in these discursive challenges, Douglass refutes scientific racism, promotes gender and racial equality, and delineates a philosophy of freedom that, in its differentiation from liberty (Gordon 2008: 50–1) prefigured later twentieth-century existentialist conceptualizations of agential action and responsibility. Gordon takes Butler's philosophical examination of Douglass's work even further by illustrating how Douglass's theorization of freedom emerged through his quest for literacy, his infamous battle with slave-breaker Covey, and his "preference for the possibility of death" over a life in bondage (ibid.: 50). These life-changing experiences led Douglass to emerge as a "philosopher of existence" (Gordon 2000: 16) whose vision and delineation of freedom is his

> primary contribution to Africana philosophy … implicit in his narratives and his radical egalitarianism. He defended the rights of women and was a known activist in the suffrage movement … [For] Douglass the distinction between liberty and freedom is crucial: the former is the absence of an impediment; the latter requires the conviction of self-worth, responsibility, and dignity in the face of death. Others could enable his liberty, as the patrons who later manumitted him attest, but only he could secure his freedom … Liberty is external; freedom is internal and constitutive of what one is or wishes to become. (Ibid.: 50–1)

Thus, Douglass's radical egalitarianism arose through an uncompromising moral and philosophical vision of freedom — a vision of freedom that became a cornerstone of progressive thought in the nineteenth and early twentieth centuries. Given the historical impact of Douglass's discourse and activism, it is safe to say that his conceptualization of freedom roused and inspired the thinkers Gordon identifies as the "three pillars of African American philosophy" (2008: 69), Anna Julia Cooper, W. E. B. Du Bois, and Frantz Fanon. These three thinkers's works span the late nineteenth, early and mid-twentieth centuries, and their varied writings have influenced every branch of Africana philosophy that has subsequently emerged.

Anna Julia Cooper (1858–1964) is most known for her 1892 collection of essays, *A Voice from the South.* In it she boldly addresses the systemic sociopolitical and cultural legacies born of chattel slavery and patriarchy—institutional racism and sexism. Using her dual commentary on anti-black racism and sexism as the organizing principle for her book's two-part structure, Cooper problematizes race and gender inequality as the starting point for a Black feminist and womanist theory that, "articulate[s] the lives of black women as a critique of racism and sexism … as the inspiration for the construction of an ethic or politics of social transformation in which racism and patriarchy are destroyed in the interest of a feminist future" (ibid.: 100). Such a future is one in which acknowledging every person's worth would be the rule rather than the exception, particularly in societies that consistently elevate the worth of the powerful and privileged—white men—over the worth of the oppressed—African American women and men.

To support her point that whites have historically imbued their race with a distorted sense of value, Cooper urges readers to consider the stark differences between poor Negroes and their white counterparts who

> were never slaves, were never oppressed or discriminated against. Their time, their earnings, their activities have always been at their own disposal; and pauperism in their case can be attributed to nothing but stagnation,—moral, mental, and physical immobility: while in the case of the Negro, poverty can at least be partially accounted for by the hard conditions of life and labor—the past oppression and continued repression which form the vital air in which the Negro lives and moves and has his being. ([1892] 1969: 253–4)

Here Cooper highlights the connections between white privilege and systemic anti-black racism, explicating the latter as the source of African American disenfranchisement and destitution. Her incisive choice of words—"the vital air in which the Negro lives and moves and has his being"—bespeaks the ubiquity of structural racism and white supremacist violence that defined Black life during the nadir period of race relations in American society in the late nineteenth and early twentieth centuries. Despite extreme levels of enforced poverty, constant threats of lynching, and razings of entire Black communities, Cooper emphasizes that African Americans made invaluable contributions to their country in the midst of the government's studied disinvestment and disinterest in their collective well-being. Gordon underscores that for Cooper "worth was a function of what an individual produced in relation to that which was invested in him or her. She pointed out that very little was invested in blacks, and even less in black women" and in spite of this neglect, black people produced inordinate amounts of slave and free labor, inventions, and scholarly innovations under extreme and often violent forms of sociopolitical and economic domination (Gordon 2008: 71). Similarly, in a chapter entitled "What Are We Worth," Cooper illustrates her point about the lack of investment in Black women through the following autobiographical comparison between herself and an average male student:

> A boy, however meager his equipment and shallow his pretensions, had only to declare a floating intention to study theology and he could get all the support, encouragement and stimulus he needed, be absolved from work and invested beforehand with all the dignity of his far away office. While a self-supporting girl had to struggle after school hours to keep up with her board bills, and actually to fight her way against positive discouragements to the higher education … ([1892] 1969: 77)

Cooper's remarkable accomplishments in the face of dissuasion and even greater personal and professional adversity confirm the logic of her value theory. Like Douglass, she was born into slavery, the child of her enslaved mother and the white slave owner who fathered her. Cooper attended the Raleigh, North Carolina St. Augustine's Normal School and Collegiate Institute for Free Blacks where she excelled so rapidly that she taught high school math to students at grade levels above her own. In 1887, Cooper graduated from Oberlin College, where she completed both her Bachelor's and Master of Arts degrees. She then took a position at the Laurence Dunbar School for Negroes and Native Americans where she rejected the prevailing Washingtonian-Tuskegee model of vocational training for Negroes and, instead, insisted on arming her students with a competitive education in "the humanities and sciences, which prepared them to go on for liberal arts degrees at some of the nation's most competitive colleges. For taking this principled stance, however, Cooper was publicly vilified and removed from her post as principal" (Gordon 2008: 70). Following her tenure at the Laurence Dunbar School, Cooper began her graduate studies in Romance languages at Columbia University in 1915, only to leave without graduating because of her familial responsibilities. However she resumed her doctoral studies at the Sorbonne and, there, completed her doctoral degree in 1925. Her dissertation, "Slavery and the French and Haitian Revolutionists" contends that the French bourgeoisie's seditious fervor was the direct result of their material enrichment from the profits of slavery. Cooper drew this astute conclusion in 1925, more than a decade before the Trinidadian philosopher C. L. R. James (1901–1989) made the same assertion in his now classic study, *The Black Jacobins* (1938). While Cooper's work does not shift the timeline, locus, or lexicon of Marxian materialism to the eighteenth-century San Domingo plantation by naming the Afro-Caribbean slaves the first "modern proletariat" as James's does ([1938] 1963, 86), Cooper condemns chattel slavery's destruction of humanity and the "moral … [and] economic order of civil societies" because it demands "[t]he exploitation of man by man … [and] … is therefore a supreme crime against humanity" (Cooper 2006: 36).

Cooper's condemnation of chattel slavery and her censure of institutional racism and sexism became two of her more widely known denunciations of structural oppression. In addition to co-organizing the inaugural Pan-African Congress in 1901, she actively engaged in the Du Bois–Washington debate on the direction of higher education for African Americans by proposing a solution to the implacable pedagogical binary of the elitist Du Boisian Talented Tenth and the accommodationist Washingtonian vocational training model. From 1907 to 1942 Cooper held a faculty position at Frelinghuysen University, a Washington DC institution that provided higher education and social services to students who needed to work in order finance their education. Frelinghuysen's early-twentieth-century model of inclusive educational opportunity laid the foundations for the community college and state college movement that came to the fore in the first half of that century (Keller 1999: 51–63). Cooper began her tenure as Freylinghuysen's president in 1930; however, the university lost its accreditation in 1937 due to racist bureaucratic policies that delegitimized and undermined Black educational institutions. Cooper was undeterred. With single-minded determination, she continued her mission to educate working class students by holding classes in her home, which also housed the university's library and admissions office; and by serving as professor, president, and registrar without pay (May 2007: 46). Cooper's staunch commitment speaks to her expansive vision of educational and societal equity; this radical egalitarianism informed her challenges to race-, gender-, and class-based oppression from the late nineteenth century onwards. Through African American public intellectuals like Cooper, Ida B. Wells-Barnett, and Mary Church Terell, Gordon effectively establishes the secular line of contemporary Black feminist thought. He then holds that twentieth-century Black feminist discourse, in this secular mode, has made its most notable impact in the works of Toni Cade Bambara (1939–1995), Angela Davis (1944–), and bell hooks (1952–2021). Gordon also traces Black feminist/womanist theory's theoretical vein through the religious-themed speeches of Maria Stewart, Sojourner Truth, and the theological writings of James Cone, along with the cultural criticism of Alice Walker. He discerns, however, that the theoretical bifurcation between the secular and the theological dissolves in the works of Black feminist theorists Patricia Hill Collins and Joy Ann James whose "standpoint epistemology" and "multitudinous" narrative and political orientations, respectively, represent a merging of secular and religious-based foci (2008: 100–3).

Among these twentieth-century Black feminist thinkers, the philosopher Angela Davis has originated an influential body of work that, like Cooper's before her, consistently links the legacies of chattel slavery and patriarchal rule to contemporary, reified structural formations that are imbricated within the hegemonic fabric of society, thereby causing their perpetuation rather than their extinction. In this regard, Davis has taken up the liberatory mantles of both Cooper and Douglass. Indeed, her foundational text of Intersectionality Studies, *Women, Race & Class* (1981), furthers Cooper's theory of worth in its call for a Black feminist future that fully acknowledges the invaluable contributions of African American club women, like Wells-Barnett, whose anti-lynching crusade fearlessly spoke truth to power, despite repeated threats against her life. And in *Are Prisons Obsolete?* (2003), one of the inaugural texts of the prison abolition movement, Davis's contention that the chattel slave system was reconfigured into the Reconstruction-era convict leasing system and the contemporary prison-industrial complex, reveals her thought as a continuation of Frederick Douglass's abolitionist/anti-slavery discourse. It is equally important to note that during Davis's incarceration as a political prisoner in the early 1970s she penned (and later revised) two lectures on liberation in direct response to Frederick Douglass's theorization of freedom in *Narrative of the Life of Frederick Douglass* (1845), and *The Life and Times of Frederick Douglass* (1881) (Ruggiero 2010: 9–21). In "Unfinished Lecture on Liberation" (1983), we see the refinement in Davis's thought from its initial expression in "Lecture One" and "Lecture Two," which were written during her sixteen-month incarceration from 1970 to 1972. In "Unfinished Lecture," Davis became the first philosopher to initiate a comparative analysis of Douglass's writings on freedom with those of the French existentialist philosopher, Jean-Paul Sartre. Davis maintains that Sartre's abstraction of freedom could not express the immediacy and gravity of freedom for those who had been enslaved and oppressed. Instead, Davis reasons that Douglass's articulation of freedom possesses greater theoretical relevance since it was informed by the materiality of bondage and subjugation. With this theoretical innovation of connecting materiality and ontology, Davis, like Douglass before her, planted the seeds for Africana existentialism that would take root in the later writings of Lewis Gordon, Paget Henry, Robert Birt, Naomi Zack, and others whose works are anthologized in *Existence in Black* (1997), as well as this author's *Being Apart* (2015). This genealogical contextualization of Davis's theoretical inheritance brings us to the second pillar of Africana philosophy, Africana existential phenomenology, and Black radical theory—the historian, sociologist, and philosopher of existence William Edward Burghardt Du Bois.

W. E. B. Du Bois: Double Consciousness, Africana Phenomenology, and Black Radicalism

Du Bois (1868–1963) is one of the most important philosophers to have contributed to the history of ideas in the twentieth century. This

Renaissance man of Africana letters created an incomparable corpus that, in and of itself, laid the transdisciplinary methodology for African American Studies, African Diaspora Studies, Black Atlantic Studies, Black Radical Studies, critical race theory, sociological inquiry, and radical historiography. Like Anna Julia Cooper, Du Bois was born in the late nineteenth-century, yet his intellectual contributions and innovations have been indispensable to twentieth-century knowledge production and intellectual history. He was born and raised in Great Barrington, Massachusetts; studied philosophy as an undergraduate at Harvard University and was dissuaded from pursuing his doctoral degree in philosophy on the grounds that "he could better serve his race through working in the discipline of history" (Gordon 2008: 74). After earning his PhD in history from Harvard and studying in Berlin, Du Bois went on to teach at Wilberforce University and Atlanta University. His career as a public intellectual also includes co-founding the Niagara Movement, the National Association for the Advancement of Colored People (NAACP) and, like Cooper, the first Pan-African Congress. Through the metatheoretical intervention of Du Bois's landmark ethnographic study, *The Philadelphia Negro* (1866), we may trace the seeds of his philosophical thought, which would germinate in his theory of double-consciousness outlined in *The Souls of Black Folk* (1903), and later become a core concept in Africana existential phenomenology.

Among those schooled in Africana Studies, it is widely known that Du Bois was commissioned by the University of Pennsylvania to undertake a study of African Americans in the closing years of the nineteenth century and that this sociological work "created urban ethnography and many of the theoretical foundations of U.S. sociology" (ibid.). However Gordon reminds us that Du Bois entered into this project with the keen awareness that African Americans could not be investigated like other subjects of research, since their humanity had been historically questioned, challenged and, in the most extreme cases of anti-black racism, fully denied. To complete his study, Du Bois had to overcome "the challenges [his study] posed to positivistic science" by "find[ing] a way to study black people without black people becoming problems in themselves" (ibid.). Like his contemporary Firmin's indictment of anthropological research, Du Bois's methodology in *The Philadelphia Negro* implicates empirical science's inextricable ties to supervening archaeologies of knowledge that created and perpetuated racist conceptions of Africana people. These findings led Du Bois to a method that was guided by an equally significant proposition, namely "that the question of black people was of philosophical importance" (ibid). This question, posed in Du Bois's *The Souls of Black Folk*, is formulated in his now famous query: "How does it feel to be a problem?" ([1903] 1997: 31). Since the question is posed to black people, Gordon emphasizes that Du Bois is actually asking how it feels to be black, which is a question that underscores ontological concerns—in its foregrounding of black being and methodological concerns in relation to Du Bois's own process of inquiry (ibid.).

Du Bois seemingly answers this question in *Souls'*, most frequently cited passage. With his trademark insight and lyricism, he explains that

> the Negro is sort of a seventh son, born with a veil, and gifted with second-sight in this American world—a world which yields him no true self-consciousness, but only lets him see himself through the revelation of the other world. It is a peculiar sensation, this double-consciousness, this sense of always looking at one's self through the eyes of others, of measuring one's soul by the tape of a world that looks on in amused contempt and pity. ([1903] 1997: 39)

Just as Du Bois attests, in a world shaped by anti-black racism, the material and existential reality for the black subject causes one's self-conceptualization to be born of an awareness that whites' scorn and judgment preclude one from experiencing the respect of an equal human being. According to Gordon, the distortion of inter-subjective relations that Du Bois describes leads to three interrelated crises of individual and societal dimensions: first, the problem of black subjectivity and self-perception emerges. The Du Boisian paradigm demonstrates the ways in which the black psyche is compromised in the form of a degraded self-image, brought about by the negative appraisals of a racist society. This, in turn, leads to the mutual exclusivity of blackness and national/social belonging, as one cannot be both black and American, or black and European for that matter. Second, and in a related vein, is the fact that consciousness and inter-subjective relations are central to phenomenological awareness since, "phenomenology examines reality as constituted by consciousness, where consciousness is understood in its intentional or directed form as always having to be of something" and that the forms of consciousness implicated in Du Boisian double consciousness are "(1) consciousness of how mainstream society sees itself (dominant 'reality') and (2) consciousness of its contradictions (subaltern reality)" (2008: 78–9). Third, in terms of mainstream society's collective self-apprehension, we must revisit the question of "problem people" and their contingent tethering to a secularized theodicean dimension of dominant reality. Gordon explains that

> in the context of modern attitudes toward and political treatment of black people, a special kind of theodicean grammar has … asserted itself. The appeal to blacks as a problem-people is an assertion of their ultimate location outside the systems of order and rationality. The logic is straightforward: a perfect system cannot have imperfections. Since blacks claim to be contradictions of a perfect system, the imperfection must … lie in black people themselves. Blacks become rationalized as the extraneous evil of a just system. (Ibid.: 76–7)

With this declaration, Gordon connects the problem of theodicy to the lived reality of anti-black racism: it perpetuates the criminalization and brutalization of Black people, even though many whites may recognize and acknowledge the "dominant reality" of systemic racism. The secularized theodicy of white domination leads to the common perception of black people as existing outside the bounds of "order and rationality;" thus, our abuse is seen as justifiable because we are seen to represent contradictions to what many whites view as an infallible democratic system. This secularized theodicean perspective leads to racial blind-spots, since many whites believe blacks to be the embodiment of "extraneous evil" that exists within an otherwise perfect system of justice.

Du Bois's *Black Reconstruction in America* (1935) also foregrounds the racial blind-spots inherent to Marxian thought. This text, along with C. L. R. Jame's *The Black Jacobins* (1938), inaugurated Africana Studies' sub-fields in Black radical and Black Atlantic studies, thereby initiating many scholars and lay people into further explorations of progressive Black thought. The works of the twentieth-century Africana philosophers Cedric Robinson and Anthony Bogues have been greatly influenced by Du Boisian thought. Robinson's *An Anthropology of Marxism* (2001) provides an indispensable critique of Marxian thought as a manifestation of bourgeois idealism, rather than the subversion of said hegemonic discourse that it is widely held to be. By deconstructing Marx's and Engels's anthropology of class struggle, focused solely on the European proletariat as a modern replication of ancient Greek societal hierarchy, which elided the socioeconomic presence of women and slaves in the Athenian polity, Marx and Engels "created a polar, dualistic, oppositional conception of man in the form of a class struggle that placed gender and race, and consequently all women and people of color, as epiphenomenal and, thus, at the periphery" (ibid.: 129–30). Furthermore, in disregarding Medieval historiographies that promulgate a radical Christian egalitarianism that defined humanity through the inclusion of women and people of color, Marx and Engels created a theory of political economy and human relations that "was part of the episteme it criticized, that it was, in effect bourgeois science" (ibid.: 130–1). In this regard, Robinson's extension of Du Boisian Black radicalism provides a most astute critique of the limitations inherent to Marxian thought, as well as its delimiting and far-reaching political repercussions. Contrary to Robinson and Gordon, however, the pragmatist philosopher Cornel West subscribes to a form of African American philosophy that combines Marxism and prophetic Christianity.[26] West also maintains that Du Bois and Alain Locke (1886–1954) should be considered pragmatists because of their association with American pragmatism. Gordon argues against this view, however, urging that it potentially reduces all Africana philosophers to pragmatists, due to Africana thought's prevailing concerns with social transformation and liberation.

Du Bois's philosophical legacy is extremely rich. It is evident in the vast number of contemporary works in social and political theory, Black radical studies, literary theory, and Africana philosophy that draw upon his timeless insights into Africana life, in particular, and the human condition in general. Following Cooper and Du Bois, Gordon's third pillar of Africana philosophy, is Frantz Fanon whose transdisciplinary investigations into the human sciences, and traditional and radical Western philosophy effectively theorized Third World decolonization while laying the basis for radical social and political theory across the globe.

Frantz Fanon: Epistemic Decolonization Through *Caliban's Reason*

Through Fanon's (1925–1961) considerable impact on the development of twentieth-century Africana thought, we may once again locate Africana philosophy's specific emergence on the African continent and witness its dissemination throughout the diaspora; in this case through Fanon's revolutionary thought on epistemic, psycho-social and material decolonization in Algeria. Although Fanon was born in Martinique, his most profound philosophical and political insights may be traced to the African continent, most specifically in his theoretical critiques of Western reason's application in the human sciences and hegemonic philosophy, and in reason's relation to the material, ideological, and psychological structures of European colonialism. Fanon's impact on the growth of Africana philosophy is perhaps best evinced in two quotes. The first quote by Karl Jaspers identifies reason as philosophy's raison d'être; the quote also reflects the extensive nature of Fanon's theoretical undertaking. Jaspers observers that "philosophy through the millennia is like one great hymn to reason—though it continually misunderstands itself as finished knowledge, and declines continually into reasonless understanding" (qtd. in Gordon 2008: 81 n.26). With this reflection on philosophy's relationality to reason, Jaspers unknowingly yet precisely outlines the interrelated contexts for professional philosophy's axiomatic dismissal of Africana thought: the Eurocentric ontologizing of the discipline, the mistaken view that philosophical knowledge is finite, and philosophical thought's paradoxical degeneration into irrationality. Thus Gordon's inclusion of Jaspers's quote prepares the reader for Fanon's equally illuminating view of reason's perceived incompatibility with blackness:

The psychoanalysts say that nothing is more traumatizing for the young child than his encounters with what is rational. I would personally say that for a man whose only weapon is reason there is nothing more neurotic than contact with unreason…when I was present, [reason] was not; when it was there, I was no longer. ([1952] 1967: 118–20)

Through this quote from *Black Skin, White Masks* (1952), Fanon presents a layered critique of Western reason that discloses its "failure," which is manifest in its epistemologically "self- [deceptive]" effort to make Europe ontological and, therefore, the embodiment of "Absolute Being" (Gordon 2015: 19). As Fanon's argument in *Black Skin, White Masks* attests, Western hegemonic domination leads to a form of self-alienation that causes black/colonial subjects to mistakenly believe that they exist apart from the realm of rationality. Through Fanon's explanation of the black subject's perceived antagonistic relationship to reason, we may locate the underlying basis of his meta-theoretical examination of the human sciences—an examination that also developed through his engagement with psychoanalysis and existential phenomenology. As a formally trained psychiatrist, Fanon effectively expanded Freudian and Lacanian therapeutic methods into his own brand of Fanonian psychoanalysis, because he recognized the fundamental inability of Western science to properly diagnose and treat the black/colonial subject. Like Firmin and Du Bois before him, Fanon subjected the epistemic bases of the human sciences to intensive evaluation and, consequently, problematized their Eurocentric orientation for positing Europe/Europeans as a false universal. In *Black Skin, White Masks*, and his expressly psychiatric writings,[27] Fanon describes Western empirical sciences' various levels of complicity in creating and perpetuating the very black subject they purported to study dispassionately and objectively.

Gordon describes this Fanonian theoretical intervention as one that reveals "epistemological colonization at the methodological level … [since] the methods have been colonized then the outcomes of inquiry could become affirmations of colonialism" (Gordon 2008: 85). Yet Fanon's apprehension of the material effects of a compromised epistemic system neither begins nor ends at the level of psychoanalysis. He arrived at this progressive therapeutic method through his keen understanding of existential phenomenology, which posits the interconnectedness of consciousness, inter-subjectivity, and socially generated internalized phenomena.

Fanon's critiques of existential phenomenology (Gordon 2015: 2–13), and his subsequent insights into its relevance for the black subject's experience of anti-black racism, inspired several aspects of his creolized methodology, which includes a sociogenic diagnosis of the colonized subject's self-alienation, a revision of the Hegelian dialectics of recognition and, much later, the Fanonian (and Du Boisian) inspired emergence of Africana existential phenomenology or what may also be termed decolonial phenomenology. Phenomenologically speaking, Fanon specifically outlined the contours of the black/colonized subject's consciousness formation through the contrasting lens of "dominant reality" (mainstream colonial society), and the "contradictions" of the black/colonized subjects' own individual, "subaltern reality" (Gordon 2008: 78–9), which led Fanon to include in his brand of psychoanalysis the variable of socially generated, or sociogenic, external forces like anti-black racism and colonialism that caused his patients' state of alienation. This merging of decolonial phenomenological and sociogenic perspectives led Fanon to make several unique contributions to Western thought, as his interposition allowed for a holistic examination and treatment of the black/colonial subject. The most progressive feature of Fanon's decolonial phenomenological model of inter-subjective consciousness is that it calls for agential action on the part of the colonized subject, both individually and collectively. Gordon stresses that Fanon's firm belief in intentional action may be "considered a fight against nihilism, a goal sought by oppressors for the minds of the oppressed; it is a goal for [the oppressed] to lose meaning, for them to lose faith in alternatives, and … eventually give up on the possibility of change" (ibid., 84–5). Thus for Fanon, psychological decolonization is the necessary precursor to the material struggle for collective self-determination and native sovereignty. Part and parcel of this mental liberation is the realization that the colonized must never look to the oppressor for acknowledgement of their humanity. Through Fanon's revision of the Hegelian dialectics of recognition, he underscores that the colonized should look within for confirmation of their intrinsic worth:

> Fanon argues that it is futile for colonized and racially oppressed peoples to seek their liberation through seeking recognition from their colonizers and racial oppressors. In doing so, they will be caught in a logic that props up their oppressor as the standard of human value. (Ibid.: 86)

In this manner, Fanon advocates for breaking the shackles of mental slavery and, in doing so, sets forth a decolonial prescription for self-determination and self-actualization for the peoples of the Global South. Fanon applies this decolonial phenomenology to the eradication of colonial rule and the construction of more humane institutions of power. He reasoned that since colonization is itself a violent historical process, the decolonization process, given the dialectics of oppression and resistance, can only be violent in kind. Following the reclamation of native rule, he envisioned the potential for new societal structures that would dispense radically egalitarian forms of power, and thereby, "set afoot a new man" (1967: 35–6, 316). In effect, Fanon recognized that individual and collective freedom could only be sustained through rigorous challenges to racist/colonialist epistemic systems in their theoretical and material manifestations:

> Fanon announces the relationship between meaning and the constitution of forms of life, and that a central role of liberation thought is the reconfiguration of concepts, including those through which practice can become praxis or freedom-constituting activity. (Gordon 2008: 86)

Through Fanon's faith in humanity's ability to overcome the hegemonic ordering of symbolic and material life, and his insistence on envisioning and fashioning liberatory praxis, we come to understand the need for decoloniality at every level of thought and action. The twentieth- and twenty-first-century philosophers William Jones, Lucius Outlaw, Lewis Gordon, Linda Martín Alcoff, Kathryn Gines, Charles Johnson, A. Shahid Stover, J. Moufawad-Paul, and Jina Fast have furthered Fanon's initial explorations of Africana existential phenomenology in a range of works that engage the thought of the European phenomenologists Husserl and Heidegger, while underscoring their own critiques of continental thought. This Fanonian discursive legacy also abounds in Afro-Caribbean philosophy and modern African political thought. Fanon's use of the Prospero-Caliban trope in *Black Skin, White Masks* has been refashioned as the theoretical crux of Afro-Caribbean philosophy in the late twentieth and twenty-first centuries; especially as Shakespeare's play *The Tempest* has become the most frequently referenced allegory for European colonial domination in the Caribbean. Paget Henry's landmark study *Caliban's Reason: Introducing Afro-Caribbean*

Philosophy (2000), theorizes that the civilizational rupture wrought by the hegemonic rise of Euromodernity in the Caribbean, through the related historical events of the European slave trade and colonial expansion, led to the establishment of culturally and racially imperialist ideological formations that degraded the native Caribbean experience and Afro-Caribbean people. Emerging out of colonial and postcolonial epistemic structures are two dominant, and sometimes overlapping, strands of Afro-Caribbean thought that, while privileging the dominant European discourse at times, also problematizes it to further native Caribbean cultural, historical, and political realities (2000: 1–8). Historicist and poeticist Caribbean philosophical discourse is the result of "the colonial situation [that] created an 'existential deviation' in the psyche of the Afro-Caribbean" (Fanon qtd. in Henry 2000: 3). The historicist Afro-Caribbean philosophers include Marcus Mosiah Garvey (1887–1940), C. L. R. James (1901–1980), George Padmore (1903–1959), Frantz Fanon, and Walter Rodney (1942–1980). The poeticist philosophers are those who have amassed oeuvres that are both creative and historical in focus. These include Nicolás Guillén (1902–1989), Aimé Césaire (1913–2008), Édouard Glissant (1928–2011), Derek Walcott (1930–2017), Kamau Brathwaite (1930–2020), Sylvia Wynter (1928–), and Wilson Harris (1921–2018) (Gordon 2008: 17). Just as Afro-Caribbean philosophers have found fertile ground in Fanonian thought for identifying and remedying the ills of mental and material colonization, thinkers from the African continent (and other regions of the Global South) have also applied Fanonian philosophy and political theory to pressing issues in more contemporary political contexts. Gordon identifies the Fanonian legacy in African political thought through the works of the East Indian-Ugandan political theorist and economist, Mahmood Mamdani (1946–); the East Indian-Kenyan political theorist, Pal Ahluwalia (1959–); the Ghanaian philosopher Kwame Gyekye (1939–2019); the Cameroonian social and political theorist Achille Mbembe (1957–); the Cameroonian philosopher and theologian Elias Bongmba (1953–); and the South African philosophers Steven Biko (1946–1977) and Rabson Wuriga (1960–2024) (ibid.: 220–48). Clearly, Fanon's philosophical and discursive interventions continue to be utilized and expanded upon today because his work is a living testament to the significance of his epistemological interpositions and their applicability to the complex social and political problems that define societal institutions and inter-subjective human relations.

Conclusion

The year 2023 marked the fifteenth anniversary of *An Introduction to Africana Philosophy's* publication, and during this decade and a half Africana philosophy's professional reception has grown to some extent. With this sweeping transdisciplinary work, Gordon has provided an indispensable theoretical and pedagogical resource to aid teachers and students alike in deepening their understanding of Black thought's central role in global knowledge production and intellectual history. This revelatory study foregrounds Africana philosophers as pivotal interlocutors in the history of ideas, Western historiography, anthropology, the social and political sciences, literary studies and, of course, philosophy itself. Within this range of academic disciplines, African and African diasporic thinkers' works have elucidated the meaning of such fundamental concepts as enlightenment, egalitarianism, and freedom. However, until Africana philosophy becomes a standard offering at all institutions of higher learning, and until the epistemological and material structures that prevent Africana people and all people of color from being fully accepted as human beings, the struggle will not be over. It will continue to rage on until thinkers and lay people grasp the wisdom of the late philosopher Drucilla Cornell's (1950–2022) admonition that encourages us to embrace Africana philosophy since all philosophers "can be committed to the best ideas of European philosophy and still [be] equally committed to the struggle against Eurocentrism for [philosophers] must do so in the name of truth … Nothing less is at stake here than the future of our humanity" (133). Cornell's exhortation is precisely what Gordon reveals in his textual survey of Black thought: We must accept the truths of Africana philosophy and Western philosophy to create an ethic of discursive inclusion and egalitarianism that Eurocentric thought has historically and consistently denied. Upholding these truths will allow us to celebrate and disseminate the philosophical legacy of our common humanity to, finally, create a more just and livable world for all.

Notes

1 *Inscription of Antef* qtd. in Théophile Obenga, "Egypt: Ancient History of African Philosophy," 35, Kwasi Wiredu, (ed.) *A Companion to African Philosophy.*

2 One of the most prevalent pseudo-scientific theories was the claim that Africans' black skin was caused by the presence of black bile, black blood, and/or a blackening of the cells' reticular membrane. Thomas Jefferson, Immanuel Kant, Georges-Louis Leclerc, and M. le Romain forwarded these notions in their respective writings. See Jefferson, *Notes on the State of Virgina,* 128–9; Kant's *Physical Geography,* quoted in Eze's *Race and the Enlightenment,* 61–2; Lecler's *A Natural History, General and Particular*, excerpted in *Race and the Enlightenment,* 24–5; and le Romain's encyclopedia entry, "Nègre," also excerpted in *Race and the Enlightenment,* 92–3.

3 Richard Popkin and Emmanuel Eze explain that disciplinary articulations of racist thought in philosophy and science are both related and overlapping. Popkin holds that the theoretical foundations of philosophical racism lie in mid-fifteenth-century Iberian debates on the biological impurity of Jewish and Muslim converts to Christianity on the Iberian Peninsula. These theories of ethno-biological determinism then led to the emergence of monogenetic and polygenetic evolutionary theories, which were used to explain the phenotypical differences among Europeans, Indigenous peoples, and Africans. He then stresses that philosophical discussions of racial difference began to proliferate during the eighteenth-century European enlightenment's science-based discussions of degeneracy theory. See Popkin, *The High Road to Pyrrhonism*, 79–87. Similarly, Emmanuel Eze stresses that European enlightenment-era philosophers utilized "identifiable scientific and philosophical vocabulary: 'race,' 'progress,' 'civilization,' 'savagery,' 'nature,' 'bile'…etc." Eze, *Race and the Enlightenment,* 5, 7.

4 Anibal Quijano and Michael Ennis, "Coloniality of Power, Eurocentrism, and Latin America."

5 See chapter 3, "Creolize the Academy," which discusses Jane Gordon's important work, *Creolizing Political Theory.* Other works on theoretical creolization include, Michael Monahan's *The Creolizing Subject* and *Creolizing Practices of Freedom,* as well as Rowman & Littlefield's *Creolizing the Canon* series, which includes *Creolizing Hegel* and *Creolizing Frankenstein.*

6 In Hegel's *Lectures on the Philosophy of World History*, he declares that "Africa consists of three continents, which are entirely separate from one another, and between which there is no contact whatsoever … The second is the land to the north of the desert … which might be described as

European Africa. And the third is the region of the Nile … which is closely connected with Asia" (173). William Stanton's, *The Leopard's Spots,* includes a thorough discussion of the American school ethnologists' spurious phrenological claims that the dynastic Egyptians were "dark skinned Europeans" (132).

7 Gordon, *An Introduction*, 23; Hugh Trevor-Roper, *The Rise of Christian Europe*, 11; Cedric Robinson, *An Anthropology of Marxism,* 29; W. Montgomery Watt, *The Influence of Islam on Medieval Europe*, 19.

8 Henri Pirenne, *Mohammed and Charlemagne,* 149.

9 Ibid., 149. See also Watt, *The Influence of Islam on Medieval Europe*, 2–9; Michael Morgan, *Lost History,* 18–21; Bernard Lewis, *The Muslim Discovery of Europe,* 18–20.

10 José Pimienta-Bey, "Moorish Spain: Academic Source and Foundation for the Rise and Success of Western European Universities in the Middle Ages," 187.

11 Ibid.

12 Dana Reynolds, "The African Heritage and Ethnohistory of the Moors," 94–5.

13 While the term "Blackamoor" refers to the Moors' black skin and "Musulmanes," "Mohammedans and Muhammadans" denote their allegiance to the Prophet, the term "Saracen" initially referred to Asian and Levantine Muslims. However Pirenne uses the term "Saracens of Africa" and, as Keita insists, all of the aforementioned terms came to be used synonymously. See Pirenne, *Mohammed and Charlemagne,* 160; and Maghan Keita, "Saracens and Black Knights," 65–77.

14 Michael Morgan, *Lost History*, 15–21; Henri Pirenne, *Mohammed and Charlemagne*, 147, 150; W. Montgomery Watt, *The Influence of Islam on Medieval Europe*, 7–19; Roberts, *The Triumph of the West*, 83; Bernard Lewis, *The Muslim Discovery of Europe*, 63.

15 The following modern sources cite the *Cantigas'* Africoid description of Yusuf ibn Tashfin: Brunson and Rashidi, "The Moors in Antiquity"; José Pimienta-Bey, "Moorish Spain"; Mamadou Chinyelu, "Africans in the Birth and Spread of Islam"; and Miriam DaCosta, "The Portrayal of Blacks in a Spanish Medieval Manuscript."

16 Michael Morgan, *Lost History,* 155–6; and W. Montgomery Watt, *The Influence of Islam on Medieval Europe,* 23–6.

17 Michael Morgan, *Lost History*, 68 and 155–6; W. Montgomery Watt, *The Influence of Islam on Medieval Europe*, 24–9; and J. M. Roberts, *The Triumph of the West*, 94.

18 Jan Carew, "Moorish Culture-Bringers: Bearers of Enlightenment," 255; Michael Morgan, *Lost History*, 69; James Brunson and Runoko Rashidi, "The Moors in Antiquity," 57.

19 See José Pimienta-Bey's "Moorish Spain."

20 Cedric Robinson, *An Anthropology of Marxism,* 32 and 39; J. M. Roberts, *The Triumph of the West,* 65–6 and 83–9; Trevor-Roper, *The Rise of Christian Europe,* 99–102; W. Montgomery Watt, *The Influence of Islam on Medieval Europe,* 48–51; Bernard Lewis, *The Muslim Discovery of Europe,* 21–2.

21 Lewis Gordon, *An Introduction*, 24–25. E. Jefferson Murphy, *History of African Civilization*; Elias N. Saad, *Social History of Timbuktu;* and Michael Gomez, *African Dominion.*

22 Samir Amin, *Eurocentrism* 151–4; Michael Morgan, *Lost History*, 33; and Watt, *The Influence of Islam on Medieval Europe*, 84.

23 Samir Amin, *Eurocentrism,* 128 and 135–6; Michael Morgan, *Lost History,* 137; W. Montgomery Watt, *The Influence of Islam on Medieval Europe*, 42, 70–1, 79; Lewis Gordon, *An Introduction*, 23–24,190; and Mourad Wahba, "Philosophy in North Africa," *A Companion to African Philosophy,* 161–2.

24 Lewis Gordon, *An Introduction,* 24 and Teodros Kiros, *Rationality of the Human Heart,* 5.

25 Truth scholars have contested the veracity of the "Ain't I a Woman" title of her famous speech. They argue that Truth, with her New York Dutch accent, would not have spoken in the southern vernacular. Instead she would have queried "Aren't I a Woman." Refer to Nell Painter, *Sojourner Truth: A Life, A Symbol.*

26 Although Gordon identifies West as a prophetic pragmatist philosopher, he has also identified an unacknowledged existential dimension in West's philosophical orientation. Refer to Gordon's *An Introduction*, 91–2.

27 See Frantz Fanon, *Écrits sur l'aliénation et la liberté.*

2
LEONARD HARRIS'S PHILOSOPHY OF STRUGGLE

To say that Leonard Harris's trailblazing work in professional philosophy made the writing of this book possible is an understatement. Absent his commitment to valorizing the historical and ideological significance of Black thought, many of the late-twentieth-century and twenty-first-century philosophical texts cited in the previous chapter could not have been published. Harris's revolutionary vision, persistent scholarly agitation, transnational organizing, and institution-building transformed late-twentieth-century philosophical discourse specifically and the US academy more generally. Harris's preeminent standing in the fields of Africana philosophy and philosophy writ large began with an intellectual journey that is representative of the intertwined cultural, pedagogical, and sociohistorical barriers that Black thinkers faced in mid-twentieth-century American society: outstanding scholarly acumen that exceeded their white professors' expectations, despite varying degrees of social alienation at predominantly white institutions.[1] In the late 1970s Harris and Lucius Outlaw[2] were fellows at the Moton Center for Independent Study in Philadelphia, where they undertook research to meet the ultimate goal of producing an anthology of Black philosophy. Harris focused on social and political philosophy, while Outlaw delved into matters of historical reconstruction. Their history-making collaboration led to six major developments that birthed Africana philosophical institutions and organizations, as well as Africana philosophy's formal recognition by the American Philosophical Association (APA) in the 1990s:

1. Outlaw's attendance at the sixth annual Pan-African Congress in Tanzania in 1975 led to his substituting the term "Africana" for "Black" as an organizing concept for philosophical thought from the African continent and the African diaspora.

2. Outlaw organized the inaugural Africana Philosophy conference at Haverford University in 1981, while Harris attended an Afro-Asian philosophy conference at the University of Nairobi in 1981.

3. In 1982, Harris organized the Africana Philosophy Research Conference at Haverford with financial support from the National Endowment for the Humanities, the Social Science Research Council, and Fund for the Improvement of Secondary Education.

4. Harris's groundbreaking collection, *Philosophy Born of Struggle: Anthology of Afro-American Philosophy from 1917* was published in 1983.

5. Harris served as editor of the APA's newsletter, *Philosophy and the Black Experience* from 1991 to 1996.

6. Harris's disciplinary expansion of professional philosophy was commemorated in the formation of Philosophy Born of Struggle conference, which had its inaugural meeting in 1993 and has met annually for the past thirty-three years.[3]

These events coincided with Harris's own curricular and pedagogical expansion while teaching African American Social and Political Philosophy and African Philosophy courses at Haverford. In addition to driving the US academy's s formalization of Africana philosophy, it is clear that Harris's and Outlaw's "meta-philosophical intervention"[4] in the late 1970s and early 1980s paved the way for the recognition of other Ethnic Studies-related sub-fields in philosophy, including, Critical Race Studies in Philosophy, Decolonial Philosophy, Feminist Philosophy, Indigenous Philosophy, and Latin American Philosophy, among others.

In taking up the mantle of the late-nineteenth- and early-twentieth-century African American philosophers Thomas N. Baker (1860–1940), Rufus L. M. Perry (1833–1895), Jerome R. Riley (1843–1949), and Alain Locke (1885–1954), Harris compiled similarly philosophical writings for his seminal collection, *Philosophy Born of Struggle* (1983).[5] He queried academic editors at the annual APA conference for two years before one editor of a leftist press informed him that none of his colleagues present (including him) "believed that white people would read what black philosophers have to say and none of them … think that they could sell such a book to white authors."[6] Harris's experience with the anti-black gatekeepers of academic publishing reflects the overarching structural and theoretical fallacies that *Philosophy Born of Struggle* refutes: pronouncements of white/European intellectual exceptionalism that are legitimized through a Eurocentric education system and its correspondingly circumscribed curricular offerings. By contextualizing late-nineteenth- and early-twentieth-century African American thinkers/ scholar-activists as philosophical interlocutors who engaged in the major sociopolitical and cultural debates of their respective times, Harris's anthology foregrounds the indispensability of Black thought to modern Western discourse. Frederick Douglass's oeuvre is a perfect example of Africana thought's vital importance to the movement and dissemination of progressive ideas. His radical egalitarian vision and committed activism—encapsulated in his hundreds (if not thousands) of speeches and articles—galvanized both the anti-slavery and women's suffrage movements in the mid-nineteenth-century. And in the early twentieth-century Du Bois's and Alain Locke's emancipatory polemics framed the literary, musical, and visual artistry of the 1920s Harlem Renaissance as epoch-defining reflections of intellectual genius that, in the service of liberation, reaffirmed African descendants' centrality to the advancement of Western civilization. *Philosophy Born of Struggle* foregrounds the philosophical innovations of Douglass, Du Bois, and Locke among others by capturing these thinkers' insights on agency, egalitarianism, justice, and freedom while highlighting these concepts' inherent contradictions in the Euromodern philosophical and sociopolitical contexts. It is fitting that *Philosophy Born of Struggle's* epigraph—"If there is no struggle there is no progress"—is an excerpt from Douglass's famed 1857 West India Emancipation speech in which he provides dialectical insights on what constitutes an emancipatory philosophy of social change:

> Let me give you a word of the philosophy of reform. The whole history of the progress of human liberty shows that all concessions yet made to her august claims, have been born of earnest struggle.

> The conflict has been exciting, agitating, all-absorbing, and for the time being, putting all other tumults to silence. It must do this or it does nothing. If there is no struggle there is no progress. Those who profess to favor freedom and yet deprecate agitation are men who want crops without plowing up the ground, they want rain without thunder and lighting. They want the ocean without the awful roar of its many waters. ([1857] 1950: 437)

Many students and scholars of Africana philosophy are familiar with Douglass's oft-quoted speech; nevertheless, the emancipatory significance of his remarks cannot be overstated. In a brief paragraph he not only outlines the dialectics of oppression and resistance, but also emphasizes that philosophies of liberation and societal reform should not be relegated to field of discourse. Rather, these philosophies must become a means of practical recourse, a methodological path towards liberation. This mission was not lost on Harris. He explains that Douglass's emancipatory thought inspired him to dispense with the Socratic method—a mainstay of philosophical dialogism— and instead embrace a philosophy of struggle that, in Harris's view, engenders the most interesting questions about the human condition.[7] Since *Philosophy Born of Struggle*'s 1983 publication, Harris has amassed an impressive scholarly corpus that intercedes in both classical and modern philosophical thought to highlight the liberationist commitments of such Black thinkers as David Walker, Maria Stewart, Douglass, and Alain Locke. His edited volume, *The Philosophy of Alain Locke: Harlem Renaissance and Beyond* (1989), was one of the first texts to introduce the Harlem Renaissance-era figure as a pragmatist philosopher and not solely a cultural critic and promoter of New Negro aesthetics.[8]

Harris's most recent work, *A Philosophy of Struggle* (2020), offers powerful arguments against romanticizing classical thought systems that elevate the attainment of wisdom to a quest for human perfection through simultaneity: a corporeal being whose consciousness is cognizant of the soul, able to observe the soul's autonomous being, while still remaining in union with the soul. In Harrisian terms this vaunted yet fantastical being heralds a monster, a "categorically impossible being" (16). With this in mind, Harris urges us to consider that "if philosophy is no longer a singularity, a well-bounded noun, a search for self and alt-self, the place to find simultaneity of the universal and the particular, philosophy's boundary would be thereby sufficiently porous and uncharted" (33). This conceptual permeability "should provide tools of poetry, imagery, evidential reasoning, inclusion of real people, and norms incommensurable with philosophy as a science," for "philosophy is not an algorithm but a walkway" (33). In this manner Harris indicts philosophy as a science that occludes material reality; he urges us to dispense with philosophy as a noun entity since the abstraction of the traditional philosophical endeavor cleaves human existence from what should be the generative relationships among human beings, their thoughts, and their actions: philosophizing on how to end human suffering. He boldly exhorts us to enter into philosophy—to linger on a path towards open possibilities that allow humankind to create a more livable world, free from the scourges of racialized oppression, enslavement, genocide, human trafficking, child abuse, and enforced poverty—all of which destroy our natural impulses to live and thrive.

A Philosophy of Struggle's discursive innovations lie in four related propositions that bespeak Harris's theoretical mission:

1. A commitment to making philosophical discourse actional in the fight for humanity's betterment;

2. Advancing an actuarial account of both structural and internalized racism as forms of necro-being,[9] or living death;

3. Applying Alain Locke's "radical pragmatism"[10] to reinvigorate pragmatist philosophy's moral imperative by;

4. proposing an abolitionist-insurrectionist ethic that reanimates pragmatism's moral center.

These concerns respond directly to two (of the three) questions Gordon identifies as the catalyzing force behind Africana thought: What does it mean to be a human being; and what are the processes of individual and collective liberation? Harris's implicit response is that philosophy must become a conceptual tool in the ongoing project of human liberation from oppression and injustice in their myriad forms. In the Harrisian spirit of philosophizing towards open possibilities, I will use two theoretical methods—namely a Black radical critique and an Africana critique of epistemic racism—to engage with *A Philosophy of*

Struggle. But before entering into my analysis, we must first highlight the importance of Harris's struggle philosophy.

Why Struggle Philosophy Matters

A Philosophy of Struggle presents a holistic reflection on human suffering and the precarious nature of our shared existence, so that we may think critically and engage collectively to improve the material conditions of our shared world. Harris's thought is meta-philosophical in its dethroning of traditional philosophy's orginary aims; his is an iconoclastic undertaking that offers a prescriptive conceptual agenda that condemns brutality, dehumanization, immiseration,[11] and all forms of unseeing that obscure the reality of human mutuality and interdependence. This Harrisian corrective underscores that in accepting our mutual humanity we must acknowledge our ethical responsibility towards each other, which behooves us to dispense with internalized biases, preconceived notions, and elitist attitudes that preclude the widespread acceptance of a liberationist imperative. Why should we philosophize in and through these processes of individual, societal, and global reassessment? Because if we don't, lauded philosophical concepts like freedom, justice, equality, and morality will remain abstractions just as those claiming to be its practitioners will remain inconscient to or disinterested in the day-to-day indignities that plague human beings. To illustrate the futility of abstractions about a distant moral universe, Harris uses the example of state-sanctioned anti-black police violence during the southern Civil Rights Movement. He asserts that Martin Luther King Jr. was wrong to claim that "The arc of the moral universe is long, but it bends towards justice."[12] Harris invokes the memory of police violence that brutalized peaceful protesters at King's nonviolent direct action campaigns, which alerted Americans to the structural anti-black racism of de jure segregation that nullified the protesters' citizenship rights:

> Those beaten may well have died before the end of *de jure* segregation, those living rarely received its benefits, and protesters often were harmed [and killed]. There is no assured justice for those suffering the agony of injustice, let alone a moral universe that would include all sentient beings everywhere receiving justice. (29)

For Harris, African American civil rights activists of the mid-twentieth-century are just one among many segments of disenfranchised humanity who received neither redress nor reprieve from the societal injustices that compromised their very lives. The activists' shared plight is one that holds no guarantee of ethical resolution in Harris estimation. By breaking with popular opinion on the efficacy of political activism driven by a belief in divine compensation, Harris reinforces his point on a distant moral universe. He holds that, rather than fostering untruths about universal justice, philosophy should offer prescriptive strategies for fashioning a world that values human life over the continuation of human degradation. For ubiquitous human misery, according to Harris, has engendered the omnipresent sorrow song:

> Sorrow songs are just that, songs that express lament, hurt, and irredeemable agony. But most philosophers do not tarry here. Instead of seeing the misery of past generations, the thought of misery disappears, and is replaced by a law, or picture of the "moral universe," as if there were such a thing, making 'justice' happen. Good philosophical magic. (29–30)

That songs of lamentation rise up among every racial and ethnic group the world over should speak to their potential for driving more hermeneutical explorations of desolation amongst philosophers. Harris contends that this is not the case; he holds that philosophers instead cling to "philosophical magic" portentous of the afore-mentioned distant and discrete moral universe. To avoid this common trap, he reminds us that "we can have hope without entrapment in undue delusions, progress without the pretense of having arrived at a location beyond provincialism ... and insurrectionist ethics without the feeling that our actions are all justified by an algorithm of pure reason ..." (31–2). Here we see that one of Harris's bequest to Africana philosophy is the framing of struggle as a conduit for purposeful reflection and intentional, inspired action. Philosophers should endeavor to transform the world through a multiplicity of conceptual methods that center the ongoing project of human liberation. To that end Harris encourages us to see that

> There is no one "philosophy of struggle," no one representative of aggregated social kind that embodies as its sole interest universal

human liberation and well-being, no one voice that is driven by its nature or its location to speak for all, that is, one voice of the people, women, men, or humanity ... Mabogo More's ... Angela Davis's [and] Rozena Maart's ... razor sharp revealing of race, class, cultural traditions, and women's and men's agency within the context of their philosophy born of struggle are not identical depictions of agency or normativity. (31–2)

The afore-mentioned thinkers all address issues of agency, class, culture and race; however, their respective meditations on these philosophical and structural formations differ. While Angela Davis's applications of Africana and feminist philosophies (as discussed in Chapter 1) laid the foundations for Africana existentialism and Intersectionality Studies, Mabogo More's engagement with Sartrean existentialism and Black existentialist thought applies Sartrean contingency to the fight against anti-black racism. Rozena Maart's application of Africana and continental philosophies furthers Black feminist thought's standpoint epistemology through her intersectional analyses of Black consciousness in the South African context. Indeed, the title of Harris's work, *A Philosophy of Struggle,* rather than "the" philosophy of struggle makes this position clear. His thought, like that of Davis, More, and Maart, reveals the transformative power of struggle philosophy's liberationist aims by disclosing the anti-human project of hegemonic domination: the continued subjugation and brutalization of groups that are fallaciously deemed less than human.

The Black Radical Tradition in Absentia

Given that Harris characterizes philosophies engendered through struggle as varied in their descriptions of agency and normativity, the passing mention of Cedric Robinson's influential work, *Black Marxism: The Making of the Black Radical Tradition* (1983) is surprising for two reasons:

1.   Robinson contextualizes Marxian thought as intrinsic to the very bourgeois science that it critiques, since it reinscribes

    rather than subverts classical philosophy's exclusionary categories of historical agents: white men are deemed agential historical actors, whereas the enslaved and women are comparatively inconsequential in Marx's science of history.[13]

2.   Robinson highlights the early twentieth-century Black radical thought of W. E. B. Du Bois and C. L. R. James as shifting the timeline and lexicon of Marx's historical materialism to the eighteenth- and nineteenth-century plantations of the Americas where Black workers and a Black proletariat,[14] respectively, used their agency to revolt against chattel slavery and, in the case of San Domingo (Haiti), overthrow French colonial rule.[15]

Robinson's seminal text is a creolized work of historiography, philosophy, political theory, and political economy that offers a meta-theoretical critique of global capitalist development and, by extension, Marxist thought. Through this catholic orientation, Robinson examines overlapping historical, sociopolitical, and epistemological developments that birthed the modern global capitalist system: European feudalism; Medieval and Renaissance-era market economies; racial capitalism (in Europe and the Americas), African racial slavery and slave insurrection; ancient Africa's erasure from the Western historiographical narrative; early twentieth-century Black radical discourse; and anti-colonial liberation movements in Africa and the Americas. Thus, he examines the geo-political events and ideological trends that arose in tandem with and in response to capitalism's growth as a global economic system. Since Marx's theoretical intervention is widely viewed as the counter-hegemonic corrective to idealist European discourses that legitimized the institutions of chattel slavery in the Americas and European colonialism in the Global South, Robinson's critique highlights Marxism's "antinomies and limitations … in the interest of its ultimate [liberationist] aims" (Gordon 2008: 131). In subjecting Marxian thought to this rigorous evaluation, Robinson shows how Marx's methodology and terms of engagement actually perpetuate patriarchal normativity[16] and further entrench Eurocentric ideological biases.

    Despite Harris's claim that Marx's thought "help[ed] to change the world … [by providing] the concepts, precepts, reasoning methods, poetic terms, and motivation that have been a resource for generations of successful activists" (28), Robinson's genealogy of the Black radical tradition shows that it was Africana philosophers' revisionist expansion of Western radical theory that actually initiated the revolutionary epistemic rupture that has mistakenly been credited to Marx. Both Du Bois and Fanon explicitly stressed that Marxism must be adapted when applied to analyses of African American oppression and European colonial domination in the Global South.[17] Robinson heeded their call by foregrounding how Du Bois's *Black Reconstruction in America 1860– 1880* and James's *The Black Jacobins* (1938) centralized enslaved African labor, agency, and mass resistance and, in so doing, Du Bois and James transformed the disciplinary fields of historiography and political theory. These Africana philosophers explicate how enslaved African labor was central to the development of modern capitalist accumulation. Their proto-decolonial shift is clear in Du Bois's estimation of how enslaved Black labor, and enforced colonial labor, fueled the "industrial empire"[18] of the Global North:

> The giant forces of water and steam were harnessed to do the world's work, and the black workers of America bent at the bottom of a growing pyramid of commerce and industry; and not only could they not be spared … but rather they became the cause … of new dreams of power and visions of empire … Black labor became the foundation stone not only of the Southern social structure, but of Northern manufacture and commerce, of the English factory system, of European commerce … The emancipation of man is the emancipation of labor and the emancipation of labor is the freeing of that basic majority of [enslaved and colonized] workers who are yellow, brown, and black. (5, 16)

Here we may see how Du Bois's radicalism surpasses that of Marx, because his call for proletarian liberation is one that makes the simultaneous demand for greater class and race consciousness. In the same manner that *Black Reconstruction* presents a reconceptualization of enslaved Black labor's indispensability to Western capitalist development, James's *The Black Jacobins* reframes the French bourgeoisie's emergent revolutionary consciousness as the result of their newfound wealth, which was gleaned through the interdependent systems of exploitation colonialism and chattel slavery: "The fortunes created at Bordeaux, at Nantes, by the slave-trade, gave to the bourgeoisie that pride which [demanded] liberty and contributed to human emancipation" (Juares qtd. in James 47). James, like Du Bois before him, integrates enslaved African laborers into the historiography of Western capitalist and political developments, so that the significance of the ancestors' toil may be recognized for what it was: the source of significant capital accumulation—rather than the primitive accumulation Marx claimed it was—that solidified the vast wealth of the United States and Europe from the sixteenth-century to the present day. In this manner, Robinson uses the works of Du Bois and James to shine a light on how the enormous capital accumulation of chattel slavery and colonial labor in the Global South fed the industrial revolution and propelled the United States and Europe to their superpower status in the Global North. *Black Marxism*'s epistemological contribution cannot be overstated. Based on Harris's classificatory terms for philosophies of struggle, the Black radical tradition that Robinson historicizes should be delineated as a philosophy of struggle. And whether one is a proponent of Marxist or Black radical thought, it is a fact of globalized economic history and political economy that Western capitalist growth was made possible through the transmogrification of African human beings into commodities. The ancestors' radical dehumanization is an example of necro-being, a concept which figures prominently in Harris's descriptive, actuarial account of racism.

Necro-being as Living Death

Harris's formulation of racism as necro-being, or living death, is a cautionary rejoinder to Africana philosophy's concerns with the meaning of human being and the processes of individual and collective liberation. For the past several centuries, humankind as a whole has failed to embrace its ethical responsibility to ensure collectivized well-being; therefore, it has also failed to realize universal egalitarianism and communalism in the fight against racism. The result of this negligence is that racism continues to cause the living death of its victims. Necro-being highlights the myriad ways in which racist social structures, discriminatory laws, and predatory economic policies make racism a life and death exchange—an exchange that creates optimal quality of life for the privileged at the expense of the downtrodden who die or barely survive. Harrisian necro-being makes it clear that the lives of the wealthy and privileged matter more than the lives of the poor and disadvantaged:

> Racism is a form of necro-being: it kills and prevents persons from being born. It is absolute necro-tragedy. There is no redemption for the worst of its victims. Dominant groups acquire longer lives, assets, and high sense of self-worth at the cost of the extinction or sustained subordination of the subjugated ... Racism persists because it works sufficiently well in an imperfect world to ensure a confluence of benefits, especially the most important benefit—namely health benefits—for enough people over generations. It effects the preconditions for the possibility of embodied well-being. (69)

Thus, the consequence of racism, be it structural or episodic, is a living death that precludes the possibility of human wellness. It is necro-being that defines the existence of millions who subsist in the midst of human-made catastrophes: genocide, enslavement, poverty, human trafficking, abuse, and more. Harris urges us to apprehend the disastrous reality of necro-being through his actuarial account of racism that describes the material conditions of the afflicted, rather than catalogues the historical causality and determinant features that have led to these conditions. This actuarial, or descriptive account, allows for "a way of morally condemning racism without the need for a corresponding explanation of its causes or ... its polymorphic array of forces" (74). Harris further argues that "morally condemning racism ... does not commit us to categorizing racial kinds as objective communities," which in Harris's social constructivist view of race, occludes the reality that "Races are ... historical contrivances, anabsolute, but have real being in each context" (76). Thus the "real being" of race, for Harris, is the facticity or actuality of human suffering—the inevitable consequence of racist policies and practices that, in turn, create a life and death exchange wherein the lives of the dominant group are exalted at the expense of the subordinated "raciated" group.

Here we can see that Harris's philosophy of struggle may be understood as a conceptual cum actional corrective to racial injustice. However, what could further animate Harris's descriptive account of racism is its contextualization as a defining and normative Euromodern episteme that continues to sanitize dehumanization, subjugation, and systemic oppression in all forms. Harris's propositions on the need for philosophy to become a discursive weapon in the service of liberation are cogent and compelling, yet his insistence on an actuarial account of racism raises a pressing question: How can this actuarial account effectively "disclose[s] the axis of power, knowledge, and ethics endemic to [racism's] reality" (87) without a corresponding delineation of epistemic racism's complicity in causing the catastrophic human suffering engendered by Euromodernity: Indigenous genocide in its related forms of conquest, settler colonialism, and cultural genocide in Indian boarding schools; the radical dehumanization of Africans during the European slave trade; the codified subjugation and torture of Africans on plantations through Slave codes; the continuation of anti-black oppression and anti-black violence in Jim Crow laws, structural discrimination, and rampant lynching; European first- and second-wave imperialist and exploitation-colonialist projects in Africa and throughout the Global South?

The Struggle Against Epistemic Racism

A Philosophy of Struggle's opening chapter argues that historicism cannot foretell evolutionary, earthly, and cosmological changes that humankind, animal life, and the planet will inevitably undergo due to ecological degeneration and subsequent physiological adaptations (15). Though historicism may not offer insights into the future biodiversity of our world, historical examinations of epistemological developments provide tools for understanding racist ideations that undergird socio-political and cultural formations, thereby perpetuatuing global injustices and human suffering. Harris provides such an historicized insight in his aforementioned critique of King's avowal on the existence of an ultimately just moral universe. His challenge to popular opinion on the efficacy of King's moralism pushes us to dispense with reassuring assumptions and, instead, forces us to ask the "who" and "what" of racism-induced suffering. But what of the "why" and "how"? In other words, what of racism's epistemic groundings and ideological expressions? Although

Harris cites the works of Edward Blyden (1832–1912), Charles Mills (1951–2021), and David Goldberg (1952–) among others, who explain racism as a "logical world system"(70), he then characterizes these thinkers' shared critical project as "misguided" (77). Harris's assessment is problematic in its implied dismissal of epistemic racism as a distinct and deliberate discursive development; this position is borne out in his appraisal of St. Clair Drake's *Black Folks Here and There* (1987) and Martin Bernal's *Black Athena* (1987). In Harris's view, these works hold that "the vicious force of white supremacy … is not a 'race' with inherent causal traits but a polymorphic arrangement of incipient variables that conjoin to make possible the completely inhumane force of white supremacist ideology and behavior" (62–3).

While Harris is correct in asserting that the white race as a whole is not intrinsically predisposed to espousing white supremacist beliefs or committing acts of racist violence, it is unsettling that Harris interprets Drake's and Bernal's texts as situating white supremacist ideology within a varied constellation of inchoate factors. Both Drake and Bernal explicitly maintain that Eurocentric historians' anti-black racism fueled their historiographical erasure of the ancient Kemites' racial, cultural, and geographical roots in the African continent, precisely because their highly advanced civilization flourished at a time when European civilization was in a primitive state. Drake and Bernal also aver that eighteenth- and nineteenth-century European thinkers' racial chauvinism drove them to erase Kemet's tremendous influence on classical antiquity, which provided the epistemological and cultural foundations in all areas of knowledge production and dissemination for Greco-Roman civilization. Moreover, both Drake and Bernal emphasize that by the mid-nineteenth-century European historians could not reconcile the Kemites' black descriptions in ancient historical sources with their high level of epistemological and cultural achievements. Consequently, nineteenth-century European historians postulated that "the original 'pure' Egyptians had been white but there had later been considerable mixture from other races, and this … miscegenation had been the major cause of their decadence" (Bernal 1987: 245). This whitening of the ancient Kemites' functioned as a historiographical parallel of the master-slave dyad of chattel slavery that rested upon the degraded condition of enslaved Africans in the Americas, a discursive revision that was not lost on Frederick Douglass. Douglass not only used his anti-slavery platform to crystallize the American republic's fundamental hypocrisy as a slaveholding "democratic" nation, but he also used his oratory skills to critique the manner in which epistemic racism served to rationalize chattel slavery. In his 1854 speech, "The Claims of the Negro Ethnologically Considered," Douglass takes a Black vindicationist stance to connect enslaved Africans in the United States to an ancestral heritage of racial and cultural achievement in ancient Kemet. Douglass refutes the American school ethnologists' argument that the dynastic Kemites were neither racially, phenotypically, nor culturally black Africans, while emphasizing the slaveholding class's affinity for the American school's anti-black views as Congress debated the 1854 Nebraska bill on slavery:

> The debates in Congress on the Nebraska Bill during the past winter, will show how slaveholders have availed themselves of this doctrine in support of slaveholding. There is no doubt that Messers. Nott, Glidden, Morton, Smith and Agassiz ... were duly consulted by our slavery propagating statesmen.
>
> Fashion is not confined to dress; but extends to philosophy as well—and it is fashionable now, on our land to exaggerate the differences between the Negro and the European. ([1854] 1950: 295, 298)

It is plain to see why the American school's racist logic held great sway over slaveholding politicians in the American south, like former South Carolina governor James Hammond who cited *Crania Aegyptica* in 1858 to proclaim that "the philosophy of subjugation lay in the doctrine of the Races" (qtd. in Stanton 1960: 53). Drake, like Douglass before him, also clarifies the white/European chauvinistic bias in his refutation of the American school ethnologists' (George Gliddon's, Samuel Morton's, and Josiah Nott's) work in the pseudo-science of phrenology, which speciously postulated that Negro skulls found in Kemet by Gliddon, and described in Morton's *Crania Aegyptica,* were those of Negro slaves who served under "*dark skinned Caucasians* ... who had developed writing, mathematics, astronomy, and lofty philosophical conceptions" which "would have been impossible had they been Negroes" (1987: 132).

Through a similar sociohistorical methodology as Drake, Bernal's "Aryan Model" of classical history underscores that European enlightenment thinkers' transfigured account of ancient Greek high civilization as autochthonous and unrelated to Kemetic influences coincided with the widespread acceptance of racial hierarchies, the Hellenomania of the Romantic era, and expanding European colonial empires in the eighteenth century. He also remarks that the anti-black writings of Hume, Hegel, and Kant postulated the moral, cultural, and intellectual inferiority of Africans ([1987] 1991: 202–6, 239–306). However, it is important to note that Hume's, Kant's, Hegel's, and the American school ethnologists' modern racism was the inevitable outgrowth of centuries-earlier proscriptions against ethno-religious difference, while also adhering to eighteenth- and nineteenth-century ideations:

1.   The codification of the Sentencia-Estatuto decree in 1449, one of the earliest *limpieza de sangre* (purity of blood) statues, preventing *conversos*, Jewish converts to Christianity, in Toledo, Spain from holding public office. These statutes were later weaponized during the Jewish (and later Muslim) purges of the Spanish Inquisition (Martinez 2008: 26–36);

2.   Seventeenth-century texts on monogenetic and polygenetic evolutionary theory, like François Bernier's "A New Division of the Earth according to the Different Species or Races of Men" (1684) and Isaac La Peyrère's *Pre-Adamitae* (1655), respectively;

3.   Eighteenth-century European enlightenment racial hierarchies, exemplified in Carrolus Linnaeus's influential *Systema Naturae* (1737); and

4.   Contemporaneous works of nineteenth-century social Darwinism, like Robert Knox's *The Races of Men: A Fragment* (1850) and Arthur Gobineau's *Essay on the Inequality of the Races* (1853).

While fifteenth-century *limpieza de sangre* statutes stigmatized Jewish and later Muslim *conversos* as impure "others," sixteenth- and seventeenth-century monogenetic and polygenetic evolutionary theories provided quasi-scientific justifications for the racialized classification of Indigenous and African peoples as subhuman. The later emergence of the eighteenth-century categorization of human beings stemmed from discourses on the "science of man" (Popkin 1980: 84) and "mastery over nature" (Kennsington 1963: 392), which is reflected in taxonomic classifications of the natural world and its anthropological corollary: the stratification of human beings through the creation of racial hierarchies. Carrolus Linnaeus's *Systema Naturae* (1737) exemplifies this ideological trend; the centerpiece of which is Linaaeus's racial hierarchy that positions Nordic-Europeans at the pinnacle of humanity and Africans at the nadir. Eze's observations on the legitimization of scientific racism bear repeating: "Enlightenment philosophy was instrumental in codifying and institutionalizing both the scientific and popular perceptions of the human race," which lent false credence to theories of white/European racial superiority and nonwhite inferiority (1997: 5). This potent blend of philosophically and scientifically-based racism has served as the epistemological justification for white racial chauvinism to thrive and adapt from the eighteenth-century onward. The aforementioned laws and texts reveal how philosophical and scientific racist discourse has served as an organizing, justificatory episteme for discriminatory sociocultural, socioeconomic, and geopolitical policies/institutions, including the manner in which Indigenous genocide and African racial slavery served as the foundations of the European settler-colonial and exploitation colonial systems. Given that epistemic racism has exerted significant influence on the history of ideas, the formation of epoch-defining, geopolitical and socioeconomic structures, and the success of Western imperialist power globally, Harris's claim that logical systems analyses of racism are ill-advised seems imprudent. This is particularly true since even a concise explanation of epistemic racism could serve as a conceptual bridge to Harris's actuarial account, allowing for a more nuanced awareness of how racist ideations have developed within the full context of six hundred years—a centurial span equivalent to the entire modern history of human ideas. Racist thought may then be apprehended in its full gravity and longevity as a defining episteme that propelled the cataclysmic nature of the Euromodern project of hegemonic domination.

Regarding Kantian ethno-biological determinism's utility in condoning the chattel slavery system's brutality, Emmanuel Eze alerts us to the German philosophe's four-decade teaching career in the twin fields of physical geography and anthropology, as well as his writings on biologically-based racial difference. Despite the fact that Kant wrote extensively on these topics, many contemporary philosophers do not consider his contributions to racist discourse deserving of the same critical scrutiny as his transcendental writings.[19] Eze reveals that Kant recommended beating the Negro with

> a split bamboo cane instead of a whip, so that the 'negro' will suffer a great deal of pains (because of the "negro's" thick skin, he would not be racked with sufficient agonies through a whip) but without dying … The African, according to Kant, deserves this kind of "training" because he or she is "exclusively idle," lazy, prone to hesitation and jealousy, and the African is all these because, for climate and anthropological reasons, … lacks "true" (rational and moral) character. (Qtd. in Eze 215)

Here we see the explicitly Kantian roots of anti-black stereotypes that reinforced slave abuse—anti-black stereotypes that are still prevalent today: innate laziness, amorality, and insensibility to pain. Kant's writings in the related fields of physical geography and anthropology support Eze's position that European philosophy codified and institutionalized scientific claims of innate racial difference. From Kant's eighteenth-century writings on African peoples' invulnerability to pain, we may infer a direct correlation to the unethical and sadistic nineteenth-century medical practices of J. Marion Sims—the so-called father of modern gynecology—who conducted experimental gynecological procedures on enslaved African women through vivisection without their consent and without anesthesia. Like Kant, Sims made assertions of innate African laziness, yet he did so to explain high incidences of neonatal tetanus among newborn slave children. Rather than making the logical deduction that the unhygienic placement of slave quarters near animal waste areas caused the infection, Sims held fast to his anti-black racist suppositions. He also followed the common nineteenth-century practice of performing operations without properly disinfecting his own hands, so his failure to self-sanitize only added to enslaved women's contagion (Washington 2006: 61–2). The preceding examples of Kantian thought and Sims's medical torture are concrete historical examples of how epistemic racism functions ideologically and culturally to inform white supremacist practices that further systemic injustice and anti-black violence. This historical reality ultimately challenges Harris's claim that logical world systems analyses of racism are somehow unconvincing. In fact the opposite appears to be true.

Harris's eschewal of framing racism as a global logical system also aligns with his view that races are not stable ontological entities and that "racial groups, as social kinds, are constructions" (57). This contention is commensurate with several modern theoretical schools, including social constructivism and critical race theory that "form a concept of the person as a dialogical and interrelated social being" (31), all of which contrast to Enrique Dussel's liberationist "self-versus other" dichotomy that, in Harris's view, "already misconstrues the human [since] [t]he 'self' is always, already, encoded in the 'other'" (ibid.). While this claim is ostensibly true, the intersubjective relationality that Harris takes as a given is one that continues to be informed through an apprehension of a "self" that exists in relation to an "other" that in many cases is racially and/or morphologically different. This is why the Dusselian "other," which is derived from Fanonian thought, is instructive: it denotes the radical separation of human selves that racist thought has normalized. White racists cannot see themselves in racialized and different "selves"; hence Dussell's "self" v. "other" specifies how racism can negate the process of encoding to which Harris refers. Explaining intersubjective relations through the racialized self-other dichotomy opens the door to critical explorations of epistemic racism's foreclosure of human recognition and mutuality. Although Harris's philosophy of struggle does not explicitly address how centuries of epistemic racism have led to the institutionalization of inequitable human relations and social structures, his insurrectionist ethic speaks to a commitment to reaffirming his scholar-activist forebears' liberationist aims of risking death and taking lives, which became instrumental in the dismantling of the chattel slavery system.

"If We Must Die": An Insurrectionist Ethic Through Lockean Pragmatism

Claude McKay's famed sonnet lyrically encapsulates Harris's insurrectionist ethic. "If We Must Die"[20] was not only penned during the infamous Red Summer of 1919 as an ode to oppressed people fighting against tyrrany, but it is also widely considered the inaugural poem of the New Negro Movement Alain Locke championed. Harris locates his insurrectionist ethic in an application of Locke's theoretical revision of pragmatism. Locke advocates for a balance between monism and value anarchy, and advised against "de-throning our absolutes" so as not to "exile our imperatives, for after all, we live by them" (qtd. in Harris 2020: 27). To live by our imperatives is to devote our life's work to a greater mission. As human liberation defines the Harrisian philosophical project, he takes Locke's guidance to heart and pointedly asks, "what are the imperatives for the meaning of a term deeply entrenched in our lexicon of being—philosophy? What should it be born of?" (27). Struggling against injustice and immiseration through the life-affirming commitment to "always make possible epistemologies, metaphysics, and aesthetics that include the excluded" (20, 22) is the answer. For its failure to actualize philosophy's discursive potential to incite socially transformative revolution in the fight for humanity's betterment, Harris indicts nineteenth-century classical American pragmatism's tethering to proprietary capitalism, which precluded its proponents, like William James, from embracing an insurrectionist ethic. Harris plaintively asks, "Would a Jamesian subject feel compelled, against popular sentiment, to promote, organize, or encourage slave escapes, knowing that they would need to kill Jim and Jane Crow slave-catchers and sellers of children, as well as cause the unintentional death of innocent bystanders?" (180). Harris then questions the theoretical basis of pragmatism itself: "Are the normative resources so deeply ingrained in classical pragmatism adequate? Is the category of *humanity* understood in a way that would justify radical action on behalf of the downtrodden, even if the consequences were likely to be harmful to the actors and others?" (181). These two questions reveal struggle philosophy's prioritization of individual and collective liberation above effete ideological allegiances that do not forward a radical understanding of humanity in its entirety, or include transforming the lives of the disenfranchised. Pragmatism, for Harris, lacks a true moral grounding because its contextualization of humanity does not accommodate acts of potential martyrdom—or the sacrifice of human life in the cause of revolutionary societal transformation. On this point, Harris and Cornel West are in agreement. Through a similarly close engagement with James's writings, West cites Jamesian pragmatism as that which is "mediating ... and promotes moral transgression based on individual conscience rather than social revolution by means of collective action" (1989: 57).

Due to Jamesian pragmatism's incompatibility with the mass insurgency required to topple chattel slavery, Harris reexamines the nineteenth-century anti-slavery struggle in the United States, by citing the insurrectionist ethics of David Walker, Lydia Maria Child, John Brown, and Henry David Thoreau to question classical pragmatism's moral assertions. Harris convincingly argues that, although these four anti-slavery activists lived during the age of classical American pragmatism, pragmatist thought had no bearing on their anti-slavery writings and political agitation. Rather, a shared reformist zeal and insurrectionist ethic defined their strident critiques of chattel slavery. For these reasons, Walker's, Child's, Brown's, and Thoreau's social and political agitation move Harris to characterize pragmatism as morally defective (179–86). Harris praises these activists for breaking with pragmatist ideals to embrace slave revolt as a conduit for the societal transformation needed to abolish the institution itself. Walker, Child, Brown, and Thoreau were committed to subverting the dehumanizing, exploitative chattel slavery system at all costs—even the cost of human life. Harris further clarifies "That the use of some methods of absolute destruction of slaveholders and bonds of servitude ... should be given meritorious ranking as a crucial feature of insurrectionist moral criteria. Moreover, advocacy representing, defending, or promoting in some form the liberation of self and other from bondage is a good that warrants special honorific status" (184).

Walker's *Appeal* (1829) encapsulates the moralism of righteous insurgency that Harris describes, for this abolitionist text presents an unparalleled combination of the following rhetorical strategies: a comparative historical analysis of ancient and modern systems of servitude, a philosophical critique of chattel slavery's inconsistency with Western enlightenment and Christian principles, a refutation of Jefferson's anti-black theses in his *Notes on the State of Virginia* (1785), and a proto-Black nationalist call for slave insurrection in the Americas. By modeling his *Appeal* on the structure of the US Constitution, Walker interpellates the enslaved Black masses throughout the Americas to fight for their liberation at all costs. His anti-slavery treatise was unprecedented and uncompromising in its rallying cry for Black unity as the emancipatory force to secure physical and psychological freedom from the tyranny of slavery, while ensuring the collectivized well being of his people:

> I advanced it therefore to you, not as a problematical, but as an unshaken and ever immovable fact, that your full glory and happiness, as well as other coloured people under Heaven, shall never be fully consummated, but with the entire emancipation of your enslaved brethren all over the world. You may therefore, go to work and do what you can to rescue, or join in with tyrants to oppress them and yourselves, until the Lord shall come upon you all like a thief in the night. For I believe it is the will of the Lord that our greatest happiness shall consist in working for the salvation of our whole body. ([1829] 2015: 29)

Walker uses prophetic Christianity to inspire feelings of mutual loyalty among the enslaved; he rouses them to see the benefit of struggling in unity and harmony to actualize their shared freedom. This method also informs his response to what he viewed as white Americans' colonizing scheme of African repatriation to Liberia. Walker chides white proponents of colonization and reminds them of the blood and toil the enslaved invested into the prosperity of the nation, while warning them of the divine retribution to be had in slave revolution:

> Remember Americans, that we must and shall be free … will you wait until we shall, under God, obtain our liberty by the crushing arm of power? Will it not be dreadful for you? I speak Americans for your good. We must and shall be free I say, in spite of you. You may do your best to keep us in wretchedness and misery, to enrich you and your children; but God will deliver us from you. And wo, wo will be to you if we have to obtain our freedom by fighting. (Ibid.: 70)

The force of Walker's moral indignation fuels his emancipatory polemic, and his renunciation of chattel slavery's exploitative barbarism bespeaks his unequivocal commitment to liberation from the physical and mental shackles of slavery. For Harris, like Walker, the processes of individual and collective liberation entail the actualization of freedom, which is inseparable from one's agency, choice, and responsibility.

Conclusion

All philosophers orient their work towards a particular telos that, in itself, defines the trajectory of their thought and their ideological objectives. In my reading of Harris, his philosophical aims have been inspired by the sociopolitical agitation of Walker, Child, Brown, Douglass, and Thoreau, as well as the critical pragmatism of Alaine Locke. Indeed, *A Philosophy of Struggle* illuminates Harrisian discourse as the product of intense dedication to the ideals of human amelioration and ascendance. Harris uses philosophy to rouse us into decisive collective action so that we may change the course of history's anti-human practices and policies. But can we truly eradicate racism without understanding its epistemological origins that, to this day, are still replicated in sociopolitical and cultural institutions? Harris and I may differ on the optimal methodologies for confronting the history of racism, yet we agree that its perpetuation into the twenty-first-century has created the disaster of necro-being for the vast majority of the world's population. Thus understanding philosophy as a walkway towards justice and liberation is to grasp Leonard Harris's commitment to human freedom: it is a beautiful struggle through which humanity embodies its lauded ideals and aspirations, and in giving our lives to this struggle we become our truest, highest selves.

Notes

1 John Capps, "I am an American Philosopher: Leonard Harris" and *Philosophy Born of Struggle*, ix.

2 Outlaw's scholarly works include, *On Race and Philosophy* and *Critical Social Theory in the Interest of Black Folks*. For discussions of Outlaw's contributions to Africana philosophy, see Paget Henry, *Caliban's Reason*, 147–8, 150–1, and 156–7; and Lewis Gordon, *An Introduction to Africana Philosophy*, 110, 120, and 136.

3 Leonard Harris, email correspondence, July 7, 2025.

4 Lewis Gordon, *An Introduction*, iv.

5 Leonard Harris, *Philosophy Born of Struggle*, xii.

6 Email correspondence, July 7, 2025.

7 Harris elaborates on his disillusionment with the Socratic method's preoccupation with expounding on the nature of reality. Rather than deal in

abstractions, he expresses the need to deal in the reality of struggle. This is why he came to embrace Douglass's philosophy of struggle. Detailed in Goyland Williams, "Philosophy Born of Struggle: An Insurrectionist Ethic."

8 Harris credits Johnny Washington's *Alaine Locke and Philosophy* as the first book-length evaluation of Locke's philosophical contributions in Harris's edited volume, *The Philosophy of Alaine Locke*, 23.

9 Harris's conceptualization of racism as necro-being highlights the myriad ways in which racist social structures, discriminatory legal statutes, and predatory economic policies make racism a life and death exchange that creates optimal conditions for well-being among privileged populations at the expense of the sufferers who either die or barely eke out an existence.

10 Leonard Harris, "Introduction." *The Philosophy of Alain Locke,* 17.

11 Leonard Harris, *A Philosophy of Struggle*, 31.

12 Martin Luther King, Jr, "Remaining Awake through a Great Revolution," 52.

13 Robinson, *Black Marxism,* 138–9; Robinson, *An Anthropology of Marxism,* 91–8, 108–99; Gordon, *An Introduction to Africana Philosophy,* 129–32.

14 In his inaugural text of the Black radical tradition, Du Bois recasts enslaved Africans as Black workers in *Black Reconstruction*, while James, three years later, refers to these workers in Haiti as a revolutionary proletariat that overthrew slavery and French colonial rule in *The Black Jacobins.* See Du Bois chapter one, "The Black Worker" and throughout subsequent chapters; as well as James chapter four, "The San Domingo Masses Begin," 86.

15 Robinson, *Black Marxism,* 184 and 199; Bogues, *Black Heretics, Black Prophets,* 74–7, 79; Fanon, *The Wretched of the Earth*; and Parris, *Being Apart,* 66–103.

16 Lewis Gordon, *An Introduction to Africana Philosophy,* 131.

17 Du Bois qtd. in Anthony Bogues, *Black Heretics, Black Prophets,* 77; and Frantz Fanon, *The Wretched of the Earth*, 40.

18 Du Bois, *Black Reconstruction,* 523.

19 Emmanuel Eze, "The Color of Reason," 200–1.

20 Claude McKay, *Harlem Shadows*, 52.

3

CREOLIZE THE ACADEMY: EMBRACING TRANSDISCIPLINARITY TO REVIVE THE HUMANITIES AND PROMOTE SOCIAL JUSTICE

For committed intellectuals whose scholarship and pedagogy embody the humanistic tradition's power to catalyze progressive discourse, the closing of various humanities departments across the United States signals the academy's acquiescence to one of neoliberalism's most insidious structural fallacies: that humanistic research no longer contributes to the productivity or betterment of society. This sea change in the perception and status of the humanities is anathema to both the mission of humanistic study and its original objectives to foster a broader understanding of the human experience in our diverse social realities, and heighten our awareness of complex historical, philosophical, and sociopolitical mechanisms that inform our understanding of human existence through various theoretical methods. In the aftermath of George Floyd's and Breonna

Taylor's murders by police (2020) and the spate of white supremacist mass shootings over the past decade in Buffalo, New York (2022); Christchurch, New Zealand (2019); El Paso, Texas (2019); Pittsburgh, Pennsylvania (2018); Charlottesville, Virginia (2017); and Charleston, South Carolina (2015), it is imperative that we continually highlight two important points about humanistic study's potential to galvanize ideological and sociopolitical transformation.

First, without the transdisciplinary probing of humanities research, it would be impossible to properly contextualize the normalization of white supremacist thought and racist violence that is continually expressed in the murder and brutality committed against Black communities. Second, it is this very type of critical reflection and rigorous intellectual inquiry into thought systems and institutions of power that lie at the heart of humanistic study. As such we cannot afford to diminish or abandon this vital intellectual work in these challenging times. This assessment is common among those dedicated to reaffirming the necessity of the humanities; nonetheless we are witnessing unprecedented assaults on national humanities funding that would have been unthinkable four decades ago. Many, if not most, academic administrators and policymakers now view the cornerstone of liberal arts education as an educational anachronism, obsolete intellectualism that holds neither import nor utility in our world of technocratic globalized markets. This crisis in higher education begs two fundamental questions: How has neoliberalism subsumed the diversifying intellectual mission of humanistic inquiry that was once the hallmark of postsecondary education? How can we use and simultaneously illuminate the ameliorative aspects of creolized humanistic knowledge production in our quest to realize a more just, egalitarian society?

I will address these questions through a discussion of creolized political theory, Africana thought, and critical pedagogy that models the transformative social and political theories of Jean-Jacques Rousseau, Frederick Douglass, Ida B. Wells-Barnett, W. E. B. Du Bois, Frantz Fanon, Paolo Friere, and Jean Anyon. Such a syncretic, theoretical approach will not only reveal these thinkers' progressive epistemological vision, but it will also disclose the pluralizing potentialities of creolization in the aforementioned fields, the humanities, and public education more generally. But before we begin this discussion, we must first address the principal antagonism between neoliberalism and the humanities.

Ideological Antagonists: Neoliberalism vs. the Humanities

Neoliberalism's prioritization of capital accumulation through market fundamentalism, and its related emphasis on quantifying societal progress through economic critical paradigms, stands in opposition to humanistic study's articulation of phenomenological complexities through multidisciplinary and transdisciplinary analyses of human reality, symbolic life, and societal structural formations. Lived experience is the most immediate plane upon which human life is theorized, explained, and apprehended. It follows, then, that we are better able to understand the specificities of our existence when we fully grasp the import of foundational historical, philosophical, and sociopolitical developments that shape our attitudes and cultures. To explain the contingency of human reality solely through the neoliberal lens of market fundamentalism is, in actuality, to delimit our lived experiences as those that emerge exclusively from market-driven phenomena that may, when positively manipulated according to neoliberals, alter social and political life in productive ways.

Given that this brand of capitalist thought lies at the heart of neoliberalism, it is natural that its basic principles would represent a counterpoint to the ethos of humanistic research in which multivalent methods of inquiry are used to enrich our understanding of human life. Neoliberal ideology's strategic elisions and studied dismissals of historical analyses, and engaged reflection on systemic power relations have effectively encouraged the embrace of solipsism, causing some to view their individual existence as separate and autonomous from others in society.[1] On the other hand, the humanities provide a fluid, multidisciplinary framework for advancing, "Dynamic, meta-critical, systemic, paradigmatic [thought] about our times ... [giving] us the language to understand the operative and abusive functioning of power and inequality" (Martín and Aguado 2017: 3) that defines our lives at both the quotidian and symbolic levels. In sum, neoliberalism encourages us to see ourselves as wholly separate and distinct beings, with no points of commonality existing outside of market-based paradigms that seek to reduce our collective identity to that of consumers and producers of capital. The humanities, in contrast, elucidate the ways in which human existence and institutions of power are mutually informed by and through various societal structures and epistemes that, while shaping our world, do not stand in absolute power, or above thoughtful critique and resistance. Is it any wonder that neoliberals are attempting to obliterate the very fields of study that problematize their insistence on prioritizing profit margins over human needs?

Educators of conscience must continue to challenge the contemporary zeitgeist, as it has negated the intrinsic value humanistic study holds for offering insights into the burning issues of freedom, justice, and equality—especially in our current moment of social and political unrest. If the humanities are to survive, it is imperative that our scholarly endeavors and pedagogical practices consistently emphasize their indispensability in furthering the project of collective progress toward the actualization of our most lauded, yet unrealized egalitarian ideals. To accomplish this crucial task, we must creolize the humanities through a broad and inclusive embrace of transdisciplinarity that will reveal humankind's enduring project of social and political amelioration through the critical evaluation of thought systems and institutions. This will enable a constructive mutuality to be realized. Examining the transdisciplinary, theoretical innovations of the eighteenth-, nineenth, and twentieth-century thinkers Jean Jacques Rousseau, Frederick Douglass, Ida B. Wells-Barnett, W. E. B. Du Bois, and Frantz Fanon will enable us to appreciate and emulate effective models of intellectual engagement that still offer relevant insights into the misuses of power, and the dialectics of oppression and resistance in our current times.

A Return to Source: Revisiting the Creolized Roots of Political Theory

Using the terms *creolization* and *transdisciplinarity* interchangeably is, as Jane Anna Gordon (2014: 6–7) argues, to announce a reimagining of humanities scholarship that will invite revisions to delimiting disciplinary terms and practices. Gordon makes a pointed contrast between transdisciplinary methods that emphasize points of thematic and theoretical fluidity among academic disciplines, and interdisciplinary approaches in which most scholars position academic disciplines as rigid, discrete fields of study. Historically speaking, creolization refers to the multiplicity of linguistic and cultural blending processes that occurred among Indigenous people, enslaved Africans, indentured Asian and European laborers, and European planters during first wave imperialism and settler-colonialism in the Americas from the late fifteenth century onward. Though creolization denotes both a history of deracination and rupture, it simultaneously connotes a distinct New World culture marked by adaptability and innovation that produced unprecedented cultural productions that, although ostensibly heretical, emerged among divergent groups of people occupying seemingly stratified racial hierarchies and social classes (ibid.: 10–11).

By recontextualizing creolization to posit the presence of an analogous methodological and theoretical practice based in transdisciplinarity, Gordon emphasizes that creolizing academic disciplines involves using a highly syncretic approach to methods of inquiry in which academic fields that were once viewed as discrete are interrogated with the aim of foregrounding their mutual constitution and convergence and, equally important, their applicability in rectifying difficult social and political problems. This suspension of rigid disciplinarity, according to Gordon, defines the works of early political theorists who culled salient facts from fields as divergent as sociology, history, and psychology to formulate their ideas on the world of politics and envision potential solutions to complex issues inherent to human relations.[2]

Gordon furthers her predecessors' transdisciplinary methods through contrapuntal readings of Rousseau's and Fanon's works by explicating the ways in which the Rousseauian formulation of "the general will" was realized in the Fanonian concept of national consciousness, as the collectivized will of the newly independent, formerly colonized masses of the Global South. Gordon makes clear distinctions between Rousseau's formulation of the "general will," which articulates and collectivizes each member of society's desires as part of a mutually implicated social gestalt, and "the will of all," which may be wielded by private citizens to establish practices that further advantage those already possessing heightened privilege (ibid.: 98–106). Gordon's creolized methodology lies in her pairing of two theorists, separated by two centuries and the polarized statuses of "colonizer" and "colonized." This unconventional coupling surpasses the heterodox methods of Gordon's predecessors because she pairs Rousseau and Fanon as kindred political thinkers whose theoretical similarities transcend their divergent status in the larger Francophone empire. As Gordon demonstrates, both Rousseau and Fanon grappled with vexing sociopolitical issues of their day, leading them to craft remedial discursive interventions that were arrived at through their privileging of problem-based inquiry, and their valorizing of creolized insights—an approach that took precedence over any fixed allegiance to their respective areas of specialization. For Rousseau and Fanon, the most pressing issue at hand was identifying conceivable solutions to abuses of political power, originating with those whose quest for dominance prevented the masses from creating and sustaining their collectivized desires and aspirations.

One of Rousseau's philosophical strengths was his role as gadfly and critic of Eurocentric trends in enlightenment thought. In that capacity he traversed the disciplinary boundaries of literature, anthropology, and science to enumerate the ways in which eighteenth-century travelogues exacerbated European cultural insularity in their promulgation of xenophobic and culturally imperialist perspectives, rather than encouraging genuine appraisals of Global South civilizations and critical self-examination among the European reading public (ibid.: 51–2). Gordon demonstrates that Rousseau was able to arrive at such probing analyses of European discourse precisely because his methods of creolized inquiry privileged the *problem* of eliminating decadent tendencies in European thought, rather than conforming to dominant ideological trends that would further legitimate them. Because a significant portion of his corpus was centered on illuminating difficult truths about European civilization, Rousseau's dissenting voice provided a measured account of European ideological practices that furthered the hegemonic aims of empire and colonization in the Global South. Nevertheless, Gordon reminds us that his critique of European ethnocentrism, his writings on Caribs, Native Americans, and Hottentots reflect an "anti-European Eurocentrism" that paradoxically contributed to the Western conceptualization of the simple-minded noble savage (ibid.: 55–7).

Yet Rousseau's work performs two related discursive functions: it reveals the fundamental utility of transdisciplinary methods in uncovering matrices of meaning that came to shape the collective consciousness of eighteenth-century European subjects, particularly their primary identification as "superior" "Selves" and those residing in French colonial regions of the Global South as distinctly "inferior" "Others" (Parris 2015: 23–7). Rousseau's critique also provides tangible proof of the manner in which creolized humanities scholarship generates inventive forms of knowledge production that are essential in their scrutiny of social and cultural particularities. For us to achieve a Rousseauian brand of shared political vision and societal unity that would neutralize the neo-fascist and white supremacist forces threatening our collective well-being, we must heed Fanon's call in *The Wretched of the Earth* to "set afoot a new man" (1963: 316). New humans are those who wield emancipatory knowledge to reconceptualize and reconstruct institutions of power into truly egalitarian formations. As an Africana philosopher and colonial subject, Fanon's formal training in psychiatry, combined with his intensive study of continental philosophy, led him to create a distinctly Fanonian method comprised of emancipatory psychiatry, sociodiagnostic critique, and existential phenomenological analysis that, together, articulated a groundbreaking theory of decolonial liberation. It is important to emphasize that although he was an advocate of psychoanalysis, Fanon did not passively embrace Freudian psychoanalytic methods. Rather he pointedly revised and expanded on these formulations to address the psychology of oppression and contributing sociogenic forces that affected colonized subjects—a comprehensive approach that traditional psychoanalysis, with its exclusive focus on the Western subject, never intended.[3] Thus Fanon's political commitment to the establishment of a liberated, sovereign Algerian state could not be divorced from his psychiatric mission to guide his North African patients toward apprehending their intrinsic freedom as human beings. His transdisciplinary background in psychiatry, psychoanalysis, and existential phenomenology led him to contextualize mental illness as a "pathology of liberty" (Fanon 2016: 419), a disorder that effectively alienated the afflicted from their immediate sense of reality and innate autonomy.

Fanon's mission to theorize and actualize liberation in the Global South was one he undertook to provide the clinical and political means of resolving the collective state of self-alienation, born of hegemonic domination, that afflicted colonized people. Together, his psychiatric and political writings attest to the efficacy of transdisciplinary approaches, as his works reveal a holistic orientation intended to foster mental emancipation and emotional well-being. Fanon's focus on improving the material and psychological condition of the colonized was arrived at through his embrace of the aforementioned disciplinary models and theoretical paradigms. His dedication to curing the psychology of oppression among colonized people led him to make seminal interventions in Western discourse that are still frequently cited to describe the persistent reality of state-sponsored, anti-black violence in our present times. Following Eric Garner's murder by New York City police officer Daniel Pantileo, social media sites echoed Garner's (and Floyd's) dying words, "I can't breathe," with those of Fanon in a later edition of *The Wretched of the Earth* ([1963] 2008: 201). As Peter Hudis observes, "they revolted … because it became impossible to breathe, in more than one sense of the word" (2015: 1). Fanon was able to initiate such timely political interpositions, while simultaneously laying the foundation for radical ethnopsychiatry (Bulhan 1985: 216–49), through his use of problem-based inquiry that generated a range of political insights and therapeutic treatments that originate in multiple fields of study.

The driving force behind Fanon's and Rousseau's work was the resolute pursuit of knowledge for the sake of subverting corrupt and oppressive forms of established power. Their discursive interventions offer potential means of improving the social and political realities of their times and, because of their expansive vision, our times as well. We would do well to revisit the goals of realizing a collectivized political will and generating societal transformation, that lie at the heart of Rousseauian general will and Fanonian national consciousness, in the conception of a new national ethos. This revitalized emancipatory consciousness speaks to the need to pointedly address the persistence of structural racism that results from the culture of historical denial about chattel slavery's enduring legacy, which has come to define American life. This new ethos has the potential to embolden people of conscience to sustain a meaningful challenge against the racist, authoritarian ideologies, policies, and practices threatening to further erode our well-being at the institutional and material levels.

Transdisciplinarity and Prescience in Africana Thought

Like Rousseau and Fanon, eighteenth- and nineteenth-century Africana thinkers also used creolized inquiry to address the most pressing sociopolitical issues of their day. Edward Blyden, David Walker, Frederick Douglass, Martin Delany, Ida B. Wells-Barnett, Anna Julia Cooper, W. E. B. Du Bois, and C. L. R. James, among others, understood the necessity of interrogating varied fields of study to address the convergence of epistemological practices, institutional policies, and social inequities that dehumanized and disenfranchised African diasporic people at the height of Western empire. These Africana thinkers used transdisciplinarity to reveal Western hegemonic domination as the manifestation of philosophical and structural formations that, in turn, perpetuated the enslavement, colonization, and subsequent socioeconomic and political oppression of Black people. In doing so their writings reveal racism, not egalitarianism, to be at the epistemic core of Western modernity's ethics and values.

Indeed, from the eighteenth century onward, Africana intellectual productions disclose the emancipatory and revelatory potential of inquiry-based scholarship, for Africana thinkers sought to elucidate the roots of anti-black racism as a defining modern ideology. I have specified these thinkers' transdisciplinary textual interpositions as "being apart" (2015: 7–8), a collective form of theoretical resistance to African negation within modern structures of meaning that effectively set African peoples apart from humanity in three related aspects of Eurocentric ideological praxis: the erasure of Africa's originary role in the birth of Western civilization, the bestialization of the African in the creation of the subhuman Negro slave, and the denial of chattel slavery's role in the birth of modern capitalism. As Black vindicationist abolitionists, both David Walker and Frederick Douglass engaged in historical, philosophical, and political analyses to craft their antislavery polemics in *David Walker's Appeal* (1832) and Douglass's "The Claims of the Negro Ethnologically Considered" (1854), as well as in the latter's three autobiographies, numerous speeches, and letters. Central to Walker's and Douglass's antislavery writings are their respective philosophical challenges to scientific racism in Thomas Jefferson's *Notes on the*

State of Virginia (1785) and Samuel Morton's *Crania Aegyptiaca* (1844). Following Walker's and Douglass's discursive interventions, W. E. B. Du Bois's *Black Reconstruction* (1935) and C. L. R. James's *The Black Jacobins* (1938) seamlessly weave radical historiography and political theory to relocate the map and timeline of Marxian revolution to the New World plantations of the enslaved African diasporic proletariat in the Americas (ibid.: 23–71).

Thus, to illustrate comprehensively the epistemological and sociopolitical assault on African people in the Americas, these thinkers' works outline the intersections of oppressive practices within thought systems and social and political institutions. In particular, the oeuvres of Douglass and Du Bois link this particular system of power relations to their lived experiences as well. Their works reveal the ways in which creolized methodologies offer the most fruitful means of engaging with the interrelationships among historical, philosophical, and sociopolitical forces that shaped the lives of nineteenth- and twentieth-century enslaved and free African Americans. Their intellectual practices and productions also initiated sustained forays into the expansion of Africana letters and discourse. How would Africana philosophers have articulated the convergence of existential, material, and political themes that arise in Douglass's anti-slavery dialectic (Stover 2019: 218) without Douglass's infamous battle with slave-breaker Edward Covey?[4] Where would Africana philosophy and literary criticism be without Du Bois's groundbreaking concept of double-consciousness? How would social, political, and literary theorists comprehensively delineate the convergence of psychological, phenomenological, and sociopolitical themes that define the lived reality of Africana people without Du Bois's innovative terminology? Douglass's and Du Bois's seminal contributions to Africana letters and discourse established the transdisciplinary foundations for Africana Philosophy, Africana Studies, Critical Race Studies in Philosophy, and Africana existentialism. In what is widely considered to be one of the inaugural works of critical race theory, *The Souls of Black Folk* (1903), Du Bois recalls his horror at witnessing the brutality of lynching. His was one among many African American works that contextualized lynching as a form of social control. Another was that of Ida B. Wells-Barnett.

Wells-Barnett's fearless antilynching campaign is articulated in her 1895 work *A Red Record,* in which she analyzes Reconstruction-era

Ku Klux Klan lynchings as a distinct form of southern barbarism and wanton murder. Cloaked in the deceptively chivalrous veil of protecting white womanhood, lynching, Wells-Barnett's research reveals, was used to obscure the consensual nature of interracial relationships and divest newly enfranchised African Americans of socioeconomic and political power. She emphasizes that the weight of the African American vote could have dismantled the white Southern power structure, just as the burgeoning prosperity of the African American middle class was a visceral affront to the former planter class's socioeconomic dominance. Her comprehensive transdisciplinary analysis of lynch law in the South presents layered historical, sociological, and political analyses to disclose the means by which lynching ensured the continued subjugation of African Americans in the wake of chattel slavery's demise (Wells-Barnett [1895] 2014: 676–86). For this reason, her prescient words bear repeating in their entirety:

> The student of American sociology will find the year 1894 marked by a pronounced awakening of public conscience to a system of anarchy and outlawry which had grown during a series of ten years to be so common, that the scenes of unusual brutality failed to have any visible effect upon the humane sentiments of the people of our land. Beginning with the emancipation of the Negro, the inevitable result of unbridled power exercised for two and a half centuries, by the white man over the Negro, began to show itself in acts of conscienceless outlawry. During the slave regime, the Southern white man owned the Negro body and soul. It was to his interest to dwarf the soul and preserve the body. … But Emancipation came and the vested interests of the white man in the Negro's body were lost. (Wells-Barnett ([1895] 2014): 677–8)

Wells-Barnett's opening paragraphs disclose the potency of creolized inquiry for explicating the complexities of post-bellum anti-black terror. She posits the practice of lynching as a sociological and political manifestation of "outlawry" that has defied moral outrage because of its prevalence. She then recalls the history of chattel slavery and its attendant entrenchment of African dehumanization and white supremacist domination, both of which reduced African American life to the status of property.

In our present historical moment of heightened racial animus, Wells-Barnett's work continues to resonate because the same white fear of Black political and socioeconomic power that was prevalent 150 years ago coincides with today's comparable increase in the number of hate groups and anti-Black, anti-immigrant, anti-Muslim, anti-Semitic violence over the past decade. In May 2024, the Leadership Conference Education Fund (the educational wing of the Leadership Conference on Civil and Human Rights) released "Cause for Concern 2024: The State of Hate," which cites that hate crimes have doubled in frequency since 2015 (4). Two years earlier, in 2022, the Senate held a series of hearings on "Confronting Violent White Supremacy: The Evolution of Anti-Democratic Extremist Groups and the Threat to Democracy." The Southern Poverty Law Center's (SPLC's) data reveals direct parallels between the election and re-election of former President Obama, and the current Trump administration, to a marked rise in white supremacist, neo-Nazi, and alt-right activity. In September 2016, Richard Cohen, president of the SPLC, testified before the House of Representatives to stress that "for the last eight years, President Obama has been a lightning rod for the radical right. He reflects our country's changing diversity and has been a target of the backlash to that change" (Cohen 2016). White supremacist activists were captured on HBO Vice News' "Charlottesville: Race and Terror" as they protested the removal of a Robert E. Lee statue by carrying tiki torches and chanting, "You will not replace us, Jews will not replace us, blood and soil, white lives matter" (Vice News Tonight 2017). Despite the widespread dissemination of the above-cited media reports alerting the public to these hate groups' murderous agendas, the sanitization of white supremacist ideologies and practices has caused these groups' numbers to swell.

In a society whose education system consistently elides thoughtful investigations into the legacy of African dehumanization, subjugation, and disenfranchisement that emerged from chattel slavery's ideological underpinnings in scientific racism, the exaltation of white life has always been the norm, not the exception. White lives have always mattered; this is one of the discursive threads in Wells-Barnett's and Du Bois's works, in particular, for Black lives were and still are extinguished at will, without due process of law, just as they both pointed out more than a century ago. Nevertheless, this logic is seen as illogic to white supremacists who view Blacks, Jews, Muslims, and all people of color as expendable impediments to the recreation of their mythic white nation. The transdisciplinary discourse of Africana thinkers has yielded seminal conceptual interventions that continually enrich our understanding of the most vital sociopolitical and cultural issues of our day. If we are to forge the type of social transformation that these thinkers advocated, we must prioritize problem-based creolized inquiry to address the issues of unfreedom, injustice, and inequality, in the same manner that Douglass, Wells-Barnett, and Du Bois did. We must also embrace the critical tools and theoretical pluralism that define the works of Fanon and Rousseau, for these thinkers' conceptualizations of national consciousness and the general will have at their core the well-being and betterment of humanity as a mutually determined collectivity. Emulating these thinkers' shared methodologies will compel us to include their works in similarly transdisciplinary curricula that will also further the progressive pedagogical aims and social critiques of Paolo Freire and Jean Anyon. These educators' foundational works shine a light on teaching practices and institutional inequities that disadvantage Global South, BIPOC and working class communities.

Critical Pedagogy and Creolized Curriculum

Paolo Freire's classic work, *Pedagogy of the Oppressed* ([1968] 2000), presents a revolutionary and creolized philosophy of education that combines Marxian critique, existential phenomenological analysis, and decolonial assessments of pedagogical practices to further the aims of liberatory praxis in the Global South. Like Rousseau, Douglass, Wells-Barnett, Du Bois, and Fanon before him, Freire implements transdisciplinarity to problematize and, thereby, decenter manifestations of institutional power that necessitate the dehumanization, subjugation, and miseducation of the masses. Freire argues against the ubiquitous banking concept of education that positions teachers and students as depositors and repositories of information, respectively, reminding us that "Liberating education consists in acts of cognition, not transferals of information" since "the humanist, revolutionary … educator['s] … efforts must coincide with those of the students to engage in critical thinking and the quest for mutual humanization" ([1970] 2000: 75, 79). For Freire, and for all radical educators, emancipatory praxis is actualized in pedagogical practices that involve students in the process of their own intellectual liberation. Thus, the learning process should be neither passive nor unilateral; it should reflect critical engagement, collaboration, and adaptation by teachers and students, as both are equally situated to become engaged learners in the ongoing project of becoming more human. To become more human, according to Freire, is to consciously reject the advancement of dehumanizing theories and practices, like racism, colonialism, and classism, which distort our shared humanity.

A decade after the publication of Freire's work, Jean Anyon's social theory of education was outlined in "Social Class and the Hidden Curriculum of Work" (1980). There, she delineates the insidiously class-based, discriminatory teaching methods guiding American primary school education. Her detailed case study presents glaring inequities in curricular and pedagogical practices that vary according to social class. Anyon's findings show that working class school curricula and pedagogy develop students' rote memorization skills, while teaching practices at the middle-class school acclimatize students to focus on formulating "correct" answers. The affluent professional school's pedagogy promotes the expression of relevant ideas through creative means, while the executive elite school hones students' intellectual acumen by way of teacher-student collaboration that promotes students' self-identification as analytical problem-solvers and potential leaders (1980: 67–92). Anyon contends that this hidden curriculum indoctrinates students into a system of social relations, and an attendant relationship to capital, that is determined by their socioeconomic status. These self-conceptions encourage a contentious relationship to capital for working class students; develop bureaucratic skills for middle-class students; elicit negotiating tendencies among upper-middle class students; and foster the manipulation of thought systems among ruling class students, thereby ensuring their future social dominance (ibid.: 87–92). Thus, while seemingly providing a thesis that answers Freire's call for the greater dissemination of critical pedagogy, Anyon's findings present us with unmistakable sociohistorical tensions: the children of the ruling class receive educational training that, although potentially emancipatory, reinforces hegemonic power by equipping them with skills that sharpen their ability to exert control over societal structural formations. Paradoxically, this is the type of pedagogical inculcation that is sorely needed among the oppressed, as Freire avers. Instead, it is being promulgated amongst those who already have access to power and privilege. Anyon does not cite Freire's work; nonetheless her examples of divergent class-based curricula and pedagogical practices provide substantiation for Freire's admonitions against the predominant banking model of education that ensures the perpetuity of ruling class hegemony.

Conclusion

The bridge of pedagogical praxis between Freire and Anyon lies in the implementation of transdisciplinary curricula that may expose all students to the emancipatory discourse of the aforementioned political theorists and Africana thinkers. Educators at all institutions of learning should reevaluate their curricular content and teaching methods to instantiate a progressive culture of learning that will empower us to achieve Freire's goal of embracing our common humanity. Elucidating the crucial works of David Walker, Jean Jacques Rousseau, Frederick Douglass, Ida B. Wells-Barnett, W. E. B. Du Bois, Frantz Fanon, and other thinkers from the Global South will enable this process of intellectual liberation to occur. As this collective transformation takes place, disciplinary divides and rigid scholarly allegiances will necessarily dissolve just as they do in the aforementioned thinkers' works, for our quest to unearth difficult truths that could prompt positive social change will take precedence for us, just as it did decades and centuries ago for them. Once this revolution in educational institutions occurs, the compelling writings of Africana thinkers will no longer be relegated to various fields within Ethnic Studies; they will be more broadly included in courses on political and social theory, and philosophy just as the works of Rousseau are. By promulgating creolized scholarship and embracing humanizing pedagogical practices, we will answer Fanon's call to set afoot a new humanity as we enact the timeless wisdom of Robert Nesta Marley to emancipate ourselves from mental enslavement (1980). Then, and only then, will we recreate the academy into a genuinely humanistic space where intellectual freedom inspires broader realizations of social justice for all.

Notes

1   Henry Giroux, *Neoliberalism's War on Higher Education* 2; Martín and Aguado, 2–3.

2   Jane Gordon, *Creolizing Political Theory,* 10–12; L. Gordon, *Disciplinary Decadence,* 33–5, 44.

3   Hussein Bulhan, *Frantz Fanon and the Psychology of Oppression,* 56, 69–73; L. Gordon, *What Fanon Said*, 70–1; Judy, "Fanon's Body of Black Experience"; and Stover, *Being and Insurrection,* 122–61.

4   For detailed discussions on the import of Douglass's battle with slave-breaker Covey to Africana/Black existential thought, see Lewis Gordon, *Existentia Africana*, 16–17 and 55–61; Cynthia Willett, "The Dialectic of Master and Slave," 166–8; and this author's *Being Apart,* 8–12.

4

THE SPECTER OF AFRICANA THOUGHT IN JULIET HOOKER'S *THEORIZING RACE IN THE AMERICAS*

Juliet Hooker's *Theorizing Race in the Americas* presents a hemispheric, juxtapositional analysis of late-nineteenth- and early-twentieth-century African American and Latin American thinkers' political theorizations of race. In this work of political theory, Hooker conducts side-by-side examinations of the writings of Frederick Douglass and Domingo Sarmiento, W. E. B. Du Bois and José Vasconcelos to argue that a thorough consideration of these theorists' discursive responses to scientific racism's hegemonic sociopolitical and cultural manifestations warrants a specifically hemispheric reading. Hooker's juxtapositional "South by South" reading demonstrates that Douglass's, Sarmiento's, Du Bois's, and Vasconcelos's respective ideas traversed the region "reveal[ing] intellectual connections and political genealogies of racial thought within the Americas … at key historical moments," while simultaneously unbinding their political thought from the strictly national contexts within which they are typically circumscribed (2017: 2–4). Thus Hooker's thesis in *Theorizing Race in the Americas* is twofold.

First, it situates thinkers from the Americas as pivotal interlocutors on discourses of race, empire, colonialism, *mestizaje*, mestizo-futurism, and

Afro-futurism. This focus is both fitting and timely since the sociopolitical and cultural formations of the Americas represent the manifold theoretical and political consequences of European imperial expansion, chattel slavery, and settler colonialism. Second, Hooker categorizes these African American and Latin American thinkers' intellectual productions as responding to three principal strains of scientific racism that peaked during the eighteenth-century European enlightenment: ethno-biological determinism, stemming from polygenetic evolutionary theories promulgated by the American school of ethnologists; the historical or civilizational school, founded on monogenetic evolutionary theories and evinced in the nineteenth-century writings of Arthur de Gobineau, also known as the "father" of modern racist theory; and social Darwinism, derived from monogenetic theories of evolutionary mutations (2017: 6–7). Hooker's historical contextualization of scientific racism's utilization of multiple and interrelated disciplinary approaches, as well as its formative impact on US domestic policy and geopolitical relations, discloses its ideological reach and centurial span—all of which influenced the trajectory of Douglass's, Sarmiento's, Du Bois's, and Vasconcelos's political writings. In this manner Hooker categorizes racist thought as a defining hegemonic discourse that is centrally implicated in the societies, politics, and cultures of the Americas. She duly emphasizes its influence in debates on chattel slavery and abolition, domestic and foreign policy, US expansionism and, as is the case with eugenics, forced sterilization of the poor, including Black, Indigenous, and people of color (BIPOC) in the United States and Latin America.

As a work of political theory *Theorizing Race in the Americas* takes disciplinary cues from conceptual developments in political science and philosophy, like Critical Race Studies, that highlight the strength of Hooker's South-by-South inquiry in its privileging of the Americas as a fecund site of theoretical probing for Douglass, Sarmiento, Du Bois, and Vasconcelos. In this regard, *Theorizing Race* propounds a creolized,[1] or transdisciplinary, method of inquiry, since the author urges political theorists and others to "mov[e] beyond what counts as a philosophical text" so that they may "think more broadly about the sites where those ideas have been formulated" (2017: 17). Paradoxically, however, Hooker's call for expansive interpretations of what constitutes a philosophical text, at times, works against the stated trajectory of her own critique. Thus, Hooker struggles to meet the very conceptual challenge she issues to readers, because her selective juxtapositions actually foreclose the broader transdisciplinary method she initially proffers. For example, her limited readings of Douglass's and Du Bois's political writings in, "What to the Slave is the Fourth of July" and *The Souls of Black Folk,* respectively, obscure the philosophical themes that are also explored in these creolized texts. Hooker impedes the stated aims of her own inquiry by overemphasizing sociopolitical themes at the expense of philosophical insight—in spite of arguing for a broader methodological approach to challenge rigid categorizations of "what counts as a philosophical text." Consequently, it becomes impossible to recognize the manner in which the political themes in Douglass's and Du Bois's works actually emerge through what we will see are Africana philosophical perspectives. The inevitable result of Hooker's circumscribed reading is that the ideological import of Douglass's and Du Bois's creolized Africana thought[2] is occluded.

For these reasons, I will use an Africana philosophical critique to underscore the utility of Fanon's, Douglass's, and Du Bois's thought to challenge Hooker's assertions about scientific racism, highlight the transdisciplinary aspects of their collective Africana liberation discourse, and bring Hooker's unrealized critique of Du Bois's own double consciousness to fruition.

Scientific Racism's Material and Epistemological Legacy

Given the extent to which Hooker astutely highlights the ideological reach of eighteenth-century enlightenment racial science into the nineteenth-, twentieth-, and twenty-first century societies, politics, and cultures of the Americas, it is surprising that her position on scientific racism is somewhat contradictory. On the one hand, Hooker states that "today … scientific racism has largely been debunked" (6), yet on the other she concludes that "older and newer forms of scientific racism … provided support for the encoding of white supremacy in public policy" (10). This speaks to the fact that, although eighteenth- and nineteenth-century scientific racism has been debunked in the name of science-based accuracy, it is still deployed in the service of hegemonic power through its ideological utilization in epistemic and societal structures. On this point, the mid-twentieth-century writings of the psychiatrist, revolutionary, and Africana philosopher Frantz Fanon, on racist dehumanization, scientific discourse, and Western imperialist power are particularly illuminating.

In "Racism and Culture" (1956), Fanon examines the sociopolitical and cultural legacy of racist thought that Hooker also addresses. As such, he explicates scientific racism's transformative movement: from representations in concrete racial hierarchies that are "genotypically and phenotypically determined" to more socially imbricated forms of racism that are manifested within specific cultures (32). He also reminds us that "racism has not managed to harden. It has had to renew itself, to adapt itself, to change its appearance. It has had to undergo the fate of the cultural whole that informed it" (ibid.). The cultural whole of which Fanon speaks is that of white/European hegemonic domination, which enforces the continued dehumanization and degradation of people of color globally. In order for scientific racism and white supremacist policies and practices to have thrived for the past four centuries, they have become malleable, taking on various disciplinary articulations and structural forms while maintaining their core tenets of white/European racial superiority. Specious though these ideations may be, they have contributed to perpetuating the racist institutional formations and practices in the United States that Hooker cites: racially discriminatory and predatory immigration laws, forced sterilization of people of color, and police violence and murders of unarmed members of BIPOC communities. These Draconian measures point to the fact that racist thought is continually reified and actuated at the material level, thereby perpetuating the subjugation and murder of people of color. Yet despite Hooker's lengthy citations of the aforementioned examples of racialized injustice and dehumanizing violence, her conclusion reasserts that "while scientific notions of nonwhite racial inferiority have been abandoned, the continuity and resurgence of racism today reveals the inadequacy of arguments about race as social construction to dismantle racial power and global white supremacy" (2017: 200). Aside from the fact that no "arguments about race" can "dismantle racial power and global white supremacy," don't Hooker's examples of racist violence reveal that the material violence expressed in the dehumanization and criminalization of BIPOC communities is premised upon the epistemic violence of scientific racism itself?

What is more the popularity of twentieth- and twenty-first-century texts that justify epistemic and structural racism further substantiates Fanon's aforementioned claims about the ideological and cultural fixity of racist thought in Western discourse. Richard Hernnstein's and Charles Murray's *The Bell Curve,* a *New York Times* bestseller (1994) and more recently, Nicholas Wade's *A Troublesome Inheritance* (2014), which went into a second printing despite a *New York Times* review characterizing Wade's arguments as "deceptive" and "dangerous,"[3] prove that racist discourse is comparable to a hydra. For every head that is decapitated through sound refutation, yet another springs forth. Although these texts do not further seventeenth- and eighteenth-century polygenetic arguments, Hernnstein and Murray rely on racially biased data that supports the preeminence of a white "cognitive elite" (1994: 25–75), while Wade reinterprets the human genome experiment's findings to reestablish monogenetic (evolutionary) degeneracy theory (2014: 67–122). The reputable presses that published these works, in addition to their popularity amongst contemporary readers, further substantiate the ideological predominance of scientific racism and its continued validation as a "legitimate" theory of knowledge (and by default humanity), which is imbricated within every facet of Western social, cultural, and political life. It was this thought system's entrenchment during the mid-nineteenth century that served to shape the philosophical and political content of Frederick Douglass's anti-slavery agitation.

Frederick Douglass: Abolitionist and Africana Philosopher of Existence

In his 1854 speech, "The Claims of the Negro Ethnologically Considered," Douglass identifies the racist polygenetic claims of the American school ethnologists, outlined in Samuel Morton's *Crania Americana* (1839) and *Crania Aegyptiaca* (1844), as evidence that:

It is the providence of prejudice to be blind; and scientific writers, not less than others, write to please, as well as to instruct, and even unconsciously to themselves, (sometimes) sacrifice what is true to what is popular. Fashion is not confined to dress; but extends to philosophy as well—and it is fashionable now, in our land, to exaggerate the differences between the Negro and the European. ([1854] 1950: 298)

In Douglass's view, the American school ethnologists' employment of biological determinism was proof of said hyperbolized racial difference, for it not only posited the false notion of innate African inferiority but also promulgated a Eurocentric, hegemonic revision of the Western historiographical narrative that erased the ancient Kemites' African racial and cultural identity. Though Hooker correctly cites "Claims" as a direct refutation of the American school ethnologists' findings, there is no mention of the nuanced transdisciplinary argument Douglass used to, at once, prove the Kemites' African racial, morphological, and cultural identity while furthering his anti-slavery argument.[4]

Additionally, in Hooker's examination of his famed "What to the Slave is the Fourth of July?" address, she avers that Douglass problematizes conceptualizations of democracy, fugitivity, and liminal citizenry. She posits that fugitive slaves' liminal citizenship imbued them with heightened "democratic subjectivities" (2017: 30). Although this is ostensibly true, enslaved people do not first arrive at this level of inter-subjective political awareness and contingent national identification without first apprehending their intrinsic freedom as human beings in spite of their material condition in bondage. It is this inherently existential claim that Douglass outlines in his infamous battle with slave-breaker Covey in *Narrative of the Life of Frederick Douglass*: "This battle with Covey was the turning-point in my career as a slave. It rekindled the few expiring embers of freedom, and revived within me a sense of my own manhood. It … inspired me again with a determination to be free … It was a glorious resurrection, from the tomb of slavery, to the heaven of freedom" ([1845] 1987: 29). Penned nearly a decade before his famed fourth of July address, these words clarify that Douglass—despite his legal and social status as another man's property—became free when he grasped the veracity of his inherent freedom as the key to fighting for his physical liberation and choosing death, if necessary, to maintain and defend said freedom. Douglass's battle with Covey shows that ideological justifications for chattel slavery legitimized the system's brutality, further sanctioning slave-owners' mission to strip the enslaved of their humanity while attempting to squelch their sense of agency. Hooker seems unwilling to deem Douglass's *Narrative* as an encapsulation of the hemispheric political concerns central to *Theorizing Race in the Americas*, yet a thorough understanding of Douglass's evolution as a thinker rests on appreciating his political awakening as emergent through an awareness of his ineluctable human freedom. Indeed, it was Douglass's apprehension of the universality of human freedom that served as the grounding for his philosophy of existence.[5]

Just as Douglass understood philosophy's epistemological and material impact on the anti-slavery struggle, he was also aware that his lived experience in bondage gave him the moral authority to challenge anti-black biases, particularly as his former Garrisonian abolitionist allies also proved susceptible to them.[6] During this time of intellectual expansion, Douglass further delineated his conception of human freedom—a theory that would later become a cornerstone of Africana existential thought. His definition of freedom, in "Lectures on Slavery No. 2," expresses the ontological claim that freedom is an innate feature of our human existence: "Such is the truth of man's right to liberty. It existed in the very idea of man's creation. It was his even before he comprehended it. He was created in it, endowed with it, and it can never be taken from him" ([1852] 1950: 140). Here we can see how Douglass's political commitments and tireless agitation as a freeman were arrived at and determined through a distinct awareness of his existential freedom. Although Hooker cites Douglass's Fourth of July speech, and other political writings, as a cornerstone of Black fugitive thought and the encapsulation of what she terms "a radical black fugitive democratic ethos" (2017: 29), establishing a conceptual bridge between this ethos and Douglass's incipient Africana existential concerns is imperative for highlighting the philosophical significance of his writings. Such an analysis would allow the author and her readers to consider "Douglass's autobiography and lectures" as encapsulating "what counts as a philosophical text" (2017: 17). For Douglass's existential explorations of agency, being, and freedom[7] served as the conceptual foundation for a radical race- and gender-based formulation of egalitarianism (as discussed in Chapter 1) that became the defining feature of his political thought. As such it should be acknowledged that the theoretical inspiration for Douglass's political work lies in his existentialist orientation, as the awareness of his intrinsic freedom impelled his physical liberation from the shackles of slavery to then agitate tirelessly for justice and equality. Douglass's rigorous and transformative process of existential self-actualization made him the groundbreaking philosopher and life-long political theorist and activist that he became.

Unrealized Critiques of Du Bois's Double-consciousness

While Hooker contextualizes the early-twentieth-century writings of both Vasconcelos and Du Bois as responses to the white supremacist terror of rampant lynchings and razing of Black communities during the nadir era of anti-black violence in US history (1877–1940s), her side-by-side probing of internalized racism is solely limited to Vasconcelos's works, *The Cosmic Race* (1925) and *Indología* (1926). What issues come to the fore, however, when we subject Du Bois's *Dark Princess* (1928) to a similar critique? After all, Du Bois originated the theory of double consciousness, which Hooker uses to explain the psychopathology of internalized racism in the works of Vasconcelos. Doesn't Du Bois's *Dark Princess* warrant a more in-depth reading that focuses on the very psychological and inter-subjective effects of white supremacist domination that his theory of double consciousness illuminates? Hooker cites Vasconcelos's portrayal of Afro-Latinx and Indigenous populations in *Indología* as "active co-contributors in the development of the region's mestizo identity" (2017: 174) in direct contrast to the relative absence of Afro-Latinx and Indigenous people in Vasconcelos's earlier work, *The Cosmic Race*. she also highlights Vasconcelos's disdain for ruling Latin American elites who deny their own African and Indigenous roots (2017: 175). This pigmentocracy, or rule by a white and/or light-skinned elite, is not unique to Latin America. While it is manifested in varying degrees and may characterize individualized and collectivized sociopolitical struggles related to assimilation and/or separation, it informs the lived experience of people of color throughout the Global South, the United States, and the world. Irrespective of this fact, Hooker unceremoniously contends that the conceptual and thematic content of Du Bois's *The Souls of Black Folk* (1903) is not representative of his later Pan-African, internationalist, and anti-colonial commitments. Ostensibly, this may appear to be true. However like Douglass, whose politicization was rooted in an existential apprehension of human freedom, Du Bois's cognizance of African Americans' bifurcated ontology is what forms the basis of his theory of double consciousness in *Souls*. Thus, Du Boisian double consciousness, however ironically, provides the very critical lens to critique Du Bois's (and the NAACP's) intra-racial color conflict with Marcus Mosiah Garvey and his Universal Negro Improvement Association (UNIA), as well as Du Bois's choice of female protagonist in *Dark Princess*.

David Levering Lewis cites numerous references to Du Bois's contrary opinions of Garvey's leadership and followers, all of which appear to be rooted in Du Bois's elitism, classism, and colorism. On the one hand Du Bois praised Garvey's Back to Africa Movement for electrifying the masses, yet on the other hand, he disparagingly characterized Garvey as a "very dark-skinned man,"[8] and "demagogue"[9] whose followers were "the lowest type of Negroes, mostly from the West Indies."[10] Hooker is quite right in her assertion that there was no "love lost" between Du Bois and Garvey (2017: 129). Though they both embraced Pan-Africanism, Garvey's earlier program of African repatriation, combined with the UNIA's mission of instilling racial pride through its valorization of African history and culture, uplifted the Black masses in unprecedented and revolutionary ways. Garvey's timeless symbols and sayings of Black Nationalist and Pan-African unity—the Red, Black, and Green flag of Black liberation; and his mottos "Up ye mighty Race" and "A people without knowledge of their history is like a tree without roots"—became badges of racial honor that Black people sorely needed and still need today. Popularizing these timely cultural nationalist symbols and affirmations made Garvey an incomparable charismatic leader and a radical, albeit contradictory race man.[11] Du Bois's and Garvey's disagreements ran the ideological gamut—from the NAACP's intergrationist aims versus the UNIA's program of African repatriation, to more practical tactics for implementing day-to-day programs of social transformation. Nevertheless one would be remiss to discount the extent to which Garvey reawakened African people around the world to the vital importance of valorizing our ancestors' historical significance, as well as our innate human dignity.

In the same manner that Garvey seized opportunities to instill race pride in African people, Du Bois could have used his 1928 novel, *Dark*

Princess, as a literary expression of Pan-African unity. Instead, however, Du Bois crafted his fictitious narrative of Global South unity through the romance between the African American protagonist, Matthew Townes and his East Indian lover and intellectual equal, Princess Kautilya. This work is widely cited as presaging both the 1955 Bandung Conference of African-Asian anti-colonial alliance, and Afro-futurism—and rightfully so. Yet, two pertinent questions remain: why didn't Du Bois choose to depict an African princess as Matthew's lover during an era of such heightened Pan-African consciousness? And how does this apparent disavowal reflect Du Bois's own internalized racism? For example, Lewis also underscores Du Bois's self-identification as a mulatto, distinct from "full-blooded Negroes," to support his point that "proud hybridization is so prevalent in [Du Bois's] sense of himself that the failure to notice it in the literature about him is as remarkable as the complex itself."[12]

Remarkable indeed, but many Du Bois scholars focus exclusively on his prodigious epistemological contributions that run the gamut from establishing our interdisciplinary fields of Africana and African American Studies, to more the more specialized areas of Black Radical and Black Atlantic Studies, and laying the foundations for modern sociology and ethnographic study. Indeed, Du Bois's contributions to the history of ideas are too numerous to count; nonetheless the effects of his own intra-racial blindspots upon his work should also be interrogated. In failing to subject *Dark Princess* to the same scrutiny that is given to Vasconcelos's *The Cosmic Race* and *Indología,* Hooker perpetuates this critical avoidance. Utilizing double consciousness to underscore Du Bois's blindspots may reveal his human frailty; however, we would not even have the conceptual framework of double consciousness without his original insights. This fact alone should remind us that it is nearly impossible to detract from his groundbreaking discursive legacy.

Conclusion

The aforementioned points of contention stem from Hooker's theoretical oversights: contradictory claims about scientific racism, undeveloped transdisciplinary analyses of Douglass's, and Du Bois's works, and what appears to be an epistemic indifference to the discursive scope of Africana philosophy in general. If Hooker had undertaken truly creolized examinations of "What to the Slave is the Fourth of July?" and *The Souls of Black Folk*, she might have identified how Douglass's and Du Bois's Africana existential/philosophical concerns lent even greater depth and nuance to their political thought. Douglass's oeuvre delineates a radical theory of freedom that animated his commitment to both the anti-slavery struggle and the women's suffrage movement, and later established the contours of twentieth-century Africana/ Black existential thought. Du Bois's aforementioned scholarly legacy paved the way for legions of twentieth- and twentieth-century scholars to highlight the importance of Black thought, for he understood that "the creation of an African-American population through the institution of enslavement, create[d] radically unique opportunities for human study—a clarifying mirror into the nature of the human species through studying it in the fullest range of predicaments."[13] Examining Black humanity through the dialectical lens of enslavement and liberation, subjugation and freedom compelled Douglas, Du Bois, and Fanon to pen a range of discursive responses through creolized inquiry that gathered wisdom from a range academic disciplines, including historiography, philosophy, psychology, and the social sciences. Their shared mission of challenging and subverting European enlightenment-era and subsequent nineteenth- and twentieth-century racist discourse led to their embrace of disciplinary plurality that, in turn, led to their becoming pillars of Africana philosophy.

As thinkers indebted to Douglass's, Du Bois's, and Fanon's shared emancipatory vision, our own research can only be enriched by interrogating and then disseminating their ideas as thoroughly as possible, because these philosophers understood that dismantling racist structural formations begins with correcting the ideological fallacies that initially engendered their entrenchment at the epistemic level. They grasped that changing the world truly begins with changing ideas, particularly those dehumanizing structures of meaning that continually threaten to destroy us. Indeed, Black thought matters and as theoretical heirs to Douglass's, Du Bois's, and Fanon's liberatory discourse, should we not honor their shared legacy of committed intellectual engagement by illuminating the full breadth of their revolutionary philosophical vision?

Notes

1 Jane Gordon, *Creolizing Political Theory.*

2 Chapter 1 details Africana philosophy's inherently creolized methodology.

3 David Dobbs, "The Fault in Our DNA."

4 For a detailed discussion of the ancient and modern historiographical, linguistic, and cultural sources from Herodotus and Diodorus, to Denon and Volney (among others) that Douglass cites in "Claims," see this author's *Being Apart*, 47–65.

5 In all three of Douglass's autobiographies—*Narrative of the Life of Frederick Douglass* (1845), *My Bondage and My Freedom* (1855), and *Life and Times of Frederick Douglass* (1881)—he recounts the battle with Covey. The first iteration of the struggle depicts the fight's existential gravity. However, in his subsequent autobiographies Douglass places even greater emphasis on his ineluctable agency, stating that "I had reached the point at which I was *not afraid to die. This spirit made me a freeman in fact*, though I still remained a slave in *form*." See *My Bondage* 186–7 and *Life and Times* 143–4. On Douglass as a philosopher of existence, see Lewis Gordon, *Existentia Africana*, 7–11, and Chapter 3.

6 Douglass's break with William Lloyd Garrison's American Anti-Slavery Society was due to Garrison's and his colleagues' racially paternalistic demand that Douglass relegate himself to the role of "talking chattel" to narrate the events of his life, and to "leave the philosophy" to them. Douglass, *My Bondage and My Freedom*, 271–2; *The Life and Times of Frederick* Douglass, 259–61; and Parris, *Being Apart*, 49–50.

7 Broadus Butler, "Frederick Douglass"; Lewis Gordon's *Existentia Africana* chapter 3; and this author's *Being Apart*, 8–11, and 47–60.

8 David Levering Lewis, *W.E.B. Du Bois: Biography of a Race*, 456.

9 David Levering Lewis, *W.E.B. Du Bois: The Fight for Equality and the American Century*, 62.

10 Ibid, 62.

11 It is well known that Garvey met with Ku Klux Klan leaders in 1922.

12 David Levering Lewis, *W.E.B. Du Bois: Biography of a Race*, 148.

13 Jane Gordon, *Creolizing Political Theory*, 42.

5

"YOUNG, GIFTED" AND WOMAN, READING ROSA LUXEMBURG THROUGH LORRAINE HANSBERRY AND THE BLACK RADICAL TRADITION

In Lorraine Hansberry's unfinished book review "Simone de Beauvoir and *The Second Sex:* An American Commentary" ([1957] 1995: 133), Hansberry praises Beauvoir's philosophical intervention while lamenting the limits of Beauvoir's middle-class perspective. While Beauvoir is somewhat hopeful about the changing status of women in the Soviet Union[1] and her brief chapter "The Point of View of Historical Materialism" examines both Engels's and August Bebel's writings on female subordination (1974: 59–63), for Hansberry *The Second Sex* lacked a comprehensive, historical-materialist analysis that would foreground the rebellion, political agitation, and eventual transcendence of enslaved African American women and working class European women (Hansberry [1957] 1995: 133). Beauvoir's work impressed and fascinated Hansberry,[2] but it also left her wanting much more. Interestingly, the historical-materialist feminism that Hansberry yearned to see unfold in Beauvoir's work had already been voiced in the writings of the formidable Marxist theorist and revolutionary Rosa Luxemburg, whose inimitable leadership of Germany's Spartacus League is mentioned in *The Second Sex* (Beauvoir 1974: 141).

If Hansberry had gone on to publish observations on Luxemburg's transdisciplinary writings, we would be graced with an early/mid-twentieth-century creolized feminist discourse that simultaneously centralizes proletarian struggle, European imperialism and Global South decolonization, and the Black freedom struggle in the African diaspora. Both Luxemburg's and Hansberry's egalitarian feminism emanates from problem-based inquiry geared towards solving the vexing sociopolitical challenges of racial and economic injustice. This transdisciplinary approach, combined with their apprehension of European imperialist-capitalist expansion in the Global South, led both Hansberry and Luxemburg to articulate a theoretical solidarity with Black radical and Black feminist thought several decades before these ideologies were formally named as such. Thus, their shared syncretic theoretical strategies led both thinkers to fruitful economic, sociopolitical, and historical reflections that were decades ahead of their respective times. To highlight Luxemburg's and Hansberry's innovative discursive contributions, I will present reflections on how their writings, speeches, and letters promote Black radical and Black feminist ideals in three related ways: in their decision to privilege a life of intellectual pursuits; in their political engagement; and in their commitment to advancing an authentic humanism.

Woman's Work: A Life of the Mind and Action

Dedicating oneself to the life of the mind in order to contribute to the betterment of humanity is an altruistic pursuit. Nonetheless, the historical record shows that men, as thinkers, are consistently celebrated for this endeavor while women thinkers are generally diminished for the same. Black feminist thought challenges this patriarchal axiom. Its focus on the intersectional nature of race-, sex-, and class-based oppression includes an emphasis on Black women's empowerment through self-definition and self-valuation. Indeed, Patrice Dickerson stresses that African American women "come into being" and attain self-awareness through their own achievements and, through this process of self-actualization, their triumphs are manifested (qtd. in Hill Collins 2000: 40). Both Lorraine Hansberry and Rosa Luxemburg garnered self-worth and strength from their calling as public intellectuals and activists. Both women lived during historic times of great social and political transformation: the advent of socialist revolution in Europe; the US Civil Rights Movement (often referred to as America's Second Revolution); and Third World decolonization.[3] Although Luxemburg and Hansberry enjoyed the relative comforts of a middle-class upbringing, they shared the experience of living under hegemonic domination: Hansberry under white supremacist segregation on Chicago's South Side, and Luxemburg in Poland under Tsarist Russian occupation. Working as thinkers and activists in their societies' respective insurgencies, Luxemburg and Hansberry heeded the call to arms. Their writings reveal that these women thinkers saw themselves first and foremost as human beings who embraced their mission to write, agitate, and raise political awareness in the fight against injustice, exploitation, and oppression in its varied yet related forms: classism, racism, sexism, and anti-humanism.[4]

Luxemburg's Revolutionary Thought and Praxis

During her doctoral studies at the University of Zurich,[5] Luxemburg became involved in the local proletariat movements and went on to cofound the Social Democracy of the Kingdom of Poland (SKDP) in 1893. She later moved to Berlin in 1898 where she edited *Wirtschaftliche und sozialpolitishe Rundschau* (Economic and Social Review) (Frölich 2010: 21–31). One year later, in October 1899, Luxemburg gave a rousing speech, peppered with her trademark humor and wit, at the Hanover Congress of the Social Democratic Party of Germany. She issued a spirited challenge to her older male comrades' findings on the role of trade unions and cooperatives in working-class revolution, which garnered enthusiastic applause and shouts of agreement (Howard 1971). By this time she was already a highly sought-after speaker who moved crowds with a potent blend of logical analysis and unwavering conviction; this approach inspired her audiences to look beyond their formerly held provincial viewpoints towards more expansive possibilities (Frölich 2010: 40–1). Luxemburg penned a letter to her longtime collaborator and companion Leo Jogiches a few short months before giving her speech at the Hanover Congress. In it, she set forth her intent to galvanize the masses:

> In my "soul" a totally new, original form is ripening that ignores all rules and conventions. It breaks them by the power of ideas and strong convictions. I want to affect people like a clap of thunder, to inflame their minds not by speechifying but with the breadth of my vision, the strength of my conviction, and the power of my expression. (Hudis and Anderson 2004: 382)

The power of Luxemburg's words is undeniable. At twenty-eight, she had not only achieved a level of self-awareness beyond her years, but she also understood and relished her pivotal role in the European socialist revolution. Hers is the voice of a woman who welcomed the role of leader *and* compatriot in the struggle to realize a socialist society. Luxemburg's zeal for the realization of a classless society was rooted in a hatred of human suffering, and this is why she prioritized the sociopolitical problems of exploitation and oppression. This focus led her to entertain the woman question in a creolized manner that combined historical, sociological, economic, and political considerations. In her 1914 article, "The Proletariat Woman," Luxemburg explains the political motivations of bourgeois women as an expedient means of increasing their class privilege. She chides these women as

> nothing but co-consumers of the surplus value their men extort from the proletariat. They are parasites of the parasites of the social body … The women of the property-owning classes will always fanatically defend the exploitation and enslavement of the working people by which they indirectly receive the means for their socially useless existence. (Ibid. 2004: 240)

Luxemburg then contrasts bourgeois women's sociopolitical solipsism to the communal resistance of subjugated, colonized women of the Global South, whose economic exploitation stems from globalized capitalist expansion in the form of European imperial hegemony. She points to the suffering of Black women in German colonial Africa and that of Indigenous Colombian women under Spanish rule. At the same time, Luxemburg emphasizes that the socialist-feminist project of posterity requires the cooperation of all oppressed, exploited people:

> The workshop of the future requires many hands and hearts. A world of female misery is waiting for relief. The wife of the peasant moans as she nearly collapses under life's burdens. In German Africa, in the Kalahari Desert, the bones of defenseless Herero women are bleaching in the sun, those who were hunted down by a band of German soldiers and subjected to a horrific death of hunger and thirst. On the other side of the ocean, in the high cliffs of Putumayo, the death cries of martyred Indian women, ignored by the world, fade away in the rubber plantations of the international capitalists. (Ibid.: 244)

Luxemburg's call for an anti-imperialist, socialist-feminism establishes her as a creolized theorist who was well ahead of her time. "The Proletariat Woman" presages the decolonial turn in late twentieth-century and twenty-first-century feminist thought, as it drives home the need for interracial, transnational alliances with the women of the Global South. While this transnational, anti-imperialist perspective is mirrored in Black radical and Black feminist thought, its organizational praxis comes to pass in the activist work of the Communist Party USA's African American and Afro-Caribbean women members from the 1930s to 1950s.[6] However it was not until the formation of the Third World Women's Alliance in the late 1960s that a global socialist, anti-colonial and decolonial feminist political agenda was realized on a mass scale.

Luxemburg's 1914 critique of bourgeois women's political opportunism bears a striking resemblance to Angela Davis's assessment of the same. Davis utilizes the theoretical framework of Black radical and Black feminist thought to unveil white feminists' furtherance of late nineteenth-century white supremacist domination in their agitation for their enfranchisement to the exclusion of African Americans, immigrants, and working-class people of all races "whose labor was exploited and whose lives were sacrificed ... by the new class of monopoly capitalists who were ruthlessly establishing their industrial empires. They controlled the immigrant workers in the North as well as the former slaves and poor white laborers who were operating the new railroad, mining and steel industries in the South." (1981: 116). Both Luxemburg and Davis delineate the ways that white bourgeois women have historically sought political equality with men in order to stand as compatriots in the fight to maintain white racial predominance. Elizabeth Cady Stanton's unabashed declaration that "I will cut off this right arm of mine before I will ever work for or demand the ballot for the Negro and not the woman" (qtd. in Gates and Smith 2014: 510) best exemplifies Davis's and Luxemburg's shared position on the bourgeois white woman's predatory self-interest. Thus, Luxemburg's antipathy toward the women of the bourgeoisie reveals a feminism rooted in a global, anti-imperialist class consciousness. It is a feminism that must be understood as one facet of a radical egalitarian worldview that informed her life-long quest for a socialist democratic society in which the humanity of every individual would be deemed of equal worth.

In "The Proletariat Woman" Luxemburg injects a feminist perspective into the historical-materialist analysis that she initially proffered in *The Accumulation of Capital* ([1913] 2003). Here she surpasses Marx's analysis of European imperialist expansion by explaining that such hegemonic encroachment would inevitably lead to the economic exploitation of Europe's colonial territories: "Luxemburg sought to uncover the economic roots of imperialism by focusing on the problem of expanded reproduction" (Hudis and Anderson 2004: 32). She does precisely this in her analysis of chattel slavery's centrality to capitalist accumulation in the United States and England. Voicing a theoretical allegiance with what we now recognize as Black radical thought, Luxemburg emphasizes the indispensability of enslaved African labor in Western exploitation colonialism:

> For the first genuinely capitalist branch of production, the English cotton industry, not only the cotton of the Southern states of the American Union was essential, but also the millions of Negroes who were shipped to America to provide the labor power of the plantations, and who later, as a free proletariat, were incorporated in the class of wage laborers in a capitalist system. Obtaining the necessary labor power from non-capitalist societies, the so-called "labor problem," is ever more important for capital in the colonies. ([1913] 2003: 343)

Luxemburg's point is clear: without enslaved African labor the enormous capital accumulation of the four-centuries-long European colonial era would not have been possible. Luxemburg then applies a related economic analysis to her critique of the bourgeoisie's role in the societal devastation of Europe during and after the First World War.

In her December 1918 speech, "What Does the Spartacus League Want," Luxemburg explains how the bourgeoisie's rapacious capitalism led to the First World War, arguing that the war not only instantiated state-sanctioned mass murder, but also destroyed the means of production for the entire region. She imagistically describes international capital as "the insatiable god Baal, into whose bloody maw millions upon millions of steaming human sacrifices are thrown" (2004: 349). This vivid metaphor acts to support Luxemburg's subsequent, oft-cited declaration that only socialism can vanquish global capital, or Baal, the consumer of human souls: "In this hour, socialism is the only salvation for humanity. The words of the *Communist Manifesto* flare ... above the crumbling bastions of capitalist society: Socialism or barbarism!" (ibid.: 350).[7] Through her geopolitical economic analysis Luxemburg deduces that capitalism would lead to the inevitable destruction of human life. This certainty, according to her comrade Paul Frölich, reveals that for Luxemburg "socialism was not only a hope but the fixed object of a tremendous will to action ... There was no room for compromise in her thought, and no conflict between her theoretical work and her practical action" ([1939] 2010: 190). In our current age of advanced neo-liberal global capital, this is precisely why Luxemburg's words should inspire us to emulate her political commitment.

Quite interestingly, just decades after the peak in Luxemburg's activist work, another young woman in the 1950s and early 1960s found her political voice during the global Black freedom struggles of the American Civil Rights Movement and Third World decolonization.

Hansberry's Black Radical Politics and Art

Political commitment defined Lorraine Hansberry's work as an activist-artist and, similar to Luxemburg, there was no divergence between her radical ideas and her deeds. At the height of 1950s McCarthy era political repression, Hansberry embarked on a course of political and creative self-actualization from which a varied corpus of writings and domestic and international activism sprung forth. In the opening pages of her auto/biography, *To Be Young, Gifted and Black* ([1969] 1995), readers learn of a young woman who fully grasped the import of her intellectual and artistic vocation:

> I am audacious enough to think of myself as an artist—that here is both joy and beauty and illumination and communion between people to be achieved through the dissection of personality. That's what I want to do. I want to reach a little closer to the world, which is to say people, and see if we can share some illuminations together about each other … I think virtually every human being is dramatically interesting. Not only is he dramatically interesting, he is a creature of stature whoever he is. (Ibid.: 5)

Hansberry was an artist. But more importantly, she was a socially engaged artist who came into political consciousness through knowledge of the Black radical tradition. Robert Nemiroff described her in 1951 as "a young woman on fire with black liberation, not only here but in Africa, an insurgent with a vision that embraced two continents" (ibid.: 28). Her father, an active member of the local NAACP, challenged restrictive real estate covenants by moving the family into a white neighborhood where they stood firm against a violent white mob. Hansberry's early education in sociopolitical resistance led her to value the strength of all African Americans as they challenged structural racism and anti-black violence. Her uncle, William Leo Hansberry, was one of the nation's foremost Africanist scholars, and he instilled within her an appreciation of African history, a sense of race-pride, and an African diasporic consciousness (Carter 1991: 8–9). It was through this familial and cultural orientation that Hansberry came to view her art as both potential catalyst for progressive social change and the reflection of her highest aspirations.

This position is made clear in her 1952 speech "Tribute to Paul Robeson," her mentor, which was given at a Harlem rally to advocate for the restoration of Robeson's passport. Hansberry reminds the participants that Robeson had "accepted the greater responsibility of the artist at once—not only in [his] art but in [his] life, as artist, as private citizen and public figure—the people from whom you spring: to be voice, member and champion of the people's struggle" (Lorraine Hansberry Papers).[8] Hansberry then goes on to name the US government as complicit in the long history of tyrannical oppression that has afflicted African people around the globe:

> To the ... Department of State we say: This man is an American citizen, his forebears fought tyranny on three continents, so that he might draw breath as a free being. His is a sacred heritage. When you infringe on his liberty you tamper with the labor and lives of generations of freedom seekers. We charge you with this responsibility. (Ibid.)

Here Hansberry equates the attainment of freedom as part and parcel of the Black radical tradition of resistance to white supremacist and Western imperialist domination. Like Luxemburg, Hansberry frequently used her gifts as a speaker to rouse audiences to heightened political awareness and to embolden them to resist state-sponsored injustice. Since Robeson's passport was never reinstated, Hansberry took his place at a transnational meeting of communist activists in Uruguay, at the Inter-American Peace Conference (1952), which had to run under the guise of a large social gathering due to constant police surveillance. Hansberry participated in a women's meeting where she was honored to represent African Americans during the red-baiting McCarthy years; she also joined arms with her comrades as they marched through the streets of Montevideo, defying the menacing, sword-wielding police force that was monitoring their activities (Perry 2018: 57–8).

Two weeks before Hansberry's landmark play *A Raisin in the Sun* opened on Broadway in 1959, she delivered an address to the American Society for African Culture entitled "The Negro Writer and His Roots: Toward a New Romanticism"[9] (LHP). In her talk, Hansberry furthers the views expressed in her "Tribute to Paul Robeson." She forcefully states her position on the enduring question of whether art is meant for purely aesthetic or social purposes, and aligns herself with the latter position. Hansberry highlights the similarities between the American Civil Rights Movement and Third World decolonization struggles while stressing the Negro artist's indispensable role in "the war against the illusions of one's time and culture" (ibid.). With the same rhetorical flair that Luxemburg used to lambaste white bourgeois women's counter-revolutionary complicity, Hansberry admonishes the Black bourgeoisie's attachment to materialism, identifying it as the primary impediment to self-awareness and collective liberation: "The desire for the possession of 'things' has rapidly replaced among too many of us the impulse for the possession of ourselves, for freedom … The war against illusions must dispel the romance of the black bourgeoisie" (ibid.). To further her argument, Hansberry warns against political isolationism and apathy, urging her audience to grasp the exigency of the political moment:

> Negro people [can no longer] afford to imagine themselves removed from the most pressing world issue of our time—war and peace, colonialism, capitalism v. socialism … If the world is engaged in a dispute between survival and destruction … in a dispute between the champions of despair and those of hope and glorification of man—then we as members of the human race, must address ourselves to that dispute. (Ibid.)

Hansberry's juxtapositions of war and peace, capitalism and socialism clearly reflect her radical political leanings. Yet she takes her argument one step further by invoking the spirit of the 1955 Bandung Conference, convened four years earlier, by stressing that the bonds between African Americans and continental Africans are no longer abstract but concretized in the immediate realities of the Third World decolonization and American civil rights struggles. Hansberry underscores that

> The unmistakable roots of the universal solidarity of the colored peoples of the world are no longer "predictable" as they were in my father's time—they are here. And I for one, as a black woman in the United States in the mid-twentieth century, feel that I am more typical of the present temperament of my people than not, when I say that I cannot allow the devious purposes of white supremacy to lead me to any conclusion other than what may be the most robust and important one of our time: that the ultimate destiny and aspirations of the African people and twenty million American Negroes are inextricably and magnificently bound up forever. (Ibid.)

Hansberry's transnational anti-colonial thought reflects Nemiroff's previously mentioned statement that she was "a young woman on fire with black liberation" ([1969] 1995: 28). Hansberry understood the urgency of the historical moment as the peoples of Africa, Asia, the Caribbean, and Latin America were overthrowing centuries of European colonial rule; she also saw the domestic civil rights struggle as integral to this subversion of global Western imperialist hegemony. Thus, Hansberry was not only calling upon her people to advance the cause of racial justice, but she was also exhorting them to embrace their ethical responsibility as members of the same race within the larger human family. When Hansberry made these compelling remarks in 1959 she was in her late twenties, and through Robert Nemiroff's contextualization we are better able to appreciate the progressive nature of Hansberry's thought:

> eleven months before the Greensboro sit-ins and fifteen [months] before the formation of the [Student Nonviolent Coordinating Committee] SNCC, Malcolm X was … the leader of a [locally known] mosque in Harlem, and Martin Luther King, the great days of Montgomery three years behind, had quietly shifted the [Southern Christian Leadership Conference] SCLC headquarters to Atlanta. The Freedom Rides, Birmingham, voter registration, the Mississippi [Freedom] summer, the cry of Black Power and the slogan "black is Beautiful" … and the rise of nationalism in all its multiple forms all lay ahead. (Qtd. in Hansberry ([1969] 1995)

Nemiroff's observations bring the Black radical ethos of Hansberry's 1959 address, "The Negro Writer and His Roots," to the fore. Five years before Malcom X's delivered his anti-colonial message of Black Nationalist, Third World solidarity in his "The Ballot or the Bullet" speech (1964), and four years before Martin Luther King Jr.'s "Letter from a Birmingham Jail" (1963) compared the Black freedom struggle to African and Asian decolonization,[10] Hansberry's 1959 address had already urged African Americans to disavow bourgeois complacency and, instead, embrace a progressive Pan-Africanist agenda. And nearly a decade before the before the Black Panthers' rise to national and transnational prominence, Hansberry called for Black pride and Black power through heightened African diasporic consciousness and political solidarity.

A few years after her address to the American Society for African Culture, Hansberry published "This Complex of Womanhood," a 1963 editorial in *Ebony* Magazine (LHP). Though concise, the editorial may be read as a Black feminist treatise that foregrounds the import of Black women to and for the movement of Western history and global capitalism. Hansberry exalts the African woman as the progenitor of ancient human civilization whose reversal of fortune came with the rise of Euromodernity and globalized capital through the advent and codification of racialized slavery. Her ruminations rise to the level of theoretical discourse because they are at once historical and philosophical, invoking the Black radical tradition's focus on historical recuperation and Black feminist thought's emphasis on Black women's agency. Hansberry enlightens her readers with a historiographical overview that spans ancient and modern times:

> The African woman who first reached the shores of the New World in the 17th century was already part and parcel of the fabric of history. She was descended from women who had birthed some of the great militarists of antiquity and from whose number had come some of the most famous queens to sit upon the thrones of ancient Egypt and Ethiopia. Her exploits and beauty were remembered by semitic writers and used into Greek mythology. But for centuries in the New World she was to cut cane, pick coffee, and chop cotton in the fields of the Indies and the plantations of Brazil and the United States. For three centuries she moved in stealth beside and, sometimes, in advance of black men who wrought havoc against the slave system with musket, machete, and petition. (Ibid.)

Here readers are graced with Hansberry's insights as a Black radical feminist thinker. In her opening paragraphs on the African woman's place in the ancient and modern worlds, she reaffirms ancient Africa's pivotal role in Western civilizational development; highlights the centuries of oppression that racialized chattel slavery visited upon enslaved Africans; and stresses the "deformed equality" (Davis 1972: 8) that the labor of chattel slavery created between Black men and women, which engendered a lived, a self-affirming feminism among Black women that required neither societal nor Constitutional validation. This three-part analysis reflects Hansberry's privileging of Black feminist and Black radical histories. Quite tellingly, this article, along with Hansberry's aforementioned talks, articulates the very historical-materialist perspective that Hansberry yearned for when she first read *The Second Sex*. Hansberry herself had developed the very radical feminist ideology for which she had searched in the thought of others.

Authentic Humanism as Praxis

Hansberry and Luxemburg dedicated their lives to intellectual reflection and political agitation because they could not tolerate humankind's self-inflicted desolation. Theirs was a humanism for all, but especially for those suffering under the bootheel of exploitation, oppression, and injustice. At the same time, however, each woman held great faith in the ability to transcend this plight through realizing our potential for greatness. Consider Hansberry's closing remarks in "The Negro Writer and His Roots":

> one cannot live with sighted eyes and feeling heart and not know and react to the miseries which afflict this world. I have given you this account so that you know that what I write is not based on the assumption of idyllic possibilities … I think the human race does command its own destiny and that destiny can eventually embrace the stars. If man is as small and ugly and grotesque as his most inhuman act, he is also as large as his most heroic gesture. (LHP)

Hansberry articulates her personal, political, and artistic credo with this commentary on human nature. She was cognizant of misery, yet well aware that humanity must continually rise up and embrace its gravitas to eradicate it.

This fervent belief is evident in Hansberry's journalistic, teaching, and political commitments during her years in 1950s Harlem when she worked in the office of Paul Robeson's *Freedom* magazine, stressing that the periodical "ought to be the journal of Negro liberation … in fact it will be" (Perry 2018: 46). As a journal that chronicled independence struggles throughout the African diaspora and the Third World,

Freedom's articles placed the nascent southern Civil Rights Movement within a global context by connecting it to liberationist movements for native sovereignty on the African continent. To that end, Hansberry wrote a piece on Kwame Nkrumah and the Ghanaian independence movement in which she states "The people of Ghana clearly see their struggles and victories in connection with black folk on the rest of the continent as well as in the United States" (qtd. in ibid.: 48). Hansberry complemented her Pan-African journalistic pursuits with teaching and research duties at the Jefferson School of Social Science, which was associated with the Community Party USA (CPUSA). There she engaged in dialogues with another mentor, W.E.B Du Bois. Hansberry then shared her growing knowledge with other Harlemites, as she lectured on racial and economic justice at the famed Harlem Speaker's Corner on Lenox Avenue. At this time she also considered herself a communist and stated the following: "I am sick of poverty, lynching, stupid wars and universal maltreatment of my people and obsessed with a rather desperate desire for a new world for me and my people" (qtd. in ibid.: 48).

Hansberry's yearning for a more human world for Black people found further literary expression in her 1964 collaboration with the Student Nonviolent Coordinating Committee (SNCC) in a work of photojournalism entitled, *The Movement: Documentary of a Struggle for Equality* (1964). This atypical coffee table book chronicles the Civil Rights Movement through Hansberry's incisive sociopolitical and historical commentary: moving portraits of Black activists, like Fannie Lou Hamer and Malcolm X; arresting photographs of gleeful white southerners pointing at immolated/lynched Black people; and select quotes from Frederick Douglass, Du Bois, and James Baldwin. The book's cover photo of a white southern police officer violently choking an unarmed Black protester is a stark reminder that the Black freedom struggle is ongoing, for the cop's death grip immediately calls to mind Eric Garner's and George Floyd's shared dying words: "I can't breathe." Despite the fact that the photographs in *The Movement* depict the brutality of white supremacy and anti-black violence, Hansberry uses her socialist orientation to inform readers that working-class and poor whites suffered under the economic exploitation that defines all capitalist systems. She states that racist white police officers are "from a class of Southerners who are themselves victims of a system that has used them and their fathers before them for generations" (Hansberry and SNCC 1964: 68). And immediately following this commentary, Hansberry cites an explanatory quote from Du Bois's *Black Reconstruction* (1935) to provide further historical contextualization of poor whites' manipulation under the US capitalist system.[11] That Hansberry was influenced by Du Bois's discursive legacy is only natural. She was of an immediate post-war generation of Black thinkers for whom he was *the* father of African American, Africana, and Black Radical Studies. Hansberry elucidates Du Bois's intellectual bequest in her remarks at his 1964 memorial service in New York City's Carnegie Hall. Her lyrical and poignant comments on Du Bois's epistemological legacy bear lengthy repetition:

> I do not remember when I first heard the name Dubois. For some Negroes it comes into consciousness so early, so persistently that it is like the spirituals or the blues or discussions of oppression; he was a fact of our culture. People spoke of him as they did the church or the nation … And without a doubt, his ideas have influenced a multitude who do not even know his name … I think that [his legacy] tells us to honor thought and thinking … I think his legacy bids us to pay attention to the genuine needs of humankind … Dubois' legacy teaches us to look toward and work for a socialist organization of society as the next great and dearly won universal condition of mankind. (LHP)

Hansberry's reflections on the towering intellectual that is Du Bois are without compare. With her opening lines that liken the great philosopher to the spirituals and the blues, she vivifies his groundbreaking transdisciplinary work, *The Souls of Black Folk* (1903), as a discursive embodiment of the man himself. Similarly, Hansberry captures the vast reach of Du Bois's ideas in her assertion that so many who do not know him by name have been deeply affected by his thought. One such aspect of Du Boisian thought is the belief that only a socialist society, a truly humanistic expression of sociopolitical and economic relations, will cure the ills of capitalism, including exploitation and poverty. And though Hansberry was echoing Du Bois's thoughts on socialism, she was also echoing Luxemburg's renowned and previously quoted forewarning: "In this hour, socialism is the only salvation for humanity. The words of *The*

Communist Manifesto flare ... above the crumbling bastions of capitalist society: Socialism or Barbarism" (2004: 350).

Luxemburg on the Global South

The desire to alert the masses to the related tragedies of human exploitation and degradation drove Luxemburg to creative and political writing as well as activism. Her youth in Russian-occupied Poland was a study in contrasts between her domestic and social lives. At home she grew up under the influence of educated parents who exposed her to the beauty of both Polish and German literature. Luxemburg was so precocious and enamored with the written word that her proud parents often coaxed her to share her poetic verse with family and friends (Frölich 2010: 4–5). Nonetheless, a misdiagnosed hip injury led to a physical disability that made her even more attuned to the suffering of the poor and her fellow Jews[12] under Tsarist rule. These experiences fueled the moral indignation that led her to pen the following words as a teenager: "I want to burden the affluent with all the suffering and all the hidden, bitter tears" (Le Blanc and Scott 2010: 5). She met her charge of disturbing the conscience of the wealthy many times over.

However, as we have seen in "The Proletariat Woman," Luxemburg also had the discernment to set her sights on a particular brand of exploitative capitalists: Western imperialists with colonial dominions in the Global South. Her brief article "Martinique" may be read as a theoretical prologue to Luxemburg's explication of European imperialist-capitalist exigencies in the colonized territories of the Caribbean and Africa that is detailed a decade later in *The Accumulation of Capital* (1913). Similar in brevity and eloquence to Hansberry's "The Complex of Womanhood," Luxemburg narrates the human devastation resulting from the 1902 eruption of Martinique's Mount Pelée to expose the harsh realities of French imperialism and the historical legacy of chattel slavery and Black subjugation in the Caribbean. Luxemburg personifies Mt. Pelée as a "true giant" who, though furious, was still [g]reat-hearted enough to emit smoke and fire to "warn the reckless creatures that crawled at his feet" (2004: 123).

Luxemburg then shifts to a nuanced, anti-imperialist reading of the eruption that highlights the hypocrisy of white Europeans' uncharacteristic altruism towards the Afro-Caribbean colonial populace. Confronted with the tragedy of this natural disaster, Luxemburg avers that for these Western imperialists, racialized slavery, class hierarchies, and hegemonic systems of domination seemingly ceased to exist. Instead, Mt. Pelée's eruption announced the arrival of

> a new guest—the human being. Not lords and bondsmen, not blacks and whites, not rich and poor, not plantation owners and wage slaves—human beings have appeared on the tiny shattered island, human beings ... who only want to help and succor. Old Mt. Pelée has worked a miracle! Forgotten are the days of Fashoda, forgotten the conflict over Cuba, forgotten "la Revanche"—the French and the English, the Tsar and the Senate of Washington ... donate money send telegrams, extend the helping hand ... a resurrection of humanism among the ruins of human culture. The price of recalling their humanity was high, but thundering Mt. Pelée had a voice to catch their ear. (Ibid.)

Luxemburg then goes on to castigate European imperialists for their disingenuous compassion towards the people of Martinique through what we now identify as a Black radical critique of French colonial rule in pre-revolutionary Haiti (the late eighteenth-century colony of San Domingo), and France's late nineteenth-century annexation of Madagascar:

> But how was it then, centuries ago, when France spilled blood in torrents for the Lesser and Greater Antilles? ... Madagascar: fifty years ago there we saw the disconsolate Republic who weeps for her lost children today, how she bowed the obstinate native people to her yoke with chains and sword ... the mouths of French cannons spewed out death and annihilation; French artillery fire swept thousands of flowering human lives from the face of the earth until a free people prostrate on the ground, ... (Ibid.)

Here we may appreciate Luxemburg's rhetorical and polemical strengths. In one searing paragraph, she denounces the atypical French empathy for colonial subjects in Martinique, since these same oppressors attempted to squelch the emancipatory impulses of the

Haitian revolutionaries and then, one century later, waged genocidal military campaigns in the imperial acquisition of Madagascar. What is more, in Luxemburg's allusion to the Haitian Revolution we see glimmers of Hansberry's unfinished play *Toussaint,* penned in 1958, to honor

> the people of Haiti [who] waged a war and won. They created a nation out of a savagely dazzling colonial jewel in the mighty French empire … their achievement of wresting national freedom from one of the most powerful nations on the face of the earth by … illiterate and cruelly divided black slaves—has aside from almost immeasurable historical importance, its own core of monumental drama. ("A Note to Readers," LHP)

Hansberry's framing of the Haitian Revolution's historical significance rings with the same tenors of C.L.R. James's Black radical critique in his classic study of the San Domingo revolution, *The Black Jacobins* (1938).[13] And just as Hansberry mentioned the contemporaneous historical events of the Bandung Conference of 1955 and Third World decolonization in her talk on the Negro writer, Luxemburg furthered her anti-imperialist message in "Martinique" through the recitation of watershed moments in second-wave nineteenth-century Western imperialism and reactionary political repression: the US occupation of the Philippines; British imperial involvement in the Boer War; Tsarist Russia's colonization of Poland; and the French army's destruction of the Paris Commune. Luxemburg closes "Martinique" with a stunning prediction of global climate change and ecological disaster, declaring that retribution will be visited upon Western imperialists in the form of an extinction-level event that could end all human life. In the wake of this destruction, she avows that "only on [the world's] ruins will the nations come together in true humanity, which will know but one deadly foe – blind, dead nature."[14]

Conclusion

Given Luxemburg's level of sociopolitical and economic acumen, it is fitting that she made providential observations on the unsustainable nature of Western capitalist-imperialist global expansion—and consumption—more than two centuries ago. Similarly, Hansberry's visionary call in the post-Bandung era for the valorization of Black life through the prioritization of African diasporic unity is now manifest in the twenty-first-century Global Movement for Black Lives. Both Luxemburg and Hansberry prioritized the problems of exploitation, oppression, and human suffering in their search for potential solutions to the same. Epistemologically speaking their writings, speeches, and activism present a counter-hegemonic, transnational feminist perspective that has ideological roots in both the Black radical and Black feminist traditions, particularly because both thinkers advocate methods for enacting gender, racial, and socioeconomic equality. As Black radical and Black feminist thought are generated in the transdisciplinary convergence of historical, political, and socioeconomic inquiry, it stands to reason that Luxemburg's and Hansberry's radical discourse meets at the intersection of these insurgent thought systems. Their intellectual productions are rich with insights gleaned from a range of disciplines, including, history, sociology, economics, and political science. This is their great contribution to creolized theory and progressive humanistic study; this is the undeniable power and prescience of Hansberry's and Luxemburg's timeless works and truly radical vision.

Coda: Lorraine and Rosa in Communion

In Hansberry's undated prose poem, " A Woman" (LHP), she recalls the human ability to see art in the mundane, as she opines that the sight of a proletarian woman reminds her of *all* women:

> A woman lifts a window across the street and rests on the sill for a moment.
>
> Her hands are white against the dark blue of the working woman's sweater. She is full bodied and strong … The hands do not know that they are especially beautiful.
>
> She does not know that in this moment—perhaps never again not ever—she is the women I remember striding out in Chapala's waters in the Mexican sun certainly black mothers I have seen in Southside windows since I was very young; a Jewish woman I remember in an

East Side market when New York was new to me—she cannot know that in this moment she is sprung from Michaelangelo. (Ibid.)

In Lorraine Hansberry's moving tribute to woman, we see the spirit of Rosa Luxemburg's "Proletariat Woman," as she recalls the heroic southern African Herero women fighting German imperial soldiers and the valiant Putumayo women of Colombia resisting the Spanish. Through the breadth of Hansberry's and Luxemburg's political and creative writings, speeches, and activism, we find two gifted thinkers who stood firm in their womanhood and their love for humanity to demand a more just world for all.

Notes

1 Beauvior criticizes the Soviet Union's state-imposed "patriarchal restrictions of marriage and child-bearing." She also inveighs against the Soviets' acceptance of prostitution since it necessitates the capitalist exploitation of women's bodies. See Beauvoir (65–6, 153, 475–6).

2 Hansberry candidly states "The Second Sex may very well be the most important work of this century," and further that "it is a victim of its own pertinence and greatness" ([1957] 1995: 129).

3 The term "Third World" will only be used in reference to the period of decolonization during which Hansberry lived. Outside of this chronological maker, the term "Global South" will be used to describe the countries of Africa, Asia, the Caribbean, and Latin America.

4 Luxemburg's love for animals and natural world is detailed at length in the following works: Hudis and Anderson (2004); Adler, Hudis, and Lachitza (2011); and Frolich (2010).

5 There is some disagreement among biographers and critics as to the specific disciplinary contours of Luxemburg's PhD. Frölich maintains that Luxemburg received her PhD in Political Science, while Paul LeBlanc and Helen Scott hold that she earned her PhD in Public Law and Political Science. What is certain, however, is that Luxemburg's dissertation, "The Industrial Development of Poland," is a work of economic theory. See Frölich 22; LeBlanc and Scott 5; and Hudis and Anderson 8.

6 For a thorough discussion of committed African American and Afro-Caribbean women activists in the Communist Party USA in the first half of the twentieth century, see Eric McDuffie (2011).

7 Editors Hudis and Anderson note that Luxemburg, here, is paraphrasing from Marx's and Engel's text, not quoting directly.

8 Hereafter, the Lorraine Hansberry Papers, housed at the New York Public Library's Schomburg Center for Research in Black Culture, will be cited as "LHP."

9 This essay was published twenty-two years later in *The Black Scholar.*

10 While "Letter from a Birmingham Jail" makes brief comparative mention of Third World decolonization, Malcolm X's "The Ballot or the Bullet" explicitly terms African American oppression a form of colonial subjugation. Malcolm X furthers this point by calling all Black people in the United States to break the shackles of mental colonialism by embracing political unity with the peoples of the African continent and the Global South. See Howard Pitney, 74–80, 165–76.

11 Du Bois, Black Reconstruction, 17–31.

12 At just ten years old, Luxemburg witnessed the harrowing violence of a pogrom. LeBlanc and Scott, 5.

13 In his preface to *The Black Jacobins,* James describes San Domingo as "the pride of France, and the envy of every other imperialist nation." Furthermore, he characterizes the revolution as "The only successful slave revolt in history" and "the transformation of slaves ... into a people able to organize themselves and defeat the most powerful European nations of their day [as] one of the greatest epics of revolutionary struggle and achievement." James also describes San Domingo's colonial wealth as "dazzling." James, ix and 55.

14 Hudis and Anderson, 124–126.

PART TWO

THE BEAUTIFUL STRUGGLE: DIALOGUES IN BLACK THOUGHT

6

INTERVIEW WITH JINA FAST, AUTHOR OF *DECOLONIZING EXISTENTIALISM AND PHENOMENOLOGY* (2023)

1. What drew you to the study and practice of philosophy in your undergraduate and graduate careers? In your view, what is the dividing line between studying academic philosophy and actually creating, or doing, philosophy?

I studied philosophy as an undergraduate student at Villanova University under Dr. Pleshette DeArmitt, Dr. Sally Scholz, Dr. Thomas Busch, and Dr. Kas Sagafi, among others, but I did not begin as a philosophy student. Rather, my interests initially were in the natural sciences and mathematics, though I had been reading philosophy since high school. As I grew up in Northern Appalachia, I had intended to study the natural sciences to ensure that I could graduate with a set of skills that would provide economic stability and philosophy, literature, and religion would have to be, I surmised, disciplines I studied in my leisure time.

Yet, in the third year of my undergraduate career, I realized I was not able to ask the questions that I was most interested in regarding what I would now call the material conditions of the production of knowledge and the social and political systems that enable, prevent, and require negotiating in the processes of asking questions, staking claims, making meaning, etc. I saw philosophy as offering a space where I could ask meaningful questions about the world, myself, the relationships between self and others. At this point, I still did not intend to become a professional philosopher, but rather to attend law school and use my philosophy background to ground a practice and study of law. As I was in the process of applying to law schools, I foresaw a future that I felt disconnected from and in this crisis of confidence about my life, I talked to Dr. DeArmitt who asked me why I saw philosophy as an impossible future. She encouraged me to apply to graduate school, and to specifically apply to programs where the philosophers in those programs practiced philosophy in way that I could envision doing it.

While I did not see myself as fully, or wholly, fitting into the Western framing of the philosophical divide (analytic, continental, or pragmatic), I decided to apply to primarily "continental" focused graduate programs such as those at Temple University, DePaul University, and Memphis University. I applied to Temple explicitly because Dr. Lewis Gordon was the Laura H. Carnell Professor of Philosophy, and I was interested in studying feminist philosophy, philosophy of race, and social and political philosophy broadly construed under him. I was, and still am, drawn to the study of law, so had not abandoned the idea that philosophy might be a first step in an eventual practice in law. It was under Dr. Gordon's tutelage that I studied Africana philosophy and was able to further problematize the analytic/continental binary. Additionally, under Dr. Gordon I came to see that philosophy is not simply a discipline we study, but rather functions/can function as an embodied practice. *Bad Faith and Antiblack Racism* was the first text of Dr. Gordon's that I read as an undergraduate, but I had read it with Jean Paul Sartre and Maurice Merleau-Ponty's work and was reducing its meaning to their philosophical analyses. As a graduate student studying Drs. Frantz Fanon, Paget Henry, and Sara Ahmed and reading Dr. Gordon's work on W. E. B. Du Bois's humanistic methods and disciplinary decadence, I was able me to see philosophy as a practice rather than just a study of knowledge production. Specifically, it was through studying phenomenology as a methodological practice employed across disciplines that I was able to begin to see where I fit as a philosopher. Philosophy as a practice to me is not fully separated or distinct from its study, but it is often artificially manufactured to appear as such.

That said, I think that many people see philosophy as merely knowing what philosophers thought or argued across history. In this framing, philosophy becomes merely historical or a study of history rather than an active practice. But, for me, who understands herself to be engaged in an Africana, feminist, phenomenological practice of philosophy, it is a critical practice of seeking to understand the world and the parameters of the being of human embodied consciousness.

Thus, in my work I have used the phenomenological and existentialist methods to study university campus and classroom spaces to consider how they can be made safe(r) for students of color and queer students. Additionally, I have used philosophical methods and practices to consider why black communities in Philadelphia were explicitly concerned with the Philadelphia Immediate Transport in Penetrating Trauma (PIPT) Trial out of Temple University naming it "Tuskegee II." These questions and considerations arose not randomly but rather through living and being in community on a campus where teaching Queer Theory during a semester when there was a Donald Trump rally that impeded the students from feeling at home on campus, and when it was my neighbors and friends in my majority black neighborhood in Philadelphia who asked me if I knew anything about the Temple PIPT study. Being a philosopher and using philosophy as an active process of inquiry has functioned as one of the means through which I serve my communities and this changes over time and place as communities themselves do not remain stable or static. Thus, part of the work of philosophy is remaining open to these changes and responding to the material conditions that are emergent within the historical, social, political, and economic parameters that shape our worlds and lived experiences of the world.

2. When you initially entered into the world of philosophical discourse, who were the thinkers that exerted the most influence on your work and why?

In high school, I was exposed to philosophy of Albert Camus, Søren Kierkegaard, Richard Wright, Toni Morrison, and, Jean-Paul Sartre through their respective works *The Stranger*, *Diary of a Seducer*, *Native Son*, *The Bluest Eye,* and *Nausea*, as well as through my early years with the idea of Catholic church leaders being not just theologians but philosophers who did not take religious texts literally but as offering spaces to think about metaphysics, epistemology, and morality. This affected how I was drawn to philosophical study. Generally, I was drawn to and observant of the ways in which people whether in the classroom, from the pulpit, or in daily life were asking questions about knowledge, meaning, and being. I saw this desire to learn about the world, truth, and one's role in the world across disciplines and cultural practices, but eventually philosophy centered and grounded my practice for asking questions as open rather than closed in ways that other disciplines in the natural and social sciences and institutional spaces did not. Existentialism specifically was accessible because as an avid reader generally I could pick up the works of Wright, Sartre, Camus, etc. and feel at home, while simultaneously being challenged to think more deeply about what it means to exist as human consciousness.

As an undergraduate, feminist texts like Simone de Beauvoir's *The Second Sex*, Shulamith Firestone's *The Dialectic of Sex,* and bell hooks's *Feminist Theory: From Margin to Center* were major influences in my life and drew me in turn to the study of G. W. F. Hegel, Martin Heidegger, and Edmund Husserl as well as deeper into the histories of feminist inquiry. Phenomenology appealed to me because I was initially working in the natural sciences and in mathematics, but my experience was less centered on asking questions of my own, but rather on repeating what others had asked. Furthermore, phenomenology allowed me to more explicitly enter into an inquiry-based model of practice that was grounded in an analysis of consciousness and the multiplicity of lived experience.

I had a very Western-centric/centered undergraduate education, in part because I attended a Catholic university that was explicitly centered on and in an Augustinian model for education (generally and morally). In fact, it was in my political science courses, which was my other major as an undergraduate that I was able to take a more "multicultural"— notably multicultural does not necessarily mean anti-racist or denote an explicit consideration of global power systems/divides—approach to inquiry through courses entitled "Japan and China," "Russia Today," and "Politics in the Middle East." In my "Politics in the Middle East" class I encountered the work of Edward Said in *Orientalism* and started to think more deeply about identity and the global politics of white supremacy. Notably, these courses could have also been Western-centric, but they weren't, and what it allowed me to do was think between disciplines and develop transdisciplinary and decolonial methods for engaging in inquiry-based learning and scholarship.

Beyond these few classes, it was through my friends and our rejection of some of the politics of our classmates that led us to develop interests in Edward Said's work more generally, and feminist analyses of abortion politics, welfare rights, and lesbian identity as a political identity. Three pivotal texts at this time were Dorothy Roberts' *Killing the Black Body: Race, Reproduction, and the Meaning of Liberty* (1997), Susan Stryker's "My Words to Victor Frankenstein above the Village of Chamounix Performing Transgender Rage" (1994), and Audre Lorde's "The Uses of Anger" (1984). I do not remember the order in which I read them, but that I was reading them outside of class, with my friends, as I was reading Aristotle's *Politics* and Plato's *Republic*, which I enjoyed, but which I thought would be deeply enriched by reading together with or by considering Lorde, Stryker, and Roberts' arguments. These texts, however, and my engagement with them, with others, with my friends, influenced how I lived my politics. It was not just enough to object to the crosses signifying the number of abortions in the United States in front of the student center or to help a friend access an abortion when they needed it, rather I had to take a holistic approach, what I would learn to name an intersectional or multidimensional approach to issues of reproductive justice.

3. In your view, what are the major distinctions between philosophy of race and Africana philosophy, or philosophical thought from the African diaspora? In what ways does philosophy of race subsume or negate the theoretical innovations of philosophers from the African diaspora?
While both philosophy of race and Africana philosophy are immensely important and rich frameworks for studying metaphysics, epistemology, ethics, and social and political philosophy, they tend to be collapsed. The effect is that Africana philosophy is taken to be merely offering commentary or study on race, racialization, and racism (specifically anti-black racism). This collapse has profound effects on the way in which peoples of the African diaspora are encoded as philosophical, as thinkers, as subjects. If Africana philosophy is only about race, then it is reduced in its importance and its expanse—though in saying this, I do not intend to assert that philosophy of race is not important, but in collapsing them, which is often done I would assert, one misses the

conversations, theories, and analyses that aren't centered on race/racialization/racism. Such a collapse also has the effect of nullifying the existence of a history of Africana philosophy in that people of African descent didn't always think of themselves as African in racialized terms. Rather this self-understanding is produced through a Western, white settler colonialist framework (Gordon 2022). If philosophy of race and Africana philosophy are understood as one and the same, then the philosophizing of people of the African diaspora has no history. In this way, rendering Africana philosophy as philosophy of race becomes another way in which peoples of the African diaspora are rendered non-historical and non-human.

As such, philosophy of race is the study of race, racialization, and racism. Philosophy of race allows us to understand the social, political, and cultural formations of race in history as well the ways in which the construction(s) of race are intended in the foundations of the natural, medical, and social sciences, in law, and education. Africana philosophy is grounded in African thought and the theoretical questions raised by critical engagement with ideas that emerge within African cultural frameworks (African-continent centric, Caribbean, creolized contexts, diasporic contexts, etc.). Africana philosophy can be further subdivided, though these lines are not perfect or meant to enact absolute distinctions, into African American philosophy, Afro-Caribbean philosophy, etc. in the modern period. And even further divided into Yorùbá, Akan, Ethiopian, Jamaican, etc. Philosophy of race and Africana philosophy intersect, of course, in important ways, such as in the fact that who is African, who is European, etc. are evolving concepts that are comingled/codeveloped and serve political purposes. Also, to understand the racism of claims that African humanism(s) was (were) imported from Europe rather than emergent from Akan, Yorùbá, and other cultures and religious conceptions, one must both understand African/a philosophy and philosophy of race.

Inevitably, it is reductive to say that Africana philosophy is simply offering a philosophy of race, although philosophy of race is not simple. To reduce people engaged in scholarly pursuits to one component of identity, their own or another's, in their studies functions to flatten the work itself and to quite frankly miss what philosophy of race and Africana philosophies bring into view on their own and when read together. But the question of subsuming and the way in which Black philosophers, to the greatest extent, and all philosophers working on Africana philosophy and/or philosophy of race are presumed to only be competent in philosophy of race, is troubling. To study Africana philosophy and to practice it is to be a metaphysician, an epistemologist, a logician, and/or a moral philosopher. Yet, these terms—metaphysician, epistemologist, logician, moral philosopher—seem only to apply to or to signify people working in Western philosophy. At the same time, because anti-black racism is so prevalent, encoded in the historical and contemporary discourses and practices across institutions and across the globe, defending against it feels like not simply a moral imperative but a literal life and death struggle. Thus, I find it imperative for there to a be a shift in the way we understand contemporary philosophers' engagements with race, gender, sexual orientation, class, disability, etc. I ask my students all the time what they think or know to be the lived reality of having to always first defend your very existence (to engage in this defensive grounding of why what you have to say matters) before you make your positive argument for (or against) something or about something. This taxes your resources: energy, time, creativity, the resilience you have built up. To always have to be on the defensive is to also not have the space to engage in creative and generative work of constructing positive arguments in philosophy. If I have to first show you I am human before you see me as capable of philosophizing, then I have to always preface my arguments with an act of translation, namely a translating for you that I am human. And while there has been undeniably important work here, in these processes of asserting the subjectivity, agency, and the very humanity of people of color, Indigenous peoples, and Black people, there have been developments in philosophy of mind, moral philosophy, environmental ethics, and epistemology. It is a specific kind of epistemological theft to bar the free pursuit of inquiry for people of color.

4. What prompted you to expand the theoretical boundaries of existentialism and phenomenology in Decolonizing Existentialism and Phenomenology? What is it about existentialism's and phenomenology's shared focus on lived experience that compelled you to engage in such a rigorous critique of these schools of thought?

I think primarily I see *Decolonizing Existentialism and Phenomenology* as a practice of love. I have always been influenced in my writing by

Sartre's argument regarding the purpose of writing and of scholarship generally. In "For Whom Does One Write?" Sartre writes, "The book, serving as a go-between, establishes an historical contact among the men who are steeped in the same history and who likewise contribute to its making. Writing and reading are two facets of the same historical fact, and the freedom to which the writer invites us is not a pure abstract consciousness of being free. Strictly speaking, it is not, it wins itself in an historical situation; each book proposes a concrete liberation on the basis of a particular alienation" (Sartre [1949] 1962: 72). Existentialism and phenomenology provided a specific kind of freedom to me by enabling a recognition and ultimately confrontation with the kinds of alienation that human consciousness experiences, both those that are components of the human condition and those that emerge resulting from social, political, and economic systems—anti-black racism, patriarchy, extractive capitalism, etc. But, as I engaged more deeply with black feminist writing and feminist of color critique, through the work of Patricia Hill Collins, Hortense Spillars, Saidiya Hartman, Angela Davis, Ruth Wilson Gilmore, Linda Martín Alcoff, Gloria Anzuldúa, Audre Lorde, and Sylvia Wynter, it became clear that the construction of consciousness from which experience is understood to unfold has been deracialized and degendered.

I was especially inspired by more recent works such as your work Dr. Parris in *Being Apart: Theoretical and Existential Resistance in Africana Literature* (2015), Nathalie Nya's *Simone de Beauvoir and the Colonial Experience: Freedom, Violence, and Identity* (2019) and Nathalie Etoke's *Melancholia Africana: The Indispensable Overcoming of the Black Condition* to engage in a critical appraisal of the limitations of European existentialist thought and how it emerges from and reinforces white normative constructions of human consciousness and coloniality in philosophy. This is not to imply that philosophers like Hegel, Heidegger, and Husserl aren't important, but when we overconcentrate on these figures in canonical framings and the teaching of phenomenology, for example, then we miss a great deal of what has been generative in the practices of philosophical methods. In reflecting, I think also my teaching, as belonging to an inquiry-based model of education, begins with the questions I have and the questions my students have about the world, their experiences, others, what they ought to do to live well, have meaning in their lives, and create just worlds, etc. Thus, I start my courses that center themes and methods from existentialism and phenomenology with student-generated questions about histories of race and power, how medicine functions as an institution, and experiences of alienation. It has been Beauvoir's work, Fanon's work, Dr. Gordon's work, Spillers's work, etc. that have initiated processes for understanding the questions students ask and from which their learning unfolds. And then we get to Hegel, Heidegger, and Husserl, but they aren't the starting point. So, I thought, what would it be to start from the students' and my shared point of inquiry, not where I was "supposed" to start? Similarly, I came to Critical Theory in the Frankfurt School—work by people like Herbert Marcuse, Theodor Adorno, and Max Horkheimer—through my engagement with and love for Angela Davis's work. And I wrote about this in an essay entitled "Marcuse, Feminism, and Intersectionality" in *The Marcusean Mind*. Did learning Marcuse benefit me in my inquiry, yes, but the idea that I, or anyone, cannot fully understand Davis without knowing Marcuse—and then Hegel, Marx, and Freud—is to render philosophy as being about the past and as akin to archeology rather than an open question posed to the future.

5. In the introduction to Decolonizing Existentialism and Phenomenology, you challenge the moralistic foundations of diversity initiatives as a means of critiquing prevailing notions of socio-cultural diversity as a panacea that can eliminate institutionalized forms of racism, misogyny, and bigotry in academia and beyond. Could you elaborate on your point that the moralism of diversity efforts is, in fact, antithetical to anti-racist praxis?

I would assert most plainly that being identified or self-identifying as belonging to a specific group does not in and of itself entail anti-racist politics or praxis. I think Dr. Gordon's distinction between black and Black consciousness in *Fear of Black Consciousness* (2022) provides a clear and useful example of showing how being racialized black and developing Black consciousness are not one and the same. One who has Black consciousness lives and constructs a Black point of view, Black agency and recognizes anti-black racism for what it is, but Black consciousness requires a critical turn, a leap into a kind of practice of agentic action and commitment to fighting oppression, including anti-black racism. The former, black consciousness with a lower case "b," I understand to be more palatable to white normative, white-serving, and even white supremacist institutions, while the latter, Black consciousness threatens oppressive forces and refuses assimilation. Similarly, being assigned female at birth and self-identifying with the gender woman is neither necessary nor sufficient to the development of feminist consciousness. Being racialized black or being a woman does not automatically entail progressive, humanistic, anti-racist politics or practices, because these are developed, active, and intentional. One of the most important examples of this for me, that has been instructive in both my teaching, my scholarship, and the way in which I operate generally in my work life and home/community life, is from bell hooks' *Black Looks: Race and Representation* (1992). Chapter 7, entitled "The Oppositional Gaze: Black Female Spectators" engages in dialogue with Laura Mulvey's analysis of "the male gaze", both problematizing the white normativity of the subject and object of "the male gaze", and extending Mulvey's analysis by considering via an intersectional lens the ways in which conceptions and practices of gazing are political and indicative of power/power relations. Yet, as hooks notes, to say that an oppositional gaze of a black woman develops *naturally* or emanates from her existence as a black woman is to fail to recognize her agency in its development. She can laugh at and subvert the racist representations of black women not because of some genetic predisposition or essential characteristic of blackness or womanhood, but because as a subject she developed critical ways of looking that function to deconstruct, analyze, and subvert dominant and dominating representations of herself, others, and systems. Via this oppositional gaze new understandings are created and reductive conceptions, such as "universal womanhood," have been problematized. But again the oppositional gaze is not essential to black womanhood, it is emergent, and it emerges as, hooks writes, "a site of resistance only when individual black women actively resist the imposition of dominant ways of knowing and looking (1992: 128). In fact, hooks observes, even though every black woman she knows is aware of racism, it doesn't necessarily mean she has developed an active critical resistance to racism. I understand hooks' point here to be quite important, a poignant analysis and commentary upon the difference between knowing and doing. Knowing can be part of doing, but it isn't sufficient just to know. Knowing isn't transformative, it doesn't produce critical engagement, and it certainly does not require acting/living the body in a transformative and/or anti-racist manner.

In writing about the ways in which diversity has been taken up as shorthand for anti-racism, I seek to draw attention to and encourage deep thinking about the ways that diversity under systems of white supremacy, heteropatriarchy, racialized capitalism, etc. is not necessarily anti-racist. I have been on hiring committees that laud themselves for the diversity of their pool of final candidates as though this indicates not just something deep and meaningful about the scholarship and politics of the candidates themselves, but also something about the committees themselves as capable of encouraging "diversity." Even as I write this, I hesitate, because these conversations are difficult today on the left, owing to the bad faith of the right. But, if we try to close ranks around diversity as it has tended to be practiced, I think we make the mistake of not following empirically and theoretically what is true. And like any concept or practice, anti-racism can be coopted and emptied of its meaning, and arguably I would say there is some evidence that this is occurring. Any term can become an empty signifier; thus we can create new terms, or resist the emptying or flattening of our terms, but there is not going to be the discovery of a new term that can function in itself as resistant to this kind of co-opting. Thus, politics and how we live as embodied subjects are always going to be more important than the language we use to describe what it is we are doing.

6. The first chapter presents a discussion of Beauvoir's delineation of female alterity in The Second Sex. Building on Margaret Simons's Beauvoir and The Second Sex: Feminism, Race, and the Origins of Existentialism, you stress that Beauvoir arrived at her thesis of woman as Absolute Other by engaging with Richard Wright's phenomenological analyses of anti-black racism's impact on Black subjectivity. Given that Simons's book was published nearly 30 years ago, and Intersectionality Studies is now an established academic field, could you elaborate on how we should account for the fact that Wright's influence on Beauvoir's thought remains relatively undertheorized?

This is such a great question, with many layers. My first response would be that I think there are specific theorists that are reading people like Beauvoir and Wright together, Jane Anna Gordon, Lewis Gordon, and Kathryn Sophia Belle in addition to Simons, but this is done by scholars who are transdisciplinary or interdisciplinary in their approaches to research and teaching. And this is part of the issue. Beauvoir is taught and theorized about in philosophy and Women's and Gender Studies and Wright in English literature and Black/African American Studies and rarely is the history of their encounters covered meaningfully. In part, perhaps because there is a tendency to reduce women and people of color—including women of color—to the biographical details of their lives. But there is a way to teach, study, and theorize about connections, those that occurred and those that were missed that leaves open historical realities.

Yet, instead of reading Beauvoir through her engagement with Wright, she has historically been reduced to her relationship with Jean-Paul Sartre, and to a lesser degree Nelson Algren. In the 1990s and early 2000s, there was a Beauvoir-renaissance so to speak, with re-readings of Beauvoir and the construction of her as a philosopher in her own right, separate, and distinct from Sartre. Thus, I think there has been a hesitancy by especially white feminist theorists to recast Beauvoir as indebted to the work of anyone else. The problem, however, is that this reinforces the idea of great thinkers as solitary, singular, and wholly responsible for themselves and the work they produce. I would assert this to be historically false in relation to Beauvoir; she was influenced by and influenced many other scholars, activists, writers, etc. including Sartre, Algren, and Wright. Additionally, this failure to take seriously Wright's influence on Beauvoir's conception of woman as Absolute Other rather than mundane other misses important, generative connections that were made between leftist thinkers in their own times, and that still provide models for thinking about engagement today.

The disciplinarity of academia and where we are turned through our disciplines to look is certainly affecting this, but it is still surprising to me when it occurs in interdisciplinary frameworks like Women's and Gender Studies and African American Studies. But maybe this points us to the fact that as we codify disciplines to make them appear more serious and grounded in methods and practices that are specific to them, as we develop PhDs and people earn them in Women's and Gender Studies and African American Studies, we introduce an aspect of decay to them. Now this isn't to suggest that there should not be PhDs in African American Studies or that we should burn Women's and Gender Studies textbooks, but that in thinking about what these inter- and transdisciplinary disciplines enable we have to attend to the ways in which systems close off rather than open up the possibilities of what we can do within systems and practices of inquiry.

7. In that same chapter you aver that "Beauvoir identifies patriarchy's idea of women's sexualized, objectified, and subordinated status as that which connects women to the static, thick, object-like facet of the human condition" (18). Existential discourse describes this static, objectified state as "being-in-itself." Could you elaborate more on how the normative gaze of patriarchy poisons the way we women see ourselves, view one another, and engage in a world that reduces "woman-as-human subjectivity" to "woman-as-facticity"? How does this internalized patriarchal gaze manifest itself in the lived experience of everyday people?

One might think that over seventy-five years after the publication of *The Second Sex* (1949), after decades of feminist activism across the world, that the analysis of patriarchy Beauvoir provides would appear outlandish. Yet, Adriana Smith, a black woman who was pregnant and experienced a medical emergency that left her brain-dead is being kept on life support to maintain the pregnancy. This is required—or is interpreted to be required by Emory University Hospital—per the state of Georgia's fetal 'personhood' law. While this may be an extreme example of the rendering of a woman to the status of a static object, the fact that this can be done to women in the United States indicates both the status women hold under patriarchy as never fully free and the truth to women that they can never fully assume their rights as subjects. The fact that Smith is a black woman should not be lost on anyone either and I can imagine important essays written about the reality that is unfolding in front of us all using Gordon's *Fear of Black Consciousness* and Robert's *Killing the Black Body* in addition to Beauvoir's work. But this example shows any woman watching that the reality of her subjecthood and personhood is dependent, rather than absolute. In the United States, it depends on which state you reside, it depends on your race, your class, your sexual orientation, and your gender identity, both identified and observed by others. Perhaps the medical staff and institution that is keeping Smith's body functioning to support her pregnancy would have engaged in an act of civil disobedience if Smith were white. We will never know, but these are questions that arise, and that are rendered problematic, paranoid, under as system that denies women's agency and subjectivity; while simultaneously telling them they benefit from the benevolence of patriarchy.

I think that patriarchy certainly affects the ways in which women interact with one another, and awareness of it does not negate the harms it engenders. For example, in academia I regularly observe women who identify as feminist—to some degree—undermining one another, talking about the fact that they know someone may have had a difficult time coming up into academic leadership as a black woman, but that she does not know how to lead, manage, or communicate with her subordinates. Or they pit supports for students of color against supports for students with disabilities. And so the recognition of the dehumanization and objectification of marginalized people, including women, exists, but it does not transform meaningfully the way in which these women engage in the world with other women and other non-women who experienced marginalization. I see feminism and anti-racism at their cores as being about how we engage with one another, how we open ourselves up to being affected by and in relationship to one another, and yes, part of this is recognizing how racism and sexism, and sexist-racism/misogynoir operate, but simply knowing this does not entail cooperation and collaboration and it certainly does not necessitate care for the other.

And this is key to understanding what patriarchy does and how it shapes our actions. Rather than being open to the other, I internalize that to be a subject I must be in control. I must control my environment so that I can externalize my will and my desires, without reference to or consideration of the subjectivities of others that I exist with. Patriarchy, then, even as it oppresses women, instills in them the idea that maybe they can win if they make enough money, make all the right choices, bank enough power, have control rather than are controlled. But, on this model, in this practice, patriarchy still exists as an operating system.

8. *In chapter 5, "Audre Lorde's Decolonial, Queer, Black Feminist Phenomenology," you highlight Lorde's self-affirming identification as an Afro-Caribbean lesbian who drew strength from a queer, feminist identity that was rooted in solidarity with other lesbian feminists of color. In what sense do you think Lorde's praxis may be echoed in the twenty-first-century activism of Alicia Garza and Patricie Cullors, the queer*

Black women who founded Black Lives Matter in the wake of Trayvon Martin's 2012 murder?

This is a great question in relation to the diversity question above as well. At Hampshire, as the Co-Director of the Learning Collaboratives we work to bring together scholars, activists, artists, etc. who are asking and seeking to address important historical and contemporary questions. Last year, we invited three of the Concerned Student 1950 activists, Storm Ervin, Andrea Fulgiam, and Ayanna Poole, who worked to make the University of Missouri attendant to the experiences of black students. All three are black women, one of whom self-identifies as queer, and like Garza and Cullors, spoke about the fact that when one is looking to build community, one can draw strength from organizing with other black women and black people's organizing efforts and then look outward. But they also noted that there were some black men involved who centered themselves rather than the group, and even others who aligned themselves with conservative politicians including Donald Trump after graduating from college. Thus, I think a lesson that one ends up learning is that solidarity can often be found by creating communities where recognition and reciprocity is key and some of that can begin and be grounded in shared experiences. But, this is not always enough. Other people have to want to be in solidarity with you and have to have community, rather than prioritizing wholly or fully self-interested goals of elevating their own power and/or position.

That said, Lorde's point as I understand it, is that for queer women of color, there is respite in being with one another. And what is left unsaid, but implied, is that the community that can be held as a space for respite is one that is actively produced as queer, black/people of color centric, and feminist in its organizing principles. But, there are other times where a version of this space can be signified say in Lorde's experiences of simply walking around in Mexico and being surrounded by other people of color. She was not walking up to everyone she saw and asking about their politics, but there is meaning in an anti-black world/white supremacist world in experiencing oneself as part of the majority, especially for a black, queer, woman who wasn't regularly afforded that in her schooling or experiences in New York City. I was listening to Natasha Rothwell, a black actor and writer, describe something similar on *Fresh Air* on National Public Radio (NPR) the other day. She noted that she had taken some solo vacations as a black woman and that it was always exciting and a relief to see other black tourists/travelers. In Ireland she was at a castle on a tour and was the only person of color in sight, but then she saw a black family walking up a hill or on the grounds and smiled and waved even though she did not know them. She had the writer/director of *The White Lotus*, Mike White, write a similar experience for her character in season three when she was a tourist/traveler because she understands this to be an important experience for black/people of color tourists. And this point can appear, at first, to contradict some of what I noted earlier about "diversity" not being enough. Rothwell and Lorde do not know the politics of their fellow black or people of color travelers, thus their feeling of being seen, of some semblance of safety, or of not being alone, indicates something deep and important about what it means to be racialized Black, Brown, Indigenous in white space(s), namely that if the other who is a person of color like me, then I am safer than I would be otherwise. So, "diversity" and sharing the same identity are not going to be enough to produce new futures and community visions held together by politics, but sometimes sharing an identity, being marked together, can produce a positive affective experience in an otherwise lonely landscape. I see it as our job as philosophers to attend to these seeming contradictions to understand what they indicate about race, power, human consciousness, backgrounds, and horizons.

9. As a white woman who writes both eloquently and extensively on Black philosophical thought, what processes of mental decolonization have you undertaken to free yourself from racial blind spots that cause many white people to minimize and/or deny the pernicious effects of anti-black racism on the individual and societal levels?
This is an important question for me personally in ensuring that I never become stagnant in considering the effects of whiteness on me and how easily it is when one is covered by the protections of whiteness to slip into seeing and acting 'whitely' (to borrow a term from Drs. George Yancy and Charles Mills), as well as pedagogically in modeling to students across racialized identities what it means to study, write about, and live a life engaged with Black philosophical thought as a white woman. Studying Marxian and feminist philosophy was certainly a first step for me in coming to understand the connections between the personal and the political, and then engaging with Black feminist thought that was

in dialogue with, but also critical of the assumptions, foundations, and exclusionary effects of white feminist thought and Marxist theory and practice helped me to understand that the universalizing tendencies of (white) critical theory obscured racialization and racism in logically and practically problematic ways.

I have also been quite influenced by where I have lived and with whom I have been in community primarily in multiracial and multicultural communities in Philadelphia and Baltimore. Thinking about race along with other academics has always been important to me, but for the most important lessons about whiteness and what it means to challenge the license and entitlement that whiteness promises white people has happened in community and how I live as embodied consciousness in the world.

Part of my philosophy practice is one of working to retain openness to arguments made by others. In my early career, the place that was the hardest for me was in seeing the limitations of Beauvoir's work and Fanon's work from the perspectives of Black feminists. I had this inclination to defend Beauvoir and Fanon, even as I saw myself as respecting the criticisms offered by Black feminists like Nathalie Nya and Kathryn Sophia Belle. And even in looking at Chapter 1 of *Decolonizing Existentialism and Phenomenology*, I see myself engaging in an attempt to square both of these things, and I have to be attendant to the fact I am a white woman and while I actively attend to the development of a radical feminist, anti-racist, queer consciousness, part of this has to be a self-consciousness and a recognition of my limitations and where growth has to occur to not simply be qualified to engage with the works of Africana philosophers, theorists, etc. but to live according to an anti-racist politics.

Finally, as someone who grew up in Northern Appalachia, I have been influenced by the ways in which Appalachian people have dismissed, overwritten, and experienced ontological collapse whereby their very being has been rendered problematic. Reading Du Bois's work in and about Philadelphia while in college, I was exposed to both the specificity of anti-black racism as it operates ontologically, epistemologically, and politically, and I would never attempt to extend in a reductive manner the effects of anti-black racism, but it inspired me to think about the ways in which Appalachians are treated, including the explicit erasure of BIPOC Appalachians. I was able to make connections among Du Bois's experiences in Philadelphia with the University of Pennsylvania and the City of Philadelphia, and the Philadelphia police's bombing of their own citizens in West Philadelphia some eight decades later—in what came to be known as the MOVE bombing in that MOVE was the Black community organization/family that was bombed. I was able to think about the stigma of being from Appalachia, of having classmates and in-laws who would tell me about, "hillbillies" from Idaho they had read about or heard about, confusing Ohio and Idaho. I would read about how stupid the people from the hill towns or hollers were and that they were tricked into selling their land to the government or private mining companies. The central lesson shared in these examples being that the people who were harmed deserved it; they were/are troubled from the start and very few deserve to be treated as human.

10. When teaching and engaging with your students, how do you use existential and phenomenological themes—like being, freedom, responsibility, agency, and lived experience—to explain how the extreme ideological polarization of mainstream partisan politics has affected our understanding of the war on truth and reality?

I have taught at three very different institutions over my career thus far. For example, my first academic appointment was at a large, public, white-serving institution located in the outer suburbs of Philadelphia. Classroom sizes were quite large (45+ students for some general education classes; 25 for writing-focused courses) and the students were predominantly white, heterosexually oriented, cisgender, and belonged to the middle to upper-middle class. All the classes I taught were those that counted toward the "diverse communities" requirement and I often encountered students that were actively hostile to the course materials, especially those materials that centered Black, Brown, and Indigenous peoples, queer folks, and were decolonial in their methodologies. The second university at which I had a professional appointment was an historic women's college classified as a minority-majority university. It was/is not an Historically Black College and University (HBCU), an Hispanic Serving Institution (HSI), or a Tribal College and University (TCU), but the majority of students were students of color. Perhaps unsurprisingly the kind(s) of resistance that I faced from students at my first institution were now absent among the student population, and the kinds of texts that I could teach in depth with a student body that identified as Igbo, Dominican, Amhara, etc., sometimes as Black also, but other times as not, and who wished each other Happy New Year, say for *Enkutatash* changed as well.

My current institution is Hampshire College, and while it is a white-majority/white-serving institution, there have been important anti-racist curricular and institutional changes made. For one, we have few requirements at Hampshire—there is not a general education curriculum—but one of them is a race and power requirement at every divisional level. Secondly, institutionally there is attention not to "diversity" but to justice and anti-racism at the executive administrative level. This is signaled by the fact that we do not have a Diversity, Equity, and Inclusion executive administrator or dean, but rather a senior vice president for justice, equity, and anti-racism. Now, this is not to suggest that racism has been "solved" at Hampshire, but rather to point to some important components of Hampshire's organizing principles that intend to impart anti-racism in the culture and the curriculum. That said, there tends to be more white students than students of color in the classes I have taught thus far, this includes requiring students to consider where, how, why, and in what forms race and power enter into their lives and the selves/experiences they bring to the classroom, as well as the ways in which race and power organize the classroom itself. For example, I employ feminist pedagogical practices such as speaking from lived experiences, drawing connections between the personal and the political, and engaging in phenomenological analysis of discursive and material realities. However, in classes where white people are the dominant group, whiteness can become dominating if white people/students/faculty uncritically express their lived experiences. Drawing attention to these lived realities of the spaces, places, and communities that we create is almost always instructive because even if whiteness is taking over, or dominating, it becomes a space for students to reflect and to think about what that means, implies, signifies, and produces in terms of the relationships among race, power, freedom, liberation, responsibility, and agency.

11. When you're not reading and/or writing philosophy, who are the authors you find yourself drawn to and why?
I love reading. I was drawn to the life of the academic, even with all its trappings and difficulties, because of my love of reading, even more than writing! I am drawn to books in the social sciences, natural

sciences, and works of literature and poetry that expand my conception of what it means to be human, as well as my moral considerations. My favorite books I have read this past year include: *Salt Houses* by Hala Alyan*, Against the Loveless World* by Susan Abulhawa, *The Lighteaters: How the Unseen World of Plant Intelligence Offers a New Understanding of Life on Earth* by Zoë Schlanger, *Hard by a Great Forest* by Leo Vardiashvli, *The Audition* by Katie Kitamura, and *The Message* by Ta-Nehisi Coates. I am generally drawn to fictional work that draws out important humanist themes that can then be used to enlarge my understanding and affective attunement to the world. I also love writers who write about loving to read and write, which gives voice to my experience in ways perhaps I cannot articulate. Coates' first chapter in *The Message,* "Journalism Is Not a Luxury," is an homage to Audre Lorde's 1985 essay "Poetry Is Not a Luxury" and details not simply the importance or necessity of journalism as a form of writing life and experience for marginalized subjects, but as connected to a love of writing, reading, and a search for truth. And Coates is someone who I believe belongs to the tradition and practice of Africana existentialism and phenomenology and with whom one can draw connections to Beauvoir, Fanon, Sartre, Wright, Lorde, and Wynter.

Also, my daughter is six-years-old and just learned to read so I am being read to as well. As I have watched and participated in her development, I have been thinking about philosophy for children and how to structure an inquiry-based model for education for her as part of our life together. We are reading lots of *Itty Bitty Princess Kitty* books which center friendship and community in interesting ways—to maybe stretch out some themes, here. But, then some really great books with philosophical themes such as Lenny Hort's *How Many Stars in the Sky?*, Shel Silverstein's *The Giving Tree*, and children's books written by bell hooks and Toni Morrison.

12. What is the subject of your next book?
I am currently working on a book on creolizing aesthetics. Two essays that I have recently worked on read together critical theorists of the Frankfurt school like Herbert Marcuse and Theodor Adorno with Africana philosophers Sylvia Wynter, Christina Sharpe, and Lewis Gordon to understand aesthetics, as a branch of philosophy, more broadly in its connections to social and political life, as well as in analyzing specific

works of art like the television show *The White Lotus.* Like existentialist literature, televisual art, film, museums, and contemporary literature are spaces where people encounter analyses and arguments regarding meaning and being, have their politics, points of view challenged and enlarged. To not attend to the aesthetic dimension, which includes contemporary popular culture is to miss a place or space for engagement with the public regarding philosophy and philosophizing.

ural# 7

INTERVIEW WITH A. SHAHID STOVER, AUTHOR OF BEING AND INSURRECTION (2019) AND EPISTEMIC RUPTURES, INSURGENT PHILOSOPHY (2022)

1. As an autodidact and independent scholar traversing the discursive terrain between Black radical thought and critical theory, what initially drew you to the discipline and practice of philosophy? How has your background as an autodidact informed the trajectory of your philosophical pursuits?

Excellent questions, especially in the sense that I didn't initially realize when I decidedly dropped out of college to embark on the path of an intellectual outsider, that the discursive trajectory of my work would manifest itself as philosophy. You have to understand, I committed to writing as a way of *being-in-the-world* the moment I left the journalism school at the University of North Carolina at Chapel Hill and started writing as a freelance journalist for *The Carolina Times*. Within a year or so after that, I moved to New York City to pursue my literary ambitions where I would eventually freelance for *The Source Magazine of Hip Hop Music, Culture and Politics*. Still under the considerable intellectual influence as set forth by the literary examples of fellow autodidacts like

Richard Wright, Harold Cruse, and Eldridge Cleaver, although I may have even had the ambition to eventually write fiction, at the time I was still writing journalism while working constantly and creatively testing out how to best hone my thoughts in essay form.

However, once *The Brotherwise Dispatch* launched as a progressive hip-hop webzine in 2001, and I started writing music criticism by drawing from hip-hop aesthetics as cultural resistance to sociohistorical oppression, the Black radical edge of my thought became sharper, and even more pronounced. It got to a point where I had to be very honest with myself about the way that I sought to engage intellectually with the world as a writer and thinker.

Basically, because of the *structural-inert violence, miseducation of soul* and global injustice that define our contemporary geohistorical situation, if I was going to write, and very much like Frederick Douglass understood long before me, I realized that I would never be satisfied as someone who just traffics in information and facts about obvious and ongoing oppression. For no matter how urgent and important providing such information and facts to people is, I felt spiritually compelled to write and think against oppression, so as to be able to confront established power through my work.

This especially, insofar as it became evermore clear to me that the problem is not so much that people don't have access to information and facts about what is going on. Think about it, right now, everyday people have all the information and facts needed to identify the ongoing genocide against Palestinian people. The facts are also readily available to anyone interested to know that this genocide is being carried out internationally by the armed forces of a Zionist settler colonial outpost of Empire who have unsurprisingly been engaged for decades in exchanges of counterinsurgent training and *biopolitical pacification* tactics with the same neocolonial police forces who systematically violate Black humanity and suppress Black liberation praxis here domestically.

No doubt, the normative gaze of western imperialist power violently constitutes both Black and Palestinian populations as amongst the *underground of modernity*, and therefore unworthy of ethical regard, legal redress and human consideration whenever it suits the needs of established power.

And yet, the truth is that information and facts about contemporary social injustice are more accessible now than they have ever been in the history of the world. Although certainly accompanying this hyperproliferation of information itself, the problem lies more in the way that information and facts are presented, organized and curated by the normative gaze of a *western imperialist continuum* for general consumption by everyday people.

This is how terms like "radical chic," "politically correct," "woke," etc. become part of a vast rhetorical lexicon of Bad Faith that allows the *imperial mainstream-as-civil society* to lie to itself about its lived structural relation to the *underground of modernity* as manifest in racist dehumanization and *coloniality in the Raw*, no matter the scope, be it disclosed in the mass incarceration and accumulative slaughter of Black people by neocolonial police violence or the programmatic displacement and wholesale slaughter of Palestinian people by a Zionist settler colonial army. The normative gaze constantly works towards undermining lived potentialities of spiritual unity and emancipatory solidarity experienced amongst everyday people over their shared plight and the common structural source of their suffering.

As such, there is no need to argue against the fact that knowledge is power, but we also should come to terms with the fact that power legitimates what is considered as knowledge as well. This brings us face to face with the problem of the normative gaze. Now, the normative gaze functions ideologically as an unquestioned background framework, violently imposed upon us by Western imperialist power, that provides the lived context from which we see ourselves, look at one another and engage the world around us.

That is why confronting the normative gaze speaks to the need for engaging in emancipatory thought at a philosophical register. This is because it actually requires of us more than just the very important informative work of a journalist, it requires of us more than just the invaluable organizational work of an activist, and it requires of us more than just the indispensable research work of an academic. To be clear, confronting the normative gaze means we must resist the journalistic, academic, and activist temptations towards any kind of epistemic closure, because we in fact have to be able to draw from the emancipatory relevance of discursive ruptures against the normative gaze of established power towards the conditions of possibility for enunciations of Revolt.

The thing is, back then, as a journalist and cultural critic, I found myself writing and hence thinking within established structures of meaning that I found incompatible with emancipatory imperatives that speak to the need for a more fundamental register of social change and geohistorical transformation. As a consequence, the more and more I wrote, the more and more my writings defied any rigid academic disciplinary characterization as sanctioned and ratified by the very structures of established power that my thought began calling into question. As my literary endeavors continuously resisted any comfortable arrangement and intellectual conformity within established structures of meaning, I decided I could no longer ignore certain emancipatory intellectual imperatives that soon led me to unapologetically embrace the Promethean scope and insurgent trajectory of my discourse as philosophy.

2. In the ten years between the publication of Hip Hop Intellectual Resistance (2009) and Being and Insurrection (2019) through which your "existential liberation critique" is introduced, what (a) catalyzed your interest in writing philosophy; and (b) which thinkers inspired you to expand the philosophical canon by highlighting the theoretical and practical connections between existential thought and Black liberation discourse?

The truth is, I often find myself being very critical of my first book which, as you mentioned, is entitled *Hip Hop Intellectual Resistance*. However, as literarily flawed and discursively uneven as I regard it, I also recognize just how necessary it was for me to begin with an original work that challenged the reader with prose as rugged and raw as hip-hop at its best, and that no one foresaw coming out of the hip-hop generation, precisely because of its searing philosophical commitment to a Black liberation discourse of hip-hop sociocultural criticism. It is unfortunate, but certainly predictable, that within the context of an advanced neoliberal capitalist society leaning towards fascism, that such hip-hop sociocultural criticism no longer holds as much weight as it once did within the imperial mainstream's remnants of how the hip-hop culture now sees itself. Remember, as I somewhat alluded to earlier, even at a time when hip-hop culture was already losing way too much ground to the hip-hop culture industry, the focus of my thought unrepentantly went against the grain, as I was still very much intent on cultivating hip-hop aesthetics with an edge of cultural resistance to sociohistorical oppression.

Now, although *Hip Hop Intellectual Resistance* was eventually published in 2009, that book was actually written from 2001 through 2004, when I was in my late twenties and just starting to come into my own as a writer and thinker. That post-9/11 era saw further justifications for increasing intrusions of totalitarian security culture as a means of not only reconfiguring Empire, but further consolidating Western imperialist power through advanced neoliberal capitalist globalization. However, little did we know that grassroots movements of *protest-as-resistance* against the legal lynching of the Jena 6 and the blatant human rights violations and *structural-inert violence* against the Black community in the aftermath of Hurricane Katrina were right around the corner.

When I was writing the essays that would eventually become that book, I was a hip-hop intellectual through and through, steeped in Bahai Faith, Malcolm X, the Black Panthers, progressive Afrocentricity and the Black radical imagination as musically mediated through Boogie Down Productions/KRS-One, Nas, Eric B. & Rakim, Public Enemy, Queen Latifah, N. W. A./Ice Cube, Native Tongues, the Dungeon Family, Lauryn Hill, Hieroglyphics, Dead Prez, Ras Kass, Tragedy Khadafi, and the mighty Wu-Tang Clan.

Quiet as is kept, I was also an eMCee in the Durham-Chapel Hill, North Carolina underground hip-hop scene, with only just a couple notable battles and a few mixtape appearances and features to show for it however. Even back then though, I understood that I was an intellectual ambitiously expressing myself as an eMCee, rather than an eMCee with intellectual ambitions. And so, in a sense, for my first book, how could I not begin with hip-hop? Of course I had to begin there, because for my generation, hip-hop at its best, and I guess even at its worst, reveals our zeitgiest on so many levels, especially because it artistically speaks to our cultural contributions as a social manifestation of the Blues metaphysic.

Now, just to clarify, the Blues metaphysic, as I've defined and formulated it in dialogue with LeRoi Jones/Amiri Baraka, Angela Y. Davis and Cornel West, speaks to the possibility of a radical beginning as a vast reservoir of emancipatory creativity, imagination, aesthetics and discourse initiated through the call and response of lived Black experience to the disaster of history as a constant improvisational search for provisional foundations of upheaval from which to approach questions of the human condition, freedom, liberation, Justice, universality and the Divine without recourse to equilibrium, guarantee of stability or necessity of resolution, completion or wholeness.

And without coming to terms with that, without returning to source, without unapologetically grappling with the Blues metaphysic, my thought wouldn't have been able to disclose an authentic upheaval; it wouldn't have been enough of a fundamental beginning to epistemologically sustain my growth and development from hip-hop intellectual concerns to Black radical intellectual engagement.

Don't forget that as an existential philosopher, the most important questions that concern philosophy arise from life itself, from our lived experience, not from the repetition or transmission of neatly polished analytical systems of well-rehearsed doubt, as sanctioned by schools of thought that exist in comforting harmony with the normative gaze of established power.

To be clear, it's not an exaggeration to say that by the time I finished *Hip Hop Intellectual Resistance*, my thought could no longer find any peace within established structures of meaning. Rather, I found my voice as an unrelenting movement of thought that strives to unsettle any epistemic arrangement of reason, whenever such reason legitimates itself solely based upon a harmonious relation to the normative gaze of Empire. Indeed, that work introduced enough of an epistemic rupture against the normative gaze of established power that, for me to continue writing at all, I found myself committed to a process of beginning again from a more radical point of departure, at a different, more insurgent register of philosophical thought.

You see, my initial attempts at cultural criticism and social commentary were strained to the limit under the epistemic pressure of needing to fulfill the emancipatory demands of Black liberation exclusively through means of hip-hop culture in the face of a western imperialist continuum. Indeed, writing *Hip Hop Intellectual Resistance* set me off on an unforgiving discursive pace of Black radical thought that would eventually culminate in my second work, *Being and Insurrection*, which is already having a significant impact upon the radical imagination of our time as what David L. Schalk, author of *Spectrum of Political Engagement* and *War and the Ivory Tower*, described during one of our many conversations over the years as "a literary molotov cocktail of philosophical engagement in unapologetic solidarity with grassroots uprisings against injustice taking place in Ferguson and Baltimore."

So, although *Being and Insurrection* is my second book, it certainly counts as my first major work of insurgent philosophy. Indeed, *Being and Insurrection* not only signaled that I had arrived as an existential philosopher and Black radical thinker, but that a literary reckoning of insurgent intellectual commitment was at hand to accompany the emancipatory momentum of *protest-as-resistance* and spontaneous rebellion disclosed as *insurrection-in-itself* in Paris, Tottenham, Ferguson, Standing Rock and Baltimore leading up to the geonational scope of the Ahmaud Arbery, George Floyd & Breonna Taylor inspired uprisings.

And yet, before we get into that, let's back up to when I had just embarked upon this new era of my writing that would eventually become exemplified in works such as *Being and Insurrection* and *Epistemic Ruptures, Insurgent Philosophy*, a time when I was initially still working through how to engage in my intellectual endeavors from an original philosophical perspective.

No doubt, as a Black radical intellectual writing outside of the Academy, unencumbered by disciplinary constraints and hierarchal institutional mandates of knowledge production and epistemic consumption, what began as a serious search for a method of philosophy that would be able to suit the growing emancipatory intentionality of my literary work, soon transformed into a weighty recognition that I would instead have to actually constitute my own thoughts as critical theory in real time, just to meet the contemporary discursive demands of Black liberation.

To be certain, the intensity of my intellectual endeavor to continue upon an emancipatory trajectory of radical thought, at the discursive pace I had already set for myself, required more of an insurgent philosophical engagement from me than just adopting already established oppositional patterns of thinking within the *imperial mainstream-as-civil* society.

And yet, from where would I begin this radical venture as an intellectual trajectory of beginning again? The thing is, at that point, I had already started an immersive theoretical engagement with Jean-Paul Sartre's *Critique of Dialectical Reason Vol.1* and Frantz Fanon's *The Wretched of the Earth* with a keen eye for prioritizing methodological questions and examples of how to translate emancipatory imperatives against western imperialist power into insurgent philosophical discourse that could hold the weight of such emancipatory imperatives until the possibility of their transformation into emancipatory praxis.

However, I still hadn't figured out a satisfying way of drawing upon Sartre and Fanon for a united emancipatory philosophical framework needed to mold a new vocabulary of critique. That all changed when I began supplementing this discursive dialogue between Fanon and Sartre with close critical readings of Mark Poster's *Existential Marxism in Postwar France,* Lewis R. Gordon's *Fanon and the Crisis of European Man*, Thomas R. Flynn's *Sartre and Marxist Existentialism*, Frank B. Wilderson III's "Gramsci's Black Marx: Whither the Slave in Civil Society?" then eventually Anibal Quijano's "Coloniality of Power, Eurocentrism and Latin America" and Sylvia Wynter's "Unsettling the Coloniality of Being/Power/Truth/Freedom: Towards the Human, After Man, Its Overrepresentation-An Argument." During this demanding stretch, when everything was at stake with regard to the future direction of my intellectual endeavors, Gordon's thought in particular served as an unparalleled conceptual catalyst, precisely because of his theoretical grasp of both Fanon and Sartre, which provided me with a necessary discursive breakthrough to unleash my own creative capacity to constitute a mode of critique that would be able to unite salient emancipatory aspects of Fanon and Sartre together in ongoing dialogue with each other as a philosophical orientation with enough of an insurgent edge and hermeneutic consistency to confront the normative gaze of a *western imperialist continuum* through my work.

I remember at one point, before the actual publication of *Being and Insurrection*, I gave Gordon a still very unrevised review copy for his thoughts and feedback, to which he responded along the lines of it being very Hegelian. Did he mean it was a dense labyrinth of original thought or was he referring to the intensity of the dialectical movement of my critique? Nevertheless, his critique drove me to revisit a classic pamphlet by Angela Y. Davis entitled *Lectures on Liberation* in which she philosophically engaged the thought of Douglass within a Marxist-Hegelian context. Realizing her thought as fundamental in illuminating a pathway forward for the Black radical imagination, still, in my view she hadn't gone far enough, so I at once set about to discursively overthrow any remnants of Hegel's *master/slave dialectic* that had infiltrated my thought by way of Sartre and Fanon. However, to initiate an epistemic overthrow of the Hegelian master/slave dialectic necessitated a philosophical return to Douglass' autobiographical trilogy as well as the five-volume collection of his lectures and essays compiled by Phillip S. Foner entitled *The Life and Writings of Frederick Douglass*. Discursively mining the work of Douglass for his vital contributions to Black liberation discourse, while still very much in dialogue with the thought of Fanon, Sartre and now Davis, introduced the conditions of possibility for a constitutive recuperation of what I now term as the Douglassian *anti-slavery dialectic*.

As such, existential liberation critique was thus born out of the insurgent philosophical tension constituted by uniting the anti-slavery dialectic of Douglass, the existential Marxism of Sartre and the decolonizing phenomenology of Fanon for what you so accurately described in your question as a "practice of philosophy" that provides me with a heuristic method, unencumbered by academic disciplinary constraints, to draw from, engage in dialogue with and push the limits of existential philosophy, Black liberation discourse and critical theory towards a discursive confrontation against Empire in all its contemporary reconfigurations.

3. Why do you refer to Being and Insurrection as a work of insurgent philosophy as opposed to a work of radical philosophy? What differentiates your theoretical orientation and philosophical perspective from what is typically considered radical philosophy?
Well, first of all, to be clear, by breaking through epistemic boundaries that often function to police the horizon of Black liberation discourse, *Being and Insurrection* is indeed a work of radical philosophy. However, I do make an effort to make sure that readers understand that it is also very much a work of insurgent philosophy. For although insurgent philosophy is always already radical philosophy, and this is the point here, not all types of radical philosophy have an insurgent relation to established power or modernity itself as imposed by a *western imperialist continuum*.

In other words, there are some forms of radical philosophy which take modernity for granted as their unimpeachable starting point for philosophical reflection. To do this however, also has the effect of sanctioning, justifying or even worse, naturalizing the forces of Western imperialist power which brought modernity into being. As such, the defining characteristic of *insurgent* philosophy, and what differentiates it from other kinds of radical philosophy that I would consider *oppositional*, is that insurgent thought does not hesitate to call the sovereign legitimacy of Western imperialist power into question in the name of emancipatory praxis.

So, on the one hand, you have oppositional philosophy that gets its fundamental epistemological precepts and core teleological conclusions from modernity itself. The problem again, is that even when unambiguously working towards radical social change, oppositional thought ultimately runs the risk of reproducing a Western imperialist continuum in the process. Even the noble and egalitarian impulse to come up with a more just distribution of the spoils of Empire amongst the *imperial mainstream-as-civil society*, does nothing to alleviate the structural injustice that is violently visited upon those for whom racist dehumanization or *coloniality in the Raw* constitutes the *socio-ontological underground of modernity*.

On the other hand, insurgent philosophy takes as its point of departure, a radical beginning arising out of the disaster of history brought about by Western imperialist power. As such, insurgent thought confronts Empire with an unprecedented emancipatory universality of the human condition toward constitutive potentialities of human "being" and human liberation that undermine a western imperialist continuum by destabilizing its claim to universality as the epistemic conditions of its possibility.

Insurgent philosophy is also defined by its twofold function of simultaneously interrogating the Real and enunciating Revolt. Some forms of radical philosophy also interrogate the Real, while still others enunciate Revolt. However, insurgent philosophy is what happens when these two dynamics unite as one and introduce epistemic ruptures against the normative gaze of established power as discursive openings towards emancipatory praxis. These epistemic ruptures introduced by insurgent philosophy not only break up, but break through classical arrangements of thought and established structures of meaning that sustain absolute claims of knowledge as set forth by scientific authority, absolute claims of truth as set forth by religious dogma, and absolute claims of sovereign legitimacy as set forth by Western imperialist power.

4. Historically and philosophically speaking, what are the major theoretical differences between your existential liberation critique in Being and Insurrection and Epistemic Ruptures *(2022), and works, like Hartman's* Scenes of Subjection *(1997) that have come to define the Afro-pessimist corpus? In your view why has Afro-pessimism gained such a degree of prominence in the academy?*

Well, as you know, my stance on Afro-pessimism isn't as critical as it is often portrayed. And where I am critical, and yes necessarily severe, it is for different reasons than most appreciate. And yet, such reasons are themselves significant. While Afro-pessimists and I may share some core premises, it is on the philosophical implications of that shared foundation of concerns over the prevalence of anti-Black racism in our contemporary world that such discursive divergences occur. This divergence exists even at a register of theoretical intentionality. For instance, Afro-pessimism promotes itself as an exclusively explanatory orientation of thought, while existential liberation critique sees itself as having a much more emancipatory imperative to interrogate the Real and enunciate Revolt.

You also mentioned Hartman in your question, who I should add, might not really consider herself an Afro-pessimist, and maybe with good reason, although it is also clear that the trajectory of her thought certainly allows for her earnest inclusion amongst a constellation of thinkers like Orlando Patterson, Hortense Spillers, Jared Sexton and Frank B. Wilderson III whose works merit consideration as theoretically constitutive of Afro-pessimism.

At the same time, it shouldn't be overlooked that regardless of what I regard as certain glaring philosophical pitfalls of Afro-pessimist thought, I feel that it should definitely be taken seriously as part of an ongoing discursive dialogue surrounding the question of Black liberation. Lest we forget, Wilderson's essay—"Gramsci's Black Marx: Whither the Slave in Civil Society," certainly exerted an important influence upon the trajectory of my own thought during crucial formative stages of what we can now recognize as existential liberation critique.

Indeed, one thing that Afro-pessimist thought and existential liberation critique share in common is an understanding of slavery as social death. Especially with regards to how, while the explicit practice of enslaving human "being" as *chattel* no longer explicitly exists on legal grounds, the ontological structure of social death that imposed 'objecthood' upon human "being" to enslave populations racialized as Black, has been continuously reconfigured as a positionality of existence that structures the Real against which Black subjectivity still relentlessly asserts itself as that *lived rhythm of praxis* which we can also describe as human "being"-in-the-world."

Now although social death originates in the imposition of Western imperialist power as it was then manifested through chattel slavery, it still shows up in contemporary sociohistorical phenomena associated with the protean proliferation of Empire like mass incarceration, cobalt mining in the Congo, and the accumulative slaughter of Black community by neo-colonial police agents. You could even argue that Douglass may have anticipated the need for an Afro-pessimist approach when he prophetically foresaw that "the slave having ceased to be the abject slave of a single master, his enemies will endeavor to make him the slave of society at large."[1] Afro-pessimist thought thus comes into its own as a theoretical orientation, by focusing its explanatory power on how the normative gaze of a Western imperialist continuum constitutes Blackness as equivalent with still being a "slave to society at large."

To do this, to explain what being a contemporary "slave to society at large" means, Hartman's thought in particular, emphasizes the savagery and barbarism against human 'being' that is indicative of slavery at its most routine, or what in existential liberationist vocabulary would be understood as *structural-inert* violence. This *structural-inert* violence refers to violence that operates at such a regularly occurring frequency that it is rendered as objective as any other aspect of the Real, and therefore almost undetectable to everyday people unless subjected to vigorous scrutiny.

Thus, according to Hartman, and on this we agree, an over-emphasis on slavery as a terrible spectacle veils the effects of racist dehumanization at its most intimate registers of lived experience and thus allows for a more effective maintenance and management of the structural subjugation of Black subjectivity by the normative gaze of a Western imperialist continuum. That to me is what Afro-Pessimism provides at its best: a thorough and comprehensive window into what that structural subjugation of Black subjectivity by the normative gaze is all about. Especially dealing in ways that such structural subjugation of Black subjectivity continued to flourish even after the juridical sanction for the institution of slavery itself was withdrawn due to the constant threat of slave Revolts, concerted everyday resistance, radical abolitionist struggle, and ultimately the American Civil War itself.

However, even with this in mind, I don't think that it's at all controversial to recognize that Afro-pessimist thought indulges in a positivist reformulation of the exceptional antagonism that exists between Western imperialist power and the assertion of Black subjectivity-as-human "being," as an irreconcilable encounter between 'the Human' and "Blackness." So what happens when, at the same time as the question of what it means to be human is being decided in the streets of Western imperialist metropoles through *geohistorical insurrection-in-itself* against the *biopolitical pacification* of Black humanity by neocolonial police violence, you have a school of thought growing within the Academy that discursively cedes the capacity to define what human 'being' means to the same Western imperialist continuum that the ascendant humanity in the streets is struggling against?

As such, if your aim is to better understand the ontological imposition of "objecthood" upon human "being" as the social death of slavery and its afterlife, then Afro-Pessimism can certainly lend the credibility of its explanatory power to such ends. However, if your concern doesn't stop there, but actually seeks to better understand potentialities of *socio-ontological* resistance to the imposition of 'objecthood' upon human "being" as slave Revolt and its contemporary implications, then existential liberation critique might have something important to contribute to the Black radical imagination as well. I actually don't even see it as an either/or situation. If anything, the explanatory power of Afro-pessimism actually enhances the emancipatory relevance of existential liberation critique. In fact, a lot of up and coming Black thinkers, artists and activists, both inside and outside the Academy, who are now beginning to gravitate towards existential liberation critique, initially went through an Afro-pessimist stage in their intellectual trajectory.

Returning to Hartman though, Afro-pessimist thinkers who draw from her work take the beating of Douglass's Aunt Hester as their point of departure, in that it depicts what they psychoanalytically describe as the primal scene that initiates Douglass into all the horrors of slavery. By contrast, existential liberation critique takes Douglass's fight against the infamous slavebreaking overseer Covey as its point of departure, in that it depicts what we phenomenologically describe as *the anti-slavery dialectic* of Revolt, resistance, struggle and progress.

As such, this question I am about to enunciate goes to the heart of the difference between Afro-pessimism and existential liberation critique. If slavery can best be understood as social death, then does not slave Revolt constitute a social rebirth of lived potentialities of human subjectivity and human community? So again, the question of slave Revolt, because it discloses the assertion of Black subjectivity as human "being" at the heart of a sociohistorical movement of emancipatory praxis against established tyranny, speaks to the most pronounced theoretical difference between Afro-pessimist thought and existential liberation critique.

For as a consequence of the cynical universality of "whiteness" that inscribes modern secular humanism, Afro-pessimist thought feels justified in effectively ceding the discursive power to pose the question of human "being" to the normative gaze of Empire.

In contrast, although existential liberation critique certainly harbors no imperial mainstream liberal illusions about the bloodbath of materialist determinism that constitutes modern secular humanism, it instead chooses to continuously call into question the sovereign legitimacy of western imperialist power upon which modern secular humanism derives its discursive authority. So, when Afro-pessimism comes to the ontological conclusion that *Blackness* is coterminous with *slaveness*, existential liberation critique reminds us that this is an accurate reading of the assumptive logic and preordained epistemic parameters of the normative gaze of modernity as imposed by a western imperialist continuum.

Let me say this, for readers that are genuinely interested in understanding Afro-Pessimism from an insurgent philosophical perspective of existential liberation critique, check out "Slave Revolt and the Exceptional Antagonism of Black Subjectivity" published in *The Brotherwise Dispatch*, Vol.3, Issue#15, March-May/2023.

Now, I think here we can delve into your following question about the popularity of Afro-pessimism within the Academy. As an intellectual outsider who has no qualms about engaging in dialogue with the Academy, even while not officially a part of the Academy itself, I don't know that my insights on the popularity of Afro-Pessimism are in any way authoritative, so I will take your word on that.

However, I do agree that any time you have a theory that claims to exhaust itself as a thorough explanation of the normative gaze of established power, without then introducing any emancipatory imperatives to confront or challenge the sovereign legitimacy of established power, well, let's just say that such a trajectory of thought is bound to be popular within imperially sanctioned institutions of higher learning.

5. Considering the alarming rise of global authoritarianism, why is it more important than ever for people to engage with the works of Africana philosophers like Douglass, Du Bois, Fanon, Anna Julia Cooper, and Malcolm X? How were these thinkers' insights ahead of their respective times?

Well, it doesn't get more authoritarian than chattel slavery that geohistorically underwrites modernity as imposed by Western imperialist power. And so, in a real sense, that "alarming rise of global authoritarianism" you described is rooted in what happens when the *structural-inert* violence that inscribes modernity with racist dehumanization starts expanding coercively from methods of oppressive coloniality reserved exclusively for the *underground of modernity*, to now encompass a burgeoning fascist repression of the *imperial mainstream-as-civil society*.

No doubt, when you have an ascendant humanity of Black community that not only has been through the racist dehumanizing violence of western imperialist power that attempted to reduce human "being" to "objecthood" through chattel slavery, but is still experiencing ongoing reconfigurations of globalized oppression due to the sociohistorical continuity of western imperialist power that guarantees our subordinate asymmetrical positionality to the imperial *mainstream-as-civil* society, we may have some insight into to what it takes to fight back against inveterate structures of global injustice.

As such, Black liberation discourse is particularly suited to meet the needs of radical sociohistorical movements of emancipatory praxis that seek to reconstitute an authentic universality of the human condition as defined through a dynamic process of long protracted struggle of resistance against a Western imperialist continuum. In particular, what does it mean to keep fighting back against an ever-changing confluence of racist dehumanization, capitalist exploitation and imperialist hegemony, even when the odds are greater than ever and there are no tangible signs of hope on the horizon that quite match the overwhelming might of Empire?

All of those thinkers you mentioned in your question have contributed significantly to the development of such Black liberation discourse. And yet, Black liberation discourse is no mere school of philosophical thought that can be simply parsed out and consumed over a semester. It must be constantly and continuously studied, revisited and vigorously engaged by anyone concerned with the question of initiating sociohistorical movements towards human liberation in our contemporary world.

You see, the conditions of possibility that make Black liberation discourse so relevant remain with us to this day. For so long as a Western imperialist continuum exists, Black liberation discourse enjoys a particular distinction, because as I mentioned earlier, modernity itself is inscribed with racist dehumanization and *coloniality in the Raw* as its *socio-ontological* conditions of historical possibility. This means that any assertion of Black subjectivity as human 'being' introduces an exceptional antagonism against Empire that speaks to the sociohistorical potentialities of its eventual overturning and emancipatory openings towards making another world order possible. Does this not then speak to the global existential relevance of Black liberation discourse, precisely because the question of Black liberation introduces a lived wager of sociohistorical freedom upon which the question of the human condition and the ontological scope and limits of its universality are staked?

So here, it's important to again rethink the Blues metaphysic, as well as Black subjectivity and lived Black experience, which are each defined by means of the social cultivation of human subjectivity in the direst of historical circumstances including chattel slavery, which again, can be characterized as the violent systematic materialist reduction of human "being" to "objecthood." And yet, in the face of such a consummate *socio-ontological* authoritarianism, the Blues metaphysic speaks to lived potentialities of spiritual upheaval towards constituting and sustaining an ascendant humanity in geohistorical Revolt against Empire.

6. In the "Emancipatory Epilogue" of Epistemic Ruptures, Insurgent Philosophy, you describe the international protests that arose in the wake of George Floyd's lynching thusly:

"The tense unity of *protest-as-resistance* and *spontaneous rebellion* globally sets in motion a geohistorical dynamic of *insurrection-in-itself* across the streets of Empire as hundreds of thousands of everyday people, students, lumpenproletariat, adults, youth, rebels, and activists rediscover ourselves as ascendant humanity and, by choosing ourselves as ascendant humanity in resistance against the normative gaze of Western imperialist power, the universality of the human condition experiences potentialities of renewal through Revolt" (115–16).

How does the realization of an "ascendant humanity" relate to and offer resolution for the materialist concerns of the Black liberation struggle?

Well again, Black liberation struggles are endowed with a global relevance precisely because of the exceptional antagonism introduced against a Western imperialist continuum by the assertion of Black subjectivity-as-human 'being' that introduces a lived social wager of historical freedom upon which the question of the human condition and the ontological scope and limits of its universality are at stake. All those hundreds of thousands who arose on a global scale and disrupted the sovereign legitimacy of structural-inert violence against Black humanity in the name of George Floyd contributed towards constituting lived social potentialities towards a new universality of ascendant humanity that defines itself in Revolt against the normative gaze of western imperialist power, rather than acquiescing anthropologically to established standards of modern secular humanism that exist in harmony with Empire.

So now, it might be important to define just what we mean by "the materialist concerns of the Black liberation struggle?" For if all we have to offer the world, after everything that we have been through, is just another racialized version of socioeconomic equilibrium suited to the American exceptionalist imagination of the upper middle class of the *imperial mainstream-as-civil society*, can we still justifiably call that emancipatory? And if so, emancipatory for whom?

However, if by "materialist concerns" we mean the Real of globalized human suffering as concretely experienced under the disaster of a Western imperialist continuum that afflicts racialized populations of ascendant humanity at spiritual, social and economic registers of existence, then we have to seriously consider, not just what we are fighting for, but whether we are open to new understandings of the human condition that will only be made readily available through sociohistorical movements of Black liberation that are geonational in scope as world encompassing struggles for social justice through the constitutive heat of emancipatory praxis against oppression that brings forth lived potentialities of ascendant humanity.

So, what does Black liberation mean as a social movement of ascendant humanity achieving geohistorical freedom against the all-pervasive context of a Western imperialist continuum? Well, what soon becomes clear is that the materialist concerns of Black liberation struggle cannot be met within an American exceptionalist context, particularly because of the way our contemporary world is geopolitically organized according to the dictates of a *western imperialist continuum*. Black liberation thus speaks to an exceptional antagonism of ascendant humanity against Empire that introduces the conditions of possibility for a fundamental egalitarian restructuring of an old world ordered according to competing nationalist projects under an advanced neoliberal capitalist hegemony, towards a new world of cooperative geonational commons of culturally diverse world communities of everyday people as an ascendant humanity awakening to the radical universality of the human condition through their own particular sociohistorical struggle for human liberation. Black liberation praxis thus exists as a potential vanguard of sociohistorical struggles of human liberation against Western imperialist power. This is not because of any cultural nationalist chauvinism associated with lived Black experience, but because of the contingency of history that situates Black community as an emancipatory Trojan Horse in the heart of Empire.

As such, a lot of what sometimes passes for Black liberation discourse is in actuality far from it. Especially in that sense that there is still a very powerful American exceptionalist narrative of assimilation into the *imperial mainstream-as-civil society* that cancerously afflicts some strains of Black oppositional thought. The Black radical imagination must ever remind us that receiving our fair share of the spoils of Empire can never be regarded as more than a means towards emancipatory praxis, rather than the point of emancipatory praxis itself.

No doubt, to truly understand that what is at stake in the struggle of Black liberation against Empire is the universality of the human condition itself, is to soberly recognize that racist dehumanization and *coloniality in the Raw* constitute the very essence of materialist concerns, the sovereign legitimacy of which is being challenged whenever *insurrection-in-itself* returns to source in the streets of Western imperialist metropoles across the world, as it did so recently in the name of George Floyd.

6. As a philosopher who has written three books outside of the academy, without being pressured by the infamous "publish or perish" dictum, what fuels your high level of productivity?
I choose to write. Writing is my calling, which means that I am driven and compelled to engage in the world through writing as my *lived rhythm of praxis*, as my way of *being-in-the-world*. However, philosophy is the particular way that my writing manifests itself in history. Furthermore, as an intellectual outsider to the Academy, and obviously aside from keeping up with a schedule of upcoming lectures and/or publication deadlines, my literary commitment isn't driven by typical institutional pressures of academic prestige and/or careerist advancement.

No doubt, what moves me to write is the spiritual intentionality of my own literary expectations and emancipatory imperatives that I have committed to, and wagered my intellectual trajectory upon, as mediated by the Real of my sociohistorical situation as a Black man writing against the violent dehumanizing gravity of a Western imperialist continuum.

However, that actually makes that dictum you accurately described as "publish or perish" even more existentially pronounced for me. Why? Well, since I do not exclusively rely on financial success or institutional sanction to validate the social relevance and intellectual rigor of my literary endeavors, if I am not consistently writing and/or publishing, then I have nothing else to stand on as a philosopher and thinker. So, for me, it actually still is "publish or perish" indeed, but for significantly different reasons.

7. What is the subject of your next book?
Well, first I'm in the process of editing and then writing the introduction to a massive one-volume anthology of Frederick Douglass's writings entitled *Anti-Slavery Dialectic* that will be published by Cannae Press in 2026. This work collects his fugitive slave lectures and radical abolitionist thought in an attempt to emphasize his singular insurgent philosophical contributions to Black liberation discourse.

However, my next work proper is tentatively entitled *Art, Aesthetics and the Blues Metaphysic*, which will also be published by Cannae Press in 2026 or 2027. This text will compile a varied assortment of my writings and lecture notes that speak to an insurgent philosophical engagement with art, music and aesthetics, with particular emphasis on what we discussed earlier about the Blues metaphysic in correlation to questions of human 'being' and human liberation.

Note

1 Frederick Douglass, "The Day of Jubilee Comes," *Douglass' Monthly*, January 1863.

8
INTERVIEW WITH LEWIS R. GORDON

Board of Trustees Distinguished Professor of Philosophy and Global Affairs and Head of Philosophy at the University of Connecticut; Honorary President of the Global Center for Advanced Studies; Distinguished Scholar, The Most Honorable PJ Patterson Centre for African and Caribbean Advocacy at the University of the West Indies at Mona, Jamaica; and Fellow of the Royal Society of Arts

1. To begin with, please explain what drew you to the discipline and practice of philosophy during the latter years of your undergraduate career. During this early stage in your development as a philosopher, who were the thinkers you found most engaging and why?

Lehman College was a wonderful place to roam through the world of ideas. I've recently been reflecting much on the concept of roaming. Many children and young adults are no longer roaming. They work their way through well organized and constrained environments. There are still places where that is not so, but they are disappearing. Roaming is an activity that is often social and offers many challenges through which roamers' cognitive capacities could grow. I experienced that as well in the jazz world, in which I performed drums and piano. That understanding was how I approached my undergraduate studies. I pursued what I liked, what stimulated my imagination, what, at the end of each semester, left me with the experience of growth. Aristotle called this "wonder." Although I always loved thinking, reading, writing, and working through ideas with a community, I in effect wondered into philosophy with a sense of wonder. It wasn't only philosophy that I loved—as literature (especially classics), politics, and physics (especially astronomy and cosmology) were among my interests—but it was the philosophical dimensions of all my other studies that I most loved. I found all the canonical thinkers—from Socrates to Plato to Aristotle to St. Augustine to the Euromoderns, exciting. I should add that I wasn't introduced to the last bunch at Lehman. I was actually introduced to Hegel and Marx in Middle School. I had an amazing social studies teacher by the name of Mr. Cirqua who engaged me regularly in debates in philosophy of history. In my undergraduate years, however, I could say without reservation that the philosopher who had the most impact on me was Jean-Jacques Rousseau. This was not only because of the power of his ideas but also because of the beauty and power of his prose. Every word, every sentence, of Rousseau's writing was extraordinary. As I love writing, Rousseau spoke to me. It was no doubt also because of his love of music and science. A shortcoming of the Lehman Philosophy Department at that time was that the faculty offered no discussion of African, Asian, nor Native American philosophers, and there was no woman philosopher who was, to my recollection, taught. This doesn't mean I was not able to learn about them and their thought elsewhere. Gary Schwartz in Classics directed the Lehman Scholar's Program, and it was through his fecund and generous mind that I was introduced to women philosophers such as Mary Wollstencraft and Susan Langer, in addition to literary intellectuals such as Mary Shelley, Gabriel José García Márquez, and Toni Morrison. As well, Africana Studies, which was at that time called Black Studies, introduced me to ancient African philosophy through to African American philosophical work, especially in aesthetics and politics.

2. What sociopolitical forces and/or historical events compelled you to write your dissertation about Sartrean bad faith and its direct connection to anti-black racism?
I went to graduate school to explore and illuminate, in philosophical terms, the concept of human potential. I quickly realized this goal was rooted in freedom and forms of dehumanization that occur in efforts to erase living freedom through flights into pleasing falsehoods. Sartrean bad faith made sense to me because it addresses not only lies but also those that involve lying to ourselves. If we are truly free, we are free to attempt fleeing our freedom. Racism involves identifying groups of human beings and then lying to ourselves and all that they are not

human beings. Anti-black racism involves denying, through a complex web of lies and institutions, the humanity of Black people.

3. How did the experience of writing Bad Faith and Antiblack Racism (1995) lead you to a) embrace transdisciplinary inquiry in all of your subsequent works; and b) create several subfields within the discipline of philosophy itself?

I immediately discovered a form of bad faith at work among practitioners of many disciplines, especially those in the human sciences. It is weird that there are even race theorists who do not address the study of race and racism as a form of human science or study. My studies of forms of bad faith revealed that no single human science incorporates all dimensions of our humanity. Attempts to do so often close off human possibilities and result in dehumanization. I therefore had to suspend any presupposition of a "complete" discipline with a perfect methodological framework to apply to human phenomena. This critical suspension led me to articulating and developing the theory of disciplinary decadence, which involves practitioners lying to themselves about their disciplines to the point of asserting forms of disciplinary solipsism. They treat their disciplines as though they were created by gods. My response was to argue for what I call "teleological suspensions of disciplinarity," which involves going beyond one's discipline for the sake of reality. This requires communicating with and appreciating contributions from other disciplines that offer connections to aspects of reality one's discipline may lack. I call this practice "transdisciplinary," because it requires letting go of disciplinary hegemony and adopting practices of co-learning and co-theorizing and nurturing the evidentiality of evidence across disciplines. Regarding philosophy, this requires rejecting disciplinary nationalism. This willingness to reach for ideas beyond philosophy also leads, ironically and paradoxically, to living philosophy, what I call "philosophy beyond philosophy." While I didn't invent Africana existentialism and Black existentialism, this approach contributed to their academic standing in contemporary philosophy. This is similar in philosophy of medicine and philosophical psychoanalysis and their fusion in philosophy of psychiatry. Fields I have invented are disciplinary decadence studies and teleological suspensions of disciplinarity studies. These connect to my work in philosophy of science. I have also been working on new understandings of "dimensions," drawing upon ideas from Ernst Cassirer, into what I call "multidimensional theory." To my knowledge, although there were phenomenological works from intellectuals in Africa and its diaspora, explicitly Africana phenomenology, including Africana existential and postcolonial forms, that were explicitly stated in writings in the 1990s, they now stand as subfields. Similarly, although I didn't coin the term "public philosophy," my work in that area transitioned from the standard model of a form of applied philosophy to the idea of the public as having philosophical importance. This links to my work in communicology, in which I argue that the idea of a nonpublic philosophy would be an abdication of the ethical core of philosophy's commitments to evidentiality and reality. This is related to my critical work against what I call "epistemic closure," which is a form of decadence in which the whole is sacrificed to a part. There is also my approach to the subfield of the history of philosophy, in which my contributions focused primarily on Africana thought. In the history of Africana philosophy, this involves my argument for engaging the ideas of Africana intellectuals instead of primarily their biographies. Although this may seem banal, part of epistemic racism—and I would add sexism—is to regard Africana intellectuals' work as mere applications of white thinkers' thought; it is a devaluing of Africana people's ideas as *thought.* For me, thought is useful if one can build on it in the pursuit of what one is trying to learn, whether that be about reality even in its metaphysical possibilities or to everyday social practices of producing meanings for livable lives. Finally, although not exhaustively, there is my work in metaphilosophy, which includes the formulations of shifting the geography of reason and shifting the geography of science. As my work is primarily dialectical and relational—in which I argue against binary oppositions or contraries—the connection with teleological suspension studies come to the fore. That facilitates asking questions that transcend closed models of various traditional philosophical subfields. For example, my Afro-Jewish writings contribute to Afro-Jewish philosophy. There is also my work in what could be called critical theodicean studies, which is critique of our tendency to transform human institutions into idols. It grows out of my critical work on disciplinary decadence. As well, the relational, communicative models join developments in Caribbean philosophy and creolizing theory. The result is an open, developmental approach to philosophy in which there is room for new subfields of it and other disciplines in which I work can come to the fore. Other subfields are coextensivity theory and irreplaceability theory as well as an area of catastrophe and disaster studies Jane Anna Gordon and I developed under the title "sign continua" studies, which involves examining the semiotic and mythopoetic aspects of disaster. As well, my work in philosophical anthropology focuses on human reality studies—namely, the significance of human beings being able to live in worlds of our making, worlds constituted by meaning in human terms. I should like to add that my current work is also exploring the implications of nonhuman forms of complex intelligence—including computer or algorithmically produced forms. I conjoin my work in philosophy of psychiatry to examine problems raised by nonempathetic—that is, psychopathological and sociopathological—forms of intelligence. It is not only that these would be forms without concern for humanity, but also that they raise possibilities of new kinds of bigotry that are not coherently forms of dehumanization.

4. In an early December 2024 talk in San Diego you revisited one of the central themes in Bad Faith and Antiblack Racism: *the responsibility of freedom. Could you explain why many people prefer to flee from this responsibility and, instead, choose to stand in bad faith? Do you think that the flight from freedom is directly related to the "fight or flight" response, and that fighting—in some people's view—requires too much concerted effort and commitment?*
It is difficult to live with freedom. Most people, nostalgic for childhood, would prefer liberty without freedom. Liberty, radicalized, becomes license. That involves doing whatever one wants without accountability. It is immature at its core and psychopathic at its worst. Freedom—whose etymology is curiously linked to friendship—is about living with others and the concomitant responsibility for which doing so calls. Freedom involves empathy (as Simone de Beauvoir observed in *The Ethics of Ambiguity*), responsibility, love, belonging, and truth. These may seem to be an odd combination but bear in mind an implication of my critique of reductive methodologies. We tend to look for a single essence of a phenomenon, when there may be a coextensive convergence of elements. Much of this comes from an insight in my early phenomenological work, in which I argue for the importance of descriptions, theorizing, and understandings that emerge from what

I call "ontological suspensions." Examining phenomena through which freedom is meaningfully lived, one would notice that hate is best suited for liberty than freedom. One could consistently hate through destroying other's freedom and dignity and destroy social relations resulting in being by oneself. It's one of the allegories in Dante's *Inferno*, in the form of Satan's frozen spot at the center of Hell. Hate destroys all. Consumed by hate, there is no room for others. Destroying relations include eliminating any meaningful form of belonging, what in prosaic language we call "home." We seek homes—whether as places of habitation or relations of flourishing, such as, for example, in disciplines, institutions, and relationships that make us grow—in which we could realize our potential. Cultivating relationships and conditions of flourishing require also celebrating others' capacities to do such. As open, others become possibilities with whom to continue growing or be at peace with what we contribute to forms of meaning that make our lives worth living. Truth, as should be obvious, involves acknowledging not only our responsibilities but also the value of so many dimensions of reality that transcend us. This leads to an important existential insight on freedom—namely, rejecting the spirit of seriousness. Simply put, part of living freely is learning not to take ourselves *too* seriously.

5. In 2003, eight years after the publication of Bad Faith and Antiblack Racism, you co-founded the Caribbean Philosophical Association in Mona, Jamaica—our native country. In the two decades since the Caribbean Philosophical Association's (CPA's) founding mission of "shifting the geography of reason" was articulated, what are the most significant strides that academic philosophy has made toward the curricular inclusion of Global South and BIPOC thinkers?

Academic philosophy hasn't done much, although it is improving. In truth, it is the institutions that many of us have built, ranging from the Caribbean Philosophical Association to others preceding it such as the Radical Philosophy Association, Social Feminist Philosophers in Action (SOFPHIA), the Phenomenology Roundtable, the Society of Africana Philosophy, the Cave Hill Philosophy Symposium, the varieties of decolonial summer schools across the globe, the African Phenomenology Center in South Africa, and many other special transdisciplinary institutions rooted in philosophical and other forms of theoretical approaches, along with what many of us have done to make our curricula more rigorous and inclusive, that are making a difference. One crucial thing is that we haven't wasted time with conventional sites of recognition. Instead of obsession over so-called masters' houses, we decided to build alternative, better homes. The livability of these alternative homes decenters prior hegemons. Increasingly, what many of us have been noticing is that hegemonic philosophy is increasingly resembling past scholasticism. They don't seem to belong to the twenty-first century. Despite their hegemony, those approaches to philosophy are increasingly suffering from something deadly: irrelevance. The result is eerie. They increasingly seem to be epistemic practices best suited for the living dead.

6. In a November 2023 interview on Overthink's podcast, you averred that Rachel Dolezal (the professor and former NAACP chapter head who was "outed" as white) had attained Black consciousness because of her political commitments and anti-racism work. However, after the interview concluded, one of the hosts posed this question: "Could Rachel Dolezal have attained Black consciousness—with an upper case 'B'—without having first traversed the psychosocial terrain from black consciousness with a lower case 'b'? Could you answer the interviewer's question and elaborate on your stance that Dolezal has arrived at Black consciousness?"

Anyone could develop a Black consciousness. I don't take the position that Black consciousness generates exclusively out of people legally designated black. There are many black people without Black consciousness. This is a position shared by Steve Bantu Biko. I don't, however, see how a non-Black person could develop a black or Black consciousness without *any* relationship with the lived-reality of black people. This includes not only anti-black racism but also the positive elements of varieties of black life ranging from those in Africa and its diaspora to those designated black peoples across South Asia through to Australasia. So, yes, relationships with lower-case "b" black consciousness is a necessary condition. I cannot say, however, what future Blackness may require in its own terms.

7. In your view why does there need to be a more emphatic distinction between studying philosophy and actually doing philosophy? As an internationally-renowned public philosopher who gives talks around the world, what do you find most gratifying and, alternately, most infuriating about doing philosophy amidst the global rise of authoritarianism?

Studying philosophy introduces one to philosophical ideas. Doctoral programs focus on professionalization and participating with the world professionals who specialize in subfields of philosophy. Such specialization is a form of epistemic capital; it basically qualifies one to assess research and scholarship in or on philosophy. Doing philosophy is another matter. It is the producing of new ideas that transform our relationship to reality. Like psychoanalysis, which attempts to unmask a disguised unconscious, doing philosophy involves clearing away what stands in the way of connecting us with reality, which includes one another. Doing that doesn't require training in professional philosophy, although the latter can help. Thinkers from other disciplines also contribute to our understanding of reality. Thus, not all professional academic philosophers actually do philosophy, and there are nonacademic intellectuals and academics who are formally philosophers who do philosophy, which here means producing work or ideas that contribute to philosophy, which I regard as first and foremost concerned with reality.

8. Over the course of your prolific career, it seems that each of your books represents a different facet of your philosophical journey. What particular aspects of this journey does each of the following works represent: Bad Faith and Antiblack Racism (1995), Fanon and the Crisis of European Man (1995), Existence in Black: An Anthology of Black Existential Philosophy (1996), Existentia Africana (2000), Disciplinary Decadence (2007), An Introduction to Africana Philosophy (2008), Freedom, Justice, and Decolonization (2020), Fear of Black Consciousness (2023).

Bad Faith and Antiblack Racism was my first book and statement on what is at stake when we fail to address displeasing truths through throwing ourselves into the arms of pleasing falsehoods such as notions of racial inferiority and superiority. *Fanon and the Crisis of European Man* was a generative work in that it introduced not only several concepts that are hallmarks of my thought—which include concepts such as disciplinary decadence, distorted anonymity, existential historicity, epistemic closure, ontological suspension, and tragic revolutionary violence—as well as the groundwork for my approach to the history of philosophy and philosophy of history. *Existence in Black* is, to my knowledge, the first collective statement of Black existentialism. I edited that work instead of writing a monograph because it struck me that an area of thought requires a community cultivating it. The results of that effort speak for themselves. *Existentia Africana* was my contribution to establishing Africana existential thought as an area of study and my articulating its distinction from, although also convergences with, Black existentialism. It offers also my critical theory of biography and experience as well as critical discussions of identity, liberation, and even incantation and a philosophy of writing. *Disciplinary Decadence* is where, after a decade of reflection, I advance my theory of living thought through introducing the concept of teleological suspensions of disciplinarity. *An Introduction to Africana Philosophy* is my statement on Africana philosophy as an intellectual enterprise. This may seem odd, but we should bear in mind that there is often more interest in lists of Africana philosophers than their thought. I introduced exploring Africana philosophy not through asking who were Africana philosophers but instead asking who—whatever their identity may be—addresses central problems of Africana philosophy such as what it means to be human, free, and justified. I talked about those in terms of philosophical anthropologies in which the construction of race and its concomitant racism are interrogated, the centrality of freedom in which enslavement and colonization are not ignored, and a metacritique of reason in which the rallying of reason in the service of dehumanization occasions a crisis that must itself receive critique, which I sometimes describe as critical examinations of justificatory practices — all of these topics come to the fore. I have subsequently added critical examinations of redemptive narratives, conceptions of dignity, and metaphysical challenges posed by uncaring forms of reality.

9. Like many of our ancestors who were great thinkers and orators— Sojourner Truth, Maria Stewart, Frederick Douglass, Ida B. Wells, Marcus Gavey, and Malcolm X to name a few—you are also a master teacher. How has your thirty-year teaching career inspired you to maintain such a high level of productivity, particularly since many academics who've attained similar levels of international recognition eschew teaching in favor of research and writing?

I'm actually in my fourth decade of teaching. Yes, I started when I was very young. For me there is no separation of researching and teaching because I regard a researcher as someone who fell in love with learning to the point of continuing to learn even if that means teaching oneself. Thus, I regard students as learners who have joined me, a long-time learner, in process of learning together. I learn from what my students bring to the classroom as they learn not only from what I share with them but also what we build together when we explore problems in real or living time. I must say I don't understand the eschewing teaching model. For me, research is heavily social. That's why, even if I weren't in a classroom, I would be in a variety of social equivalents through workshops, seminars across the globe, conferences, and more. The more includes playing music. There is no moment of making music in which there isn't co-learning. I bring the same to cooking and other activities I love to do. For me, they're all communal or social. Of course, a time will come when I'm not particularly functional and will have to end formal teaching. The same might pertain to my ability to write. That doesn't mean, however, that I won't continue to learn.

10. When teaching a range of courses—from large lecture hall courses to more intimate upper-level seminars—who are the thinkers and texts you most enjoy teaching and why? Outside the realms of philosophy and political theory, which particular authors' works resonate with you and why?

Too many to mention here. My courses include thinkers from antiquity such as Khun-Anup and Antef from Kemet 4,000 years ago as well as Plato (2,500 years ago). Imhotep, Aristotle, and other physician philosophers such as William James, Karl Jaspers, and Frantz Fanon are staples. As philosophers who are great writers go, Plato, Lucretius, St. Augustine, Zara Yacob, Jean-Jacques Rousseau, Arthur Schopenhauer, Friedrick Nietzsche, Karl Marx, W. E. B. Du Bois, Anna Julia Cooper, Sri Aurobindo, Ortega Y. Gasset, Simone Weil, Simone de Beauvoir, Jean-Paul Sartre, Albert Camus, Maurice Merleau-Ponty, Hannah Arendt, Elias Canetti, Alfred Schütz, Fanon, Ali Shari'ati, and Keiji Nishitani stand out. Although not thought of in philosophical terms, I have taught Mary Shelley, Richard Wright, Ralph Ellison, and Toni Morrison regularly, and there are other political writers such as Antonio Gramsci and the Chinese feminist social philosopher He-Yin Zhen, who are regulars in my courses on political philosophy. My courses also include so many in the Africana canon beyond Fanon, such as C. L. R. James, Steve

Biko, V. Y. Mudimbe, Chabani Manganyi, and those among the living such as Paget Henry, P. Mabogo More, and Angela Y. Davis. Of course, given the nature of the work I do, G. W. F. Hegel, Edmund Husserl, and Karl Jaspers receive annual shoutouts. So, too, do Martin Buber and Ernst Cassirer. There is also a community of contemporary, younger thinkers whose writings are great to teach. Jane Anna Gordon's and Michael Monahan's creolizing work, Nelson Maldonado-Torres's decolonial work, writings by Rozena Maart, Jean-Paul Rocchi, and Nathalie Etoke, among writings by recent existentialists such as Jina Fast, Devon Johnson, Tom Meagher, and you, regularly hit home. There is also a group of feminist philosophers/theorists whose work make their way through my courses regularly. They include Iris Marion Young, Carol Gilligan, Drucilla Cornell, Judith Butler, and Sara Ahmed. And of course, because I teach philosophical psychoanalysis, Sigmund Freud, Karl Jung, Anna Freud, Eric Fromm, Barnaby Barratt, Marilyn Nissim-Sabat, who is also included in my courses on phenomenology, make regular appearances. As I also teach courses on philosophical reasoning, I add Charles Sanders Peirce, John Dewey, Gottlob Frege, Alfred North Whitehead, Bertrand Russell, Ludwig Wittgenstein, and Susan Haack. Finally, I do include film and music as philosophical texts in my courses. I have a long list of films, from those by Ingmar Bergman and Lina Wertmuller to Charles Burnett and so many others, and given the more than 3,000 tunes and songs in rotation on my playlists, let's just say that whether European classical, African American classical (jazz), reggae, Afrobeat, hip-hop, folk, or *bhangra*, among many other kinds of music, there is much to learn, especially in tandem with reading philosophical and other kinds of theoretical texts.

11. It's fairly well-known that, in addition to being one of the most important living philosophers, you are also an avid musician and physicist. Using your prodigious pedagogical skills and transdisciplinary acumen, could you elaborate on the areas of conceptual overlap among the seemingly disparate fields of existential freedom, jazz, roots reggae, and quantum physics?

Music, especially jazz, informs my work in aesthetics, in which I argue that aesthetic dimensions of life should not be secondary because of their connection to meaning—without which life is not worth living—but also, as many other existentialists argue, freedom. Music is also very mathematical and is a wonderful entry into problems of theoretical physics. My concerns in theoretical physics connect not only to problems at quantum and macro-levels but also through reimagining physical phenomena, especially in light of developments in studies of dark energy, dark matter, and possibilities of other forms of physical phenomena not hitherto thought of. It strikes me that the creativity in music is also thematic in a way that offers theoretical reflection, as Stephon Alexander observes in his wonderful book *The Jazz of Physics*. As my position is that aesthetic reality, such as found in music and poetry, and physical reality are different aspects of reality, the question of perspectivity and thematicization comes to the fore.

12. In closing, what would you like readers to understand about the importance of doing philosophy in our present historical moment?
The importance of doing philosophy—actually *doing philosophy*—brings us in touch with what matters in life and reminds us that we shouldn't be afraid of reality but instead live it. Life, at least for most human beings, comes down to doing what we love, being with whom we love and being lucky enough to have the gift of being loved by them; learning about different dimensions of what it means to live a meaningful life, bringing dignity to the world through making our lives worthwhile through developing relationships, even with nonliving things, and not taking ourselves so seriously that we fail to experience humor, especially those moments that occasion joyful laughter, and love.

References

Adler, George, Hudis, Peter, and Annelis, Laschitz., eds. (2011), *The Letters of Rosa Luxemburg*, New York: Verso.

Amin, Samir. (1989), *Eurocentrism*, New York: Monthly Review Press.

Antef, *Inscription of*. ([1991–1782 BCE] 2006), in (ed.) Kwasi Wiredu, *A Companion to African Philosophy*, London: Blackwell.

Anyon, Jean. (1980), "Social Class and the Hidden Curriculum of Work," *The Journal of Education*, 162 (1): 67–92. Available online: https://www.jstor.org/stable/42741976 (accessed October 12, 2017).

Averroes (Ibn Rushd). ([c. 1190 CE] 1960), *On the Harmony of Religion and Philosophy*, trans. George Hourani, Oxford: Oxbow Books.

de Beauvoir, Simone. ([1949] 1974), *The Second Sex*, trans. H. M. Parshley, New York: Random House-Vintage Books.

Bernal, Martin. ([1987] 1991), *Black Athena: The Afro-Asiatic Roots of Classical Civilization*, vol. 1, New York: Random House-Vintage.

Bernal, Martin. (1989), "*Black Athena* and the APA," *Arethusa*, (22): 17–38. Available online: https://www.jstor.org/stable/26308574 (accessed January 21, 2025).

Bogues, Anthony. (2003), *Black Heretics, Black Prophets: Radical Political Intellectuals*, New York: Routledge.

Brunson, James, and Rashidi, Runoko. (1992), "The Moors in Antiquity," in (ed.) Ivan Van Sertima, *Golden Age of the Moor*, New Brunswick: Transaction.

Bulhan, Hussein. (1985), *Frantz Fanon and the Psychology of Oppression*, New York: Plenum Press.

Butler, Broadus. (1983), "Frederick Douglass: The Black Philosopher in the United States," in (ed.) Leonard Harris, *Philosophy Born of Struggle: Afro-American Philosophy since 1917*, Dubuque: Kendall/Hunt Publishing.

Capps, John. "I am an American Philosopher: Leonard Harris." *Society for the Advancement of American Philosophy*. Available online: https://american-philosophy.org/i-am-an-american-philosopher-interview-series/i-am-an-american-philosopher-leonard-harris/ (accessed June 17, 2025).

Carew, Jan. (1992), "Moorish Culture Bringers: Bearers of Enlightenment," in (ed.) Ivan Van Sertima, *Golden Age of the Moor*, New Brunswick: Transaction.

Carter, Steven. (1991), *Hansberry's Drama: Commitment and Complexity*, Chicago: University of Illinois Press.

Chinyelu, Mamadou. (1992), "Africans in the Birth and Spread of Islam," in (ed.) Ivan Van Sertima, *Golden Age of the Moor*, New Brunswick: Transaction.

Cooper, Anna Julia. ([1892] 1969), *A Voice from the South*, Westport: Negro Universities Press.

Cooper, Anna Julia. (2006), *Slavery and the French and Haitian Revolutionists* (Francis Keller Ed. & Trans.), New York: Rowman & Littlefield.

Cugoano, Ottobah. ([1791] 1999), *Thoughts and Sentiments on the Evil and Wicked Traffic of Slavery and Commerce of the Human Species*, New York: Penguin.

DaCosta, Miriam. (1975), "Historical and Literary Views of Yusuf, Conqueror of Spain," *The Journal of Negro History*, 60 (4): 480–90. Available online: https://www.jstor.org/stable/2717019 (accessed April 15, 2025).

Davis, Angela (1972), "Reflections on the Black Woman's Role in the Community of Slaves," *The Massachusetts Review*, 13 (1–2): 81–100. Available online: https://www.jstor.org/stable/25088201 (accessed October 20, 2024).

Davis, Angela (1981), *Women, Race & Class*, New York: Random House.

Davis, Angela. (1983), "Unfinished Lecture on Liberation II," in (ed.) Leonard Harris, *Philosophy Born of Struggle: Anthology of Afro-American Philosophy from 1917*, 130–8, Dubuque: Kendall Hunt Publishing Company.

Davis, Angela. (2003), *Are Prisons Obsolete?*, New York: Seven Stories Press.

Diodorus Siculus (c. 60 BCE). *The Library of History*, Book 1. 1–29, from https://penelope.uchicago.edu/Thayer/E/Roman/Texts/Diodorus_Siculus/1A*.html.

Dobbs, David. (2014), "The Fault in Our DNA." *New York Times*, July 10. Available online: December 2018, https://www.nytimes.com/2014/07/13/books/review/a-troublesome-inheritance-and-inheritance.html (accessed December 15, 2017).

Douglass, Frederick. ([1845] 1987), *Narrative of the Life of Frederick Douglass*, New York: American Library.

Douglass, Frederick. ([1852] 1950), "What to the Slave is the Fourth of July?," in (ed.) Philip Foner, vol. 2, *The Life and Writings of Frederick Douglass*, New York: International Publishers.

Douglass, Frederick. ([1854] 1950), "The Claims of the Negro Ethnologically Considered," in (ed.) Philip Foner, vol. 2, *The Life and Writings of Frederick Douglass*, New York: International Publishers.

Douglass, Frederick. ([1855] 2003), *My Bondage and My Freedom*, New York: Simon & Schuster.

Douglass, Frederick. ([1857] 1950), "West India Emancipation," in (ed.) Philip Foner, vol. 2, New York: International Publishers.

Drake, St. Clair. (1987), *Black Folk Here and There: An Essay in History and Anthropology*, Los Angeles: University of California.

Du Bois, W. E. B. ([1903] 1961), *The Souls of Black Folk*, New York: Fawcett Publications.

Du Bois, W. E. B. ([1928] 1995), *Dark Princess*, Jackson: University Press of Mississippi-Banner Books.

Du Bois, W. E. B. ([1935] 1962), *Black Reconstruction in America*, New York: Antheneum.

Du Bois, W. E. B. ([1946] 1965), *The World and Africa*, New York: International Publishers.

Dussel, Enrique. (1998), *The Underside of Modernity: Apel, Ricoeur, Rorty, Taylor & The Philosophy of Liberation*, trans. Eduardo Mendieta, Amherst: Humanities Press.

Eze, Emmanuel. (1995), "The Color of Reason: The Idea of 'Race' in Kant's Anthropology," in (ed.) Katherine Faull, *Anthropology and the German Enlightenment*, 200–41, Lewisburg: Bucknell University Press.

Eze, Emmanuel. ed. (1997), *Race and the Enlightenment: A Reader*, Oxford: Blackwell Publishing.

Fanon, Frantz. ([1952] 1967), *Black Skin, White Masks*, trans. Charles Markmann, New York: Grove Press.

Fanon, Frantz. (1963), *The Wretched of the Earth*, trans. Constance Farrington, New York: Grove Press.

Fanon, Frantz. ([1956] 1967), "Racism and Culture," *Toward the African Revolution*, trans. Hakkon Chevalier, New York: Grove Press.

Fanon, Frantz. ([1963] 2008), *The Wretched of the Earth*, trans. Richard Philcox, New York, New York: Grove Press.

Fanon, Frantz. (2016), *Frantz Fanon: Écrits sur l'aliénation et la liberté*, in (eds.) Jean Khalfa and Robert Young, Paris: Éditions la découverte.

Fast, Jina. (2024), *Decolonizing Existentialism and Phenomenology: The Liberation of Philolsophies of Freedom and Identity*, New York: Rowman & Littlefield.

Firmin, Anténor. ([1885] 2002), *The Equality of the Human Races*, trans. Asselin Charles, Chicago: University of Illinois Press.

Freire, Paolo. ([1970] 2000), *Pedagogy of the Oppressed*, trans. Myra Ramos, New York: Bloomsbury.

Frölich, Paul. ([1939] 2010). *Rosa Luxemburg*, trans. Johanna Hoornweg, Chicago: Haymarket Press.

Gates, Henry Louis and Valerie Smith. eds. (2014), *The Norton Anthology of African American Literature*, 3rd edition, New York: W. W. Norton & Company.

Giroux, Henry. (2014), *Neoliberalism's War on Higher Education*, Chicago: Haymarket Books.

Gobineau, Arthur. ([1853] 2018), *The Inequality of Human Races*, trans. Adrian Collins, London: Forgotten Books.

Goldin, Frederick. ([c. 1140 CE] 1978) trans. *The Song of Roland*, New York: W.W. Norton.

Gomez, Michael. (2018), *African Dominion: A New History of Empire in Early and Medieval West Africa*, Princeton: Princeton University Press.

Gordon, Jane. (2014), *Creolizing Political Theory: Reading Rousseau through Fanon*, New York: Fordham University Press.

Gordon, Lewis. (Ed.) (1997), *Existence in Black: An Anthology of Black Existential Philosophy*, New York: Routledge.

Gordon, Lewis. (2000), *Existentia Africana: Understanding Africana Existential Thought*, New York: Routledge.

Gordon, Lewis. (2006), *Disciplinary Decadence: Living Thought in Trying Times*, London: Paradigm Publishers.

Gordon, Lewis. (2008), *An Introduction to Africana Philosophy*, Cambridge: Cambridge University Press.

Gordon, Lewis. (2015), *What Fanon Said: A Philosophical Introduction to His Life and Thought*, New York: Fordham University Press.

Gordon, Lewis. (2022), *Fear of Black Consicouness*. New York: Farrar, Strauss & Giroux.

Hansberry, Lorraine. ([1957] 1995), "Simone de Beauvoir and *The Second Sex:* An American Commentary," in (ed.) Beverly Guy-Shetfall, *Words of Fire: An Anthology of African American Feminst Thought*, New York: The New Press.

Hansberry, Lorraine and the Student Nonviolent Coordinating Committee. (1964), *The Movement: Documentary of a Struggle for Equality*, New York: Simon & Schuster.

Hansberry, Lorraine. ([1969] 1995), *To Be Young, Gifted and Black*, adapted and edited by Robert Nemiroff, New York: Random House-Vintage.

Hansberry, Lorraine. Lorraine Hansberry Papers, Sc MG 680, Schomburg Center for Research in Black Culture, Manuscripts, Archives, and Rare Books Division, The New York Public Library. Box 42, Box 56, Box 59, and Box 61.

Harris, Leonard. ed. (1983), *Philosophy Born of Struggle: Afro-American Philosophy from From 1917*, Dubuque: Kendall-Hunt Publishing Company.

Harris, Leonard. ed. (1989), *The Philosophy of Alain Locke: Harlem Renaissance and Beyond*, Philadelphia: Temple University Press.

Harris, Leonard. (2020), *A Philosophy of Struggle: The Leonard Harris Reader*, London: Bloomsbury Academic.

Hegel, Georg W. F. ([1857] 1975), *Lectures on the Philosophy of World History*, trans. H. B. Nisbet, Cambridge: Cambridge University Press.

Henry, Paget. (2000), *Caliban's Reason: Introducing Afro-Caribbean Philosophy*, New York: Routledge.

Hernnstein, Richard and Charles Murray. (1994), *The Bell Curve: Intelligence and Class Structure in American Life*, New York: The Free Press.

Herodotus. ([*c.* 450 BCE] 1997), *The Histories*, trans. George Rawlinson, New York: Alfred A. Knopf.

HERU6200., *For the people: Black Athena Live, October 25, 1987* [Video] You Tube: https://www.youtube.com/watch?v=dt1NyAqUL6Y (accessed December 4, 2015).

Hill Collins. ([1990] 2000). *Black Feminist Thought: Knowledge, Consciousness, and the Politics of Empowerment*. New York: Routledge.

Hooker, Juliet. (2017), *Theorizing Race in the Americas: Douglass, Sarmiento, Du Bois, and Vasconcelos*, Oxford: Oxford University Press.

hooks, bell. (1992), *Black Looks: Race and Represenation*, Boston: South End Press.

Howard, Dick., ed. (1971), *Selected Political Writings of Rosa Luxemburg*. New York: Monthly Review Press.

Howard-Pitney, David., ed. (2004) *Martin Luther King, Jr., Malcolm X and the Civil Rights Struggle*, New York: Bedford/St. Martins Press.

Hudis, Peter, and Kevin Anderson.,eds. (2004), *The Rosa Luxemburg Reader*, New York: Monthly Review Press.

Hudis, Peter. (2015), *Frantz Fanon: Philosopher of the Barricades*, London: Pluto Press.

Hume, David. ([1741] 1998), "Of National Characters," in (eds. Stephen Copley and Andrew Edgar), *Selected Essays of David Hume*. Oxford: Oxford University Press.

James, C. L. R. ([1938] 1963), *The Black Jacobins: Toussaint L'Overture and the San Domingo Revolution*, New York: Random House-Vintage.

Judy, R. A. (1996), "Fanon's Body of Black Experience," in (eds.) Lewis Gordon, T. Denean-Whiting, and Renée White, *Fanon: a Critical Reader*, 53–73, Malden: Blackwell.

Kant, Immanuel. ([1764] 2011), *Observations on the Feeling of the Beautiful and Sublime and Other Writings*, in (eds.) Patrick Ferguson and Paul Guyer, Cambridge: Cambridge University Press.

Kant, Immanuel. ([1802] 1997), "From *Physical Geography*," in (ed.) Emmaneul Eze, *Race* and *the Enlightenment*, 58–64, London: Blackwell Publishing.

Kazembe, Lasana. (2021), "The Steep Edge of a Dark Abyss: Mohonk, White Engineers, and Black Education," *Journal of Black Studies*, 52 (2): 123–41. Available online: https://www.jstor.org/stable/10.2307/26985228 (accessed August 15, 2025).

Keita, Maghan. (2000), *Race and the Writing of History: Riddling the Sphinx*, Oxford: Oxford University Press.

Keita, Maghan. (2006), "Saracens and Black Knights," *Arthuriana*, 16 (4): 66–77. Available online: https://www.jstor.org/stable/27870789 (accessed May 5, 2025).

Keller, Francis Richardson. (1999), "An Educational Contreversy: Anna Julia Cooper's Vision of Resolution," *National Women's Studies Association Journal*, 11 (3): 49–67, https://www.jstor.org/stable/4316681 (accessed November 5, 2017).

Kennsington, Richard. (1963), "Rene Descartes," in (eds.) Leo Strauss and Joseph Cropsey *History of Political Philosophy*, 379–96, Chicago: Rand McNally.

King, Martin Luther. (1991), *A Testament of Hope: The Essential Writings and Speeches of Martin Luther King, Jr.*, ed. James M. Washington, San Franciscos: Harper San Francisco.

Kiros, Teodros. (2005), *Rationality of the Human Heart*, Trenton: Red Sea Press, Inc.

Knox, Robert. ([1850] 2018), *The Races of Men: A Fragment*, London: Forgotten Books.

LeBlanc, Paul and Helen Scott. eds. (2010), *Socialism or Barbarism: The Selected Writings of Rosa Luxemburg*, New York: Pluto Press.

Leclerc, Georges-Louis. ([1749] 1997), "From *A Natural History, General and Particular*" in (ed.) Emmaneul Eze *Race* and *the Enlightenment*, 15–28, London: Blackwell Publishing.

Le Romain, M. " 'Nègre' From *Encycloepédie ou Dictionnaire raisonné des sciences, des artes, et des metiers*," in (ed.) Emmaneul Eze, *Race* and *the Enlightenment*, 91–4, London: Blackwell Publishing.

Lewis, Bernard. (1982), *The Muslim Discovery of Europe*, New York: W. W. Norton & Company.

Lewis, David Levering. (1993), *W.E.B. Du Bois: Biography of a Race, 1868–1919*, New York: Henry Holt and Company.

Lewis, David Levering. (2000), *W.E.B. Du Bois: The Fight for Equality and the American Century, 1919–1963*, New York: Henry Holt and Company.

Luxemburg, Rosa. ([1913] 2003). *The Accumulation of Capital*, trans. Agnes Schwarschild, New York: Routledge.

Marley, Bob, and the Wailers. (1980). "Redemption Song," In *Uprising*, CD, Kingston: Tuff Gong-Island Records 422-846211-2.

Martín, Annabel, and Txetxu Aguado. (2017), "Crisis, Change, and the Humanities." *Humanities*, 6 (35): 1–13.

Martínez, María Elena. (2008), *Genealogical Fictions: Limpieza de Sangre, Religion, and Gender in Colonial Mexico*, Stanford: Stanford University Press.

May, Virginia. (2007), *Anna Julia Cooper, Visionary Black Feminist*, New York: Routledge.

McDowell, Deborah. ([1845] 1999), "Introduction," in (ed.) Deborah McDowell, *Narrative of the Life of Frederick Douglass*, Oxford: Oxford University Press.

McDuffie, Erik. (2011), *Sojourning for Freedom: Black Women, American Communism, and The Making of Black Left Feminism*, Durham: Duke University Press.

McKay, Claude. ([1922] 2022), *Harlem Shadows*, New York: Modern Library.

Morgan, Michael. (2013), *Lost History: The Enduring Legacy of Muslim Scientists, Thinkers, And Artists*, Washington, DC: National Geographic.

Murphy, E. Jefferson. (1972), *History of African Civilization: The Peoples, Nations, Kingdoms, and Empires of Africa from Prehistory to the Present*, New York: Dell Publishing.

Outlaw, Lucius. (1996), *On Race and Philosophy*, New York: Routledge.

Outlaw, Lucius. (2005), *Critical Social Theory in the Interest of Black Folks*, London: Rowman & Littlefield.

Painter, Nell Irvin. (1997), *Sojourner Truth: A Life, A Symbol,* New York: W. W. Norton & Company.

Parris, LaRose. (2015), *Being Apart: Theoretical and Existential Resistance in Africana Literature*, Charlottesville: University of Virginia Press.

Perry, Imani. (2018), *Looking for Lorraine: The Radiant and Radical Life of Lorraine Hansberry*, Boston: Beacon Press.

Pimienta-Bey, José. (1992), "Moorish Spain: Academic Source and Foundation for the Rise and Success of Western Universities," in (ed.) Ivan Van Sertima, *Golden Age of the Moor*, 182–247 Trenton: Transaction.

Pirenne, Henrí. ([1939] 2017), *Mohammed and Charlemagne*, Dover: Dover Publications.

Plato. ([c. 360 BCE] 2001), *Timaeus*, trans. Peter Kalkavage, Newburyport: Focus Publishing.

Popkin, Richard. (1980), *The High Road to Pyrrhonism* (eds. Richard Watson and James Force), San Diego: Austin Hill Press.

Potok, Mark. (2017), "The Year in Hate and Extremism," Intelligence Report, 15 February. Available online: https://www.splcenter.org/fighting-hate/intellige nce-report/ 2017/year-hate-and-extremism (accessed August 1, 2017).

Pressman, Jeremy and Elannah Devin. (2023), "Profile: The Diffusion of Global Protests after George Floyd's Murder," *Social Movement Studies*, 23 (4): 558–65. Available onine: https://doi.org/10.1080/14742837.2023.2171 980 (accessed June 6, 2023).

Quijano, Anibal, and Michael Ennis. (2000), "Coloniality of Power, Eurocentrism, and Latin America," *Neplanta: Views from the South*, 1 (3): 533–80. Available onine: http://muse.jhu.edu/journals/nep/summary/v001/1.3quij ano.html (accessed February 3, 2005).

Reynolds, Dana. (1992), "The African Heritage & Ethnohistory of the Moors: Background to the Emergence of Early Berber and Arab Peoples, from Prehistory to the Islamic Dynasties," in (ed.) Ivan Van Sertima, *Golden Age of the Moor*, 93–146 Trenton: Transaction.

Roberts, Dorothy. (1997), *Killing the Black Body: Race, Reproduction, and the Meaning of Liberty*, New York: Pantheon.

Roberts, J. M. (1985), *Triumph of the West: The Origin, Rise, and Legacy of Western Civilization*, New York: Little, Brown & Company.

Robinson, Cedric. (1983), *Black Marxism: The Making of the Black Radical Tradition*, Chapel Hill: University of North Carolina Press.

Robinson, Cedric. (2001), *An Anthropology of Marxism*, Chapel Hill: University of North Carolina Press.

Ruggiero, Greg. ([1845] 2010), "Editor's Note," in (ed.) Angela Davis, *Narrative of the Life of Frederick Douglass*, 9–20, San Francsico: City Lights Books.

Saad, Elias. (1983), *Social History of Timbuktu*, Cambridge: Cambridge University Press.

Saint Augustine. ([*c.* 426 CE] 1972), *City of God*, trans. Henry Bettenson, New York: Penguin Classics.

Sartre, Jean-Paul. ([1949] 1962), *Literature and Existentialism*, trans. Bernard Frechtman, New York: The Citadel Press.

Scobie, Edward. (1992), "The Moors and Portugal's Global Expansion," in (ed.) Ivan Van Sertima, *Golden Age of the Moor*, 331–59, Trenton: Transaction.

Smith, Colin. (1988), *Christians and Moors in Spain*, Oxford: Oxbow Books.

Southern Poverty Law Center. (2016), "Southern Poverty Law Center President Warns U.S. House Members about the Threat of Radical-Right Terrorism," Intelligence Report, September 14. Available online: https://www.splcenter.org/news/2016/09/14/splc-president-warns-us-house-members-about-threat-radical-right-terrorism (accessed August 2, 2017).

Stanton, William. (1960), *The Leopard's Spots: Scientific Attitudes towards Race in America, 1815–1859*, Chicago: University of Chicago Press.

Stover, A. Shahid. (2019), *Being and Insurrection: Existential Liberation Critique, Sketches and Ruptures*, New York: Cannae Press.

Stover, A. Shahid. (2022), *Epistemic Ruptures, Insurgent Philosophy*, New York: Cannae Press.

The Leadership Conference Education Fund. (2024), "Cause for Concern 2024: The State of Hate," Washington, DC: The Leadership Conference on Civil and Human Rights Available online: https://civilrights.org/edfund/wp-content/uploads/sites/2/2024/05/CauseforConcern-TheStateofHate-2024.pdf (accessed June 15, 2025).

Trevor-Roper, Hugh. ([1965] 1988), *The Rise of Christian Europe*, New York: W. W. Norton & Company.

Vasconcelos, José. ([1925] 1997), *The Cosmic Race* (Didiear Jaén, Ed. & Trans.). Baltimore: Johns Hopkins University Press.

Vasconcelos, José. (1926), *Indología: Una Interpretacíon de la Cultura Ibrero-Americana*, Madrid: Agencia Mundial de Librería.

Vice News Tonight (2017), [Charlottesville: Race and Terror] HBO, 14 August. 14

Wade, Nicholas. (2014), *A Troublesome Inheritance: Genes, Race, and Human History*, New York: Penguin.

Walker, David. ([1829] 2015), *Walker's Appeal, in Four Articles; Together with A Preamble, to the Coloured Citizens of the World, but in Particular, and Very Expressly, to those of the United States of America*, Mansfield Center: Marino Publishing.

Washington, Harriet. (2006), *Medical Apartheid: The Dark History of Medical Experimentation on Black Americans from Colonial Times to the Present*, New York: Vintage Books.

Watt, W. Montgomery. (1972), *The Influence of Islam in Medieval Europe*, Edinburgh: Edinburgh University Press.

West, Cornel. (1989), *The American Evasion of Philosophy: A Genealogy of Pragmatism*, Madison: University of Wisconsin Press.

Wells-Barnett, Ida. B. ([1895] 2014), "A Red Record," in (eds.) H. L. Gates, Jr. and V. Smith, *The Norton Anthology of African American Literature*, 670–75. New York: W.W. Norton and Company.

Willet, Cynthia. (1998). "The Dialectic of Master and Slave: Hegel vs. Douglass," in (ed.) Tommy Lott *Subjugation and Bondage: Critical Essays on Slavery*, 151–71. New York: Rowman and Littlefield.

Williams, Goyland. "Philosophy Born of Struggle: An Insurrectionist Ethic," *YouTube*, February 18, 2016, www.youtube.com/watch?v=2gVrNMaAwQA, (accessed June 1, 2025).

Woodson, Carter G. ([1933] 2012), *The Miseducation of the Negro*, Garden City: Dover Publications.

X, Malcolm. (1967), *Malcolm X on Afro-American History*, New York: Merit Publishers.

Index

activism xv, xvi, 29, 51, 55, 108,
116, 119, 120, 137, 138
activist(s) ix, xiii, 29, 55, 58, 69, 84,
96, 103, 105, 107, 109, 136,
139, 149, 159, 162
Africa xi, xii, xvi, xvii, 6, 8–11, 17,
25, 27, 45 n. 6, 57, 61, 97,
104, 108, 111, 116, 170,
172, 173
Africana existential phenomenology
15, 34, 35, 41, 42
Africana phenomenology 34–8, 170
Africana philosophy xv, xvi, 6, 13,
16, 26, 28, 29, 30, 34, 44, 49,
50, 52, 55, 82, 99, 126, 129,
130, 131, 170, 175
Africana thought, transdisciplinarity
and prescience 81–5
African cultures 7, 109
African diaspora xvii, 35, 39, 102,
114, 129, 130, 170, 173
African people xi, xii, xviii, 5, 12, 21,
25, 27, 64, 66, 81, 82, 97, 98,
109, 110
African racial deficiency 26
Africans ix, xi, xii, xviii n. 7, 10, 13,
17, 20–4, 45 n. 2, 58, 61–5,
72 n. 14, 77, 110, 112
Afro-Caribbean philosophers 15, 43
Afro-Caribbean philosophy 42, 130
Afrocentric/Afrocentricity xi, xiii,
xviii, 15, 27, 151

Afro-Jewish 170
Afro-Pessimism 157–60
agency 18, 19, 51, 56, 57, 58, 70,
95, 112, 131, 133, 134, 138,
142, 143
Ahluwalia, Pal 43
al-Andalus 8, 9, 11, 12, 16
Alfonso X 10–11
alienation 40, 41, 49, 132, 133
American Negro Academy 27
American Philosophical Association
(APA) 49–51
American pragmatism 38, 68, 69
American school ethnologists 7, 46
n. 6, 63, 64, 94
Americas 57, 62, 69, 77, 82, 89–92
Amo, Anton Wilhelm 22–4, 27
Ancient Model 170
Antef 3, 4–7, 16, 26, 176
Anthropology of Marxism, An
(Robinson) 38
anti-black racism 10, 30, 35–7, 36,
40, 41, 54, 56, 62, 81, 126,
129, 131, 132, 133, 135, 140,
141, 157, 168, 169, 173
anti-black violence xv, ix, 61, 66,
80, 96, 108, 114
anti-colonial 57, 97, 98, 105, 111
antiquity
Arab 8–10, 12, 14
Aryan Model 63
authoritarian ix, 80, 161, 162

authoritarianism 161, 162, 174
  classical antiquity ix, x, xii, 17, 62
anti-racist 128, 133–5, 141
anti-slavery struggle 28, 69, 95, 99
Arab 8–10, 12, 14
archeo-linguistic inquiry 7
Aryan Model 63
Asante, Molefi xiii, xviii, 27
Asian cultures 7
Augustine, St. 16–18, 23, 26, 31,
  168, 176
authentic humanism 113–16
Averroes (Ibn Rushd) 9, 16–22

Baker, Thomas N. 50
Baldwin, James 114
Bambara, Toni Cade 33
de Beauvoir, Simone 101, 128,
  132, 135–137, 141, 144,
  171, 176
Being and Insurrection xvi, 152–
  5, 157
Bell Curve, The (Herrnstein and
  Murray) 5, 93
Berber 9, 10, 16, 17
  Nafza 10
  North African 16
Bernal, Martin x, xiii, 7, 62, 63
Biko, Steven 43
Birt, Robert 34
Black
  Blackamoors 9, 46 n. 13
  Black freedom struggle 102,
    107, 111, 114
  Black identity 16
  Black Lives Matter xv, ix, 139
  Black nationalist xiv, 69, 97, 111
  Black radical xvi, 15, 34, 35, 37,
    38, 53, 56–9, 72 n. 14, 98,
    102, 105–13, 115, 117–19,
    148, 151–4, 159, 164
  Black radicalism 34–8
  Black Reconstruction 58,
    82, 115

Black vindicationism/Black
  vindicationist xiv, xiii, xviii,
  23, 63, 81
Black American thinkers 28
Black Athena xiii, 62
Black existentialism xvi, 169, 175
Black Jacobins, The (James) 32,
  37, 58, 72 n. 14, 82, 118,
  121 n. 12
*Black Looks: Race and
  Representation* (hooks) 134
*Black Marxism: The Making of
  the Black Radical Tradition*
  (Robinson) 56, 59
black radicalism 34–8
Black Reconstruction in America
  (Du Bois) 37, 58, 82, 115
Black Skin, White Masks
  (Fanon) 40, 42
Blyden, Edward 62, 81
Bogues, Anthony 37
Bondage and My Freedom, My
  100, n. 5, 100 n. 6
Bongmba, Elias 43
bourgeoisie/bourgoise 32, 58, 59,
  106, 107, 110
Boxill, Bernard 20
Brathwaite, Kamau 43

Cantigas de Santa Maria 10–11
capitalism xii, 57, 68, 81, 107, 110,
  112, 115, 132, 135
  neo-liberal capitalism 73, 74
  neo-liberal capitalist
    ideology 75–6
Caribbean xvii, 42, 43, 105, 111,
  116, 130, 167, 170
Caribbean Philosophical
  Association's (CPA's) 172
Caucasian xi, xii, 63
Césaire, Aimé 43
Charlemagne 12
chattel slavery xi, xiv, xii, xviii, 4, 20,
  21, 22, 24, 30, 32, 33, 57, 58,

59, 62, 63, 65, 67, 69, 83, 90, 93, 95, 107, 112, 116, 158, 161, 162
Chauvinism xiii, 13, 14, 62, 65, 164
Christendom 8, 12
Christianity 38, 45 n. 3, 64, 70
  Civil Rights Movement 54, 103, 107, 109, 114
  prophetic Christianity 38, 70
"Claims of the Negro Ethnologically Considered, The" 63, 81, 93
Clair Drake, St. 62–63
Collins, Patricia Hill 33
colonialism 14, 21, 39, 40, 41
  colonial rule 9, 20, 24, 42, 57, 111, 117
  exploitation colonialism 58, 106
  settler colonialism 61, 77, 90
colonialist xiv, xiii, xviii, 4, 5, 42, 130
colonization x, 8, 11, 12, 14, 40, 42, 43, 70, 78, 81, 118, 175
colorism 97
communalism 59
communion 108, 119–20
Complex of Womanhood, This 112, 116
conquest 8, 12, 14, 61
contact 39, 45, 132
conversos 64
Cooper, Anna Julia 27, 30–3, 35, 38, 81, 161, 176
Córdoba 11, 16, 18
counter-hegemonic 57, 119
Covey, Edward 29, 82, 94, 159
Crania Aegyptiaca (Morton) 82, 93
Crania Americana (Morton) 93
creolization xvi, 45 n. 5, 74, 76, 77
critical pedagogy 85–7
critical self-examination 19, 78
Crusades 12, 33
Cugoano, Quobna Ottobah 23, 24, 26, 27

Davis, Angela 33, 34, 56, 105, 106, 132, 133, 151, 154, 155, 177
  Women, Race & Class 33
De Bello Vandalico 10
decolonial 15, 41, 42, 50, 58, 79, 85, 105, 129, 142, 172, 177
  decolonial phenomenology 41, 42
decolonization 28, 38, 39–44, 102, 103, 107, 109, 110, 111, 118
dehumanization ix, xii, 4, 5, 22, 25, 54, 59, 61, 81, 83, 84, 85, 92, 93, 138, 149, 156, 158, 161, 162, 164, 168, 169, 171, 175
Delany, Martin 81
Dikr Bilad al-Andalus 10
double consciousness 34–8, 82, 91, 96–8
Douglass, Frederick xvi, 27–9, 31, 33, 34, 51, 52, 62, 63, 71, 74, 76, 81, 82, 85, 87, 88 n.4, 89–91, 93–7, 99, 100 n. 5, 100 n. 6, 100 n. 7, 114, 148, 154, 155, 158, 159, 165, 175
Du Bois, W. E. B. 30, 34–8, 40
  anti-black racism 36
  Black radicalism 38
  Black Reconstruction in America 37
  double consciousness 37
  humanistic methods 115, 126
  paradigm 36
  The Philadelphia Negro 35
  philosophical legacy 38
  The Souls of Black Folk 35
Dussel, Enrique 7, 13, 67

early modern period xvii, 12–14, 16
egalitarianism xv, ix, 15, 29, 33, 38, 44, 51, 59, 81, 95
Egypt xi, xii, 9, 112
Egyptology xii, xviii n. 7
enlightenment xvii, 4, 15, 20, 44, 45 n. 3, 65, 69, 78, 91

enlightenment philosophy 4
enslavement 12, 14, 20, 24, 53,
 60, 81, 87, 99, 104, 175
epistemic decolonization 39–44
epistemological ruptures 29
epistemology
 epistemic colonization x, 11
 epistemic violence xiv, 93
 epistemological erasure 8, 12
 ethno-biological determinism 45
 n. 3, 65
*Essay on the Inequality of the
 Human Races* (Gobineau) 5,
 25, 64, 90
ethics of insurrection 55, 69
ethnocentrism 12, 44, 78
Eurasian xi, xii, xiii
Eurocentricity
 Eurocentric 12
 Eurocentrism xiii, 44, 154
 European identity 8, 12
Euromodern 21, 65, 168
Euromodernity 8–15, 19, 61
Euromodern philosophy 8–15,
 19, 21, 51
Europe 4, 8, 12–14, 19, 20, 22,
 23, 27, 28, 40, 57, 59, 103,
 107, 130
existentialism
 Black existentialism xvi, 169, 175
 existential phenomenology 34,
 35, 40–2, 79
 existential thought 95, 96,
 99, 175
 exploitation xviii, 32, 58, 61,
 65, 103, 104, 106, 113–16,
 119, 161
existential phenomenology 34, 35,
 40–2, 79
Eze, Emmanuel 4, 27, 45
 n. 3, 65, 66

Fanon, Frantz 30, 58, 74, 76–81,
 85, 87, 91–3, 99, 126, 133,
 141, 144, 153–5, 161,
 174, 176
 Black Skin, White Masks 40
 epistemic decolonization 39–44
feminism
 Black feminist thought xvi, 33,
 56, 102, 105, 112, 119, 140
 first-wave feminism 77
Firmin, Anténor 24–7, 40
 awareness 26
 human categorization 26
 ideas and arguments 26–7
 Kantian critique 27
 pioneering research 27
 transcendental idealism 25
Floyd, George ix, 73, 114,
 153, 162–4
freedom 4, 17, 18, 23, 28, 29, 34,
 42, 44, 51, 52, 54, 70, 71,
 76, 79, 85, 94–7, 99, 109,
 110, 118, 132, 142, 143, 152,
 154, 162–4, 168, 171, 172,
 175, 177
Freire, Paolo 85–7
*Fundamental Constitution of
 Carolina, The* (Locke) 20

Garner, Eric 80, 114
Garvey, Marcus Mosiah 43, 97,
 98
genocide 24, 53, 60, 61, 65, 148
Gliddon, George 63
Glissant, Édouard 43
Global Movement for Black
 Lives 119
Global North 58, 59
Global South 5, 21, 28, 42, 43,
 57–9, 61, 77–9, 85, 87, 96,
 98, 102, 104, 105, 111,
 114, 116–18
Gobineau, Arthur 5, 25, 64, 90
Goldberg, David 62
Gordon, Jane Anna xv, 45 n. 4,
 76–8, 135, 171, 177

Gordon, Lewis xvi, 3, 4, 6–8, 13–16, 19–27, 29, 31, 33–44, 34, 53, 126, 133, 135, 144, 154
   An Introduction to Africana Philosophy 6, 8, 11
   Fanonian theoretical intervention 40
   Fear of Black Consciousness 137
Greco-Roman 5, 7, 13, 14, 62
Greece/Greek x, xi, xii, xvii, xvii n. 3, 7–9, 14, 22, 38, 64, 112
Guillén, Nicolás 43
Gyekye, Kwame 27, 43
gynecology 66

Haitian Revolution 32, 118
Hansberry, Lorraine xvi, 101–3, 113–16, 118–20, 120 n.2
   black radical politics and art 107–13
   A Raisin in the Sun 109
   The Second Sex 101, 113, 120 n. 2, 128, 135, 137
Harlem Renaissance 51, 52, 57
On the Harmony of Religion and Philosophy (Averroes) 19
Harris, Leonard xv, 49–57, 59–62, 65–71, 72 n. 7–11
Harris, Wilson 43
Hegel, Georg W.F. 4, 5, 7, 21, 26, 27, 64, 128, 132, 133, 168, 177
   Lectures on the Philosophy of World History 5, 26, 45 n. 6
hegemony xiii, 21, 81, 104, 111, 161, 164, 169, 173
   hegemonic domination 21, 40, 56, 65, 81, 92, 103
   systems of hegemonic domination 117
Henry, Paget 27, 34, 42, 126, 177
Hernnstein, Richard 5, 93
hip-hop culture 150, 152
historiography
   Eurocentric historiography xiii
   hegemonic historiography 99
   revisionist historiography 58
history
   historical recuperation xiii, 112
   historical restoration xiii, 108
   historicism 61
   historicist 15, 43
   history of ideas 5, 6, 15, 20, 34, 44, 65, 98, ix
   intellectual history xv
hooks, bell 33, 128, 134, 144
Hudis, Peter 80
humanistic study 73–6, 119
humanities 5, 20, 21, 23, 32, 35, 38, 41, 42, 44, 53, 54, 55, 56, 65, 68, 71, 73–6, 79, 81, 85–7, 93, 95, 99, 102, 106, 107, 115, 118, 120, 131, 148, 159, 161–4, 169, 171
humankind xv, xvii, 17, 28, 53, 59, 61, 76, 113, 115, 120
human suffering 53, 54, 60, 61, 104, 116, 119, 163
Hume, David 4, 5, 21, 24–6, 64
   Of National Characters 5

Iberian peninsula 8, 19, 45 n. 3
Ibn Rushd (Averroes) 9, 16–22
ideological antagonisms 75–6
immiseration 54, 68
imperialism 12, 77, 102, 106, 116, 118
indigenous 5, 9, 17, 24, 61, 64, 65, 77, 90, 96, 104, 131, 140, 142
innovation
   architectural innovation 12
   conceptual innovation 4
   discursive innovation 53
   engineering innovation 12
   epistemological innovation ix
   intellectual innovation 35
   philosophical innovation 51
   scholarly innovation 31

theoretical innovation 34, 40,
    76, 129
insurrection 147–66
    ethics of insurrection 55, 69
    insurrectionist ethic 55, 67–71
    slave insurrection 57, 69
insurrectionist ethic 55, 67–71
integration 17, 59
intellectualism 12, 74
intermarriage 9
intersectionality xv, 33, 56,
    133, 135
intersubjectivity
    intersubjective 67
    intersubjective relations 36, 44, 67
*Introduction to Africana Philosophy,
    An* (Gordon) 6–8, 11, 18, 44,
    174–175
irrigation systems 11
Islam 10, 12, 14
Islamic enlightenment xvii, 8–15
Islamic Golden Age 12

James, C. L. R. 32, 37, 43, 57, 59,
    63, 68, 81, 82, 118, 176
    The Black Jacobins 32, 37, 58,
    82, 118
James, Joy Ann 33
James, William 68, 176
Jaspers, Karl 39, 176, 177
Jefferson, Thomas 21, 45
    n. 2, 69, 81
Jewish 45 n. 3, 64, 120
Jews 84, 116
Jim Crow laws 61
justice 9, 17, 21, 23, 28, 37, 51,
    53–5, 71, 76, 96, 111, 114,
    129, 143, 152, 163
juxtapositional analysis xvi, 89

Kant, Immanuel 4, 5, 21, 25–7, 64–6
    Physical Anthropology 5
Kemet x, xi, ix, xii, xiii, xvii, 62,
    63, 176

Kemetic drainage 11
Kemites ix, x-xii, xvi, xii, 7, 11,
    62, 63, 94
King, Martin Luther, Jr. 54, 74
    n. 12, 111

labor 19, 30, 31, 58, 59, 105, 107,
    109, 112
labor power 106
Latin 8, 9, 12, 17, 18, 22, 23, 50,
    89, 90, 96, 111, 154
*Lectures on the Philosophy of World
    History* (Hegel) 5, 26, 45 n. 6
Levantine cultures 7
Lewis, Bernard 46 n. 9
liberation 28–34, 41, 42, 51–9, 61,
    67–71, 79, 86, 87, 91, 94,
    97, 99, 108, 110, 111, 113,
    132, 143, 148, 150, 152, 153,
    155–66, 175
*Life and Times of Frederick
    Douglass* 34, 100 n. 5
limpieza de sangre 64
Linnaeus, Carrolus 64, 65
Locke, Alain 38, 50–3, 68, 71
Locke, John
    *The Fundamental Constitution of
    Carolina* 20
    *Second Treatise on
    Government* 20
Lott, Tommy 20
L'Overture, Toussaint 118
Luxemburg, Rosa xvi, 101–3, 109,
    110, 113, 115, 118–20
    on Global South 116–18
    revolutionary thought and
    praxis 103–7
lynching 31, 61, 82, 83, 96,
    114, 151

Malcolm X xvii, 111, 114, 121
    n. 10, 151, 161, 175
marginalization ix, xvii, 138
Martel, Charles 12

Martinique 39, 116–18
Marx, Karl 38, 58, 59, 133, 154,
    157, 158, 176
  Marxian thought 37, 38,
    56, 57, 79
  Marxism 38, 57, 58, 155
  Marxist thought 57
Mauri 8, 9
Maurus 8–9
Mbembe, Achille 43
Mbiti, John 27
medieval epic poem 10
meta-philosophical
    intervention 14, 50
Mills, Charles 20, 62
modern age, theodicy 21
modern European civilization 12–13
Mohammedans/Muhammadans 9,
    46 n. 13
monogenetic 21, 45 n. 3, 64, 90, 93
Moors 10, 11, 18
  colonization 11, 12, 14
  Moorish 10–13
  Muslim 64, 84
moralism 61, 69, 133
moral universe 54, 55, 61
Morton, Samuel 63, 82
  Crania Aegyptiaca 82, 93
  Crania Americana 93
Mount Pelée 116
Mudimbe, V. Y. 27, 177
Murray, Charles 5, 93
Muslims 8–10, 12, 13, 45
    n. 3, 64, 84
  Mohammedans/Muhammadans
    9, 46 n. 13
  monogenetic 21, 45 n. 3,
    64, 90, 93
Musulmanes 9, 46 n. 13

Nafza, Berber 10
*Narrative of the Life of Frederick
    Douglass* (Douglass) 34,
    100 n. 5
  slave-breaker Covey in 94
National Association for the
    Advancement of Colored
    People (NAACP) 35, 97, 108
Of National Characters (Hume) 5
necro-being 53, 72 n. 9
  disaster 71
  disastrous reality 60
  living death 59–61
  racism 60
New World 24, 114
  cooperative geonational
    commons 164
  culture 77
  plantations 82
  17th century 112
Negro Writer and his Roots, The
    109, 111, 113
normative gaze 137
  of Empire 152, 160
  of established power 149, 152,
    156, 161
  of modernity 160
  of Western imperialist continuum
    148, 149, 154, 158, 163
North African, Berber 16, 79

Obenga, Theophile 7
oppression 24, 30, 53, 161, 163
  of African Americans xiv, 58
  of anti-black 61, 133
  class-based 33, 102
  dialectics of 42, 52, 76
  institutionalized 5
  political 81
  psychology 79, 80
  sociohistorical 148, 151
  structural 32
  systemic 21, 61
  tyrannical 109
Others 15, 23, 29, 34, 36, 50, 51,
    62, 64, 68, 75, 79, 90, 94
  identify 6
  rob and oppress 23

in society 75
Outlaw, Lucius 42, 49, 50, 71 n. 2
outlawry 83

Padmore, George 43
patriarchal
    axiom 102
    normativity 57
    rule to contemporary 33
patriarchy 30, 132, 135
    analysis 137
    women interact 138
Perry, Rufus L. M. 50
phenomenology
    decolonial
        phenomenology 41, 42
    phenomenological 41, 75,
        79, 82, 85, 127, 143, 159,
        170, 171
Philadelphia Negro, The (Du
    Bois) 35
philosophical racism 27, 45 n. 3
philosophy 7
    academic philosophy xvi, 4, 172
    Africana philosophy xv, xvi, 6, 13,
        16, 26, 28, 29, 30, 34, 44, 49,
        50, 52, 55, 82, 99, 126, 129,
        130, 131, 170, 175
    decolonial philosophy 50
    Euromodern philosophy 8–
        15, 21, 51
    hegemonic philosophy 39, 173
    philosopher of existence 29
    philosophy of existence 95
    professionalization of 4
Philosophy Born of Struggle (Harris)
    50–2, 56
Philosophy of Struggle, A xv,
    49–67, 71
Physical Anthropology (Kant) 5
Piper, Adrian 20
Pirenne, Henri 11
poeticist 15, 43
politically correct 149

polygenetic evolutionary theories
    21, 24–25, 45 n. 3, 64, 90
pragmatism
    American pragmatism 38, 68, 69
    pragmatist philosophy 53
    pragmatist thought 69
    Western hegemonic
        philosophy 40, 81
pragmatist philosophy 53
praxis xvi, 42, 81, 85–7, 103–7,
        113–16, 133, 138, 148, 156,
        158, 160, 161, 163–5
problem-based inquiry 78, 80, 102
proletarian 58, 102, 119
proletariat 32, 38, 57, 82, 103–6
Proletariat Woman, The 104–6,
        116, 120
protest-as-resistance 151,
        153, 162
psychiatry 79, 80, 169, 171
psychology of oppression 79, 80

racial hierarchies 64, 65, 77, 92
racialized slavery 112, 117
racial science 91
racism
    actuarial account of 53, 59–61
    anti-black racism 10, 30, 35–7,
        40, 41, 54, 56, 62, 81, 126,
        129, 131, 132, 133, 135, 140,
        141, 157, 168, 169, 173
    institutional racism 30, 32, 108
    philosophical racism 27, 45 n. 3
    scientific racism xii, 4, 21, 24, 29,
        65, 81, 84, 89–93, 98
    structural racism 30, 93
    systemic racism 37
radical xv, ix, xvi
    dehumanization 22, 25, 59, 61
    egalitarian 42, 51, 106
    egalitarianism 29, 33, 38
    etymological interrogation 7
    philosophy 155, 156
    pragmatism 53

sociohistorical movements 161
  Western philosophy 17, 20, 38
radical chic 149
radical egalitarianism ix, 29, 33
radicalism 34–8, 58
Raisin in the Sun, A
  (Hansberry) 109
La Reconquista 8–15
reconstruction 34, 49, 82
reform 51, 52
Renaissance
  European 8–10, 12–14, 35
  Harlem 51, 52, 57
resistance ix, 42, 52, 58, 76, 81,
  104, 108, 109, 134, 142, 148,
  151, 159, 161, 163
revolution
  Haitian Revolution 32, 118
  socialist revolution 103, 104
Riley, Jerome R. 50
Roberts, Dorothy 129
Roberts, Rodney 20
Robinson, Cedric 13, 37, 38,
  47 n. 20, 56–9, 72 n. 15,
  720 n. 13
  An Anthropology of Marxism 38
Rodney, Walter 43
Rousseau, Jean-Jacques 21, 74,
  76–81, 85, 87, 168, 176
  The Social Contract 20

Saracens 9, 14, 46 n. 13
scholar-activist xiii, 51, 67
scientific racism xii, 4, 21, 22, 25,
  29, 65, 81, 84, 89–93, 98
Second Sex, The 120 n. 2, 128,
  135, 137
  Hansberry on 101, 113
Second Treatise on Government
  (Locke) 20
segregation 54, 103
self 36, 53, 67, 69, 126
sexism 30, 32, 103, 138, 170
slave insurrection 57, 69

slavery
  chattel slavery xi, xiv, xii, xviii, 4,
    20, 21, 22, 24, 30, 32, 33, 57,
    58, 59, 62, 63, 65, 67, 69,
    83, 90, 93, 95, 107, 112, 116,
    158, 161, 162
  racialized slavery 112, 117
  slave trade xii, 22, 23, 43, 59, 61
slave trade xii, 22, 23, 43, 59, 61
Social Contract, The (Rousseau) 20
social Darwinism 64, 90
socialism 107, 110, 115, 116
socialist revolution 103, 104
social transformation 15, 28–34,
  38, 85, 97
sociodiagnostic 79
sociogenic 40, 41, 79
sociology 35, 77, 83, 98, 119
Song of Roland 10
Souls of Black Folk, The (Du Bois)
  35, 36, 82, 91, 97, 99, 115
Stanton, Elizabeth Cady 106
Stewart, Maria 27, 33, 52, 175
structural racism 30, 93
Systema Naturae (Linnaeus) 64, 65
systemic racism 37

Tarik ibn Ziyad 10
Taylor, Breonna 73, 153, 163, 164
teleological suspension 14, 169,
  170, 175
theme of invention 27
theodicy 15–23, 37
theory
  creolized theory 119
  decolonial theory 79
  evolutionary theory (monogentic
    and polygenetic) theoretical 45
  n. 3, 64, 90
  theoretical fallacy(ies) 51
Third World 28, 38, 103, 105, 109,
  110, 118, 120 n. 3, 121 n. 10
Thomas Aquinas, St. 9, 19
thought

Africana philosophical
    thought 14, 15
Africana thought 6, 14, 17, 26,
    27, 38, 39, 53, 74, 81–5,
    91, 170
Black thought xi, xv, ix, xvi, xvii,
    6, 7, 15, 16, 37, 44, 49, 51,
    99
decolonial thought 41–2
emancipatory thought 52, 149
hegemonic thought 5, 6, 9, 12–
    14, 21, 33, 38–40, 42, 43, 56,
    65, 78, 79, 81, 86, 89, 90, 92,
    94, 103, 106, 117, 119, 173
liberationist thought 52, 54, 56,
    57, 67, 70, 114, 158
liberatory thought 28, 33, 42,
    85
political thought 42, 43, 89,
    90, 95, 99
racist thought 5, 22, 24, 27, 45
    n. 3, 65, 67, 90, 92, 93
radical thought 57, 59, 106, 147,
    152, 153
Tours, Battle of 12
transdisciplinarity xix, xvi, 76,
    77, 81–5
transdisciplinary 6, 14, 24, 35, 38,
    44, 57, 74–83, 85–7, 90, 91,
    94, 99, 102, 115, 119, 129,
    136, 137, 169, 172, 177
transdisciplinary curriculum 85–7
transformation 15, 28–34, 38, 68,
    69, 74, 80, 85, 87, 97, 103,
    150, 154
*Treatise on the Art of Philosophizing
    Soberly* (Amo) 22
Truth, Sojourner 27, 28, 33, 47
    n. 26, 175

University of Halle 22

vivisection 66
Voice from the South, A 30

Walcott, Derek 43
Walker, Alice 33
Walker, David 27, 52, 69, 70, 71,
    81, 82, 87
Watt, W. Montgomery 9, 10, 13
Wells-Barnett, Ida. B. 33, 74, 76,
    81–5, 87, 175
West, Cornel 38, 68, 151
Western
    Western hegemony ix, 81
    Western imperialism xi, 118
    Western imperialist
        domination 109
Western hegemonic
    philosophy 40, 81
Western theodicy 21
West India Emancipation
    Speech 51
What to the Slave is the Fourth of
    July? 91, 94, 95, 99
white supremacist ix, xiv, 30, 62,
    66, 74, 79, 83, 84, 92, 96,
    103, 105, 109, 134, 139
white supremacy xiv, 62, 84, 91,
    92, 93, 110, 114, 128, 135
woke 149
Women, Race & Class (Davis) 33
Woodson, Carter G. xiv
Wuriga, Rabson 43
Wynter, Sylvia 43

xenophobic (xenophobia) 78

Yacob, Zara 16–18, 19, 20,
    26, 176
Yusuf ibn Tachfin 11

Zack, Naomi 34